BUSTED SANCTIONS

BUSTED SANCTIONS

Explaining Why Economic Sanctions Fail

Bryan R. Early

Stanford University Press
Stanford, California

Stanford University Press
Stanford, California

Printed in the United States of America on acid-free, archival-quality paper

Library of Congress Cataloging-in-Publication Data

Early, Bryan R., 1982– author.
    Busted sanctions : explaining why economic sanctions fail / Bryan R. Early.
      pages cm
    Includes bibliographical references and index.
    ISBN 978-0-8047-9273-8 (cloth : alk. paper)—
    ISBN 978-0-8047-9413-8 (pbk. : alk. paper)
    1. Economic sanctions, American. 2. Economic sanctions. 3. United States—
Foreign economic relations. 4. United States—Foreign relations administration.
I. Title.
    HF1413.5.E25 2015
    327.1'17—dc23

                                      2014036766

    ISBN 978-0-8047-9432-9 (electronic)

Typeset by Thompson Type in 10/14 Minion

To my parents,
Pam and Walt Early

Contents

Acknowledgments

THIS BOOK WAS WRITTEN WITH THE SUPPORT OF MANY GEN-erous contributors who provided their encouragement, feedback, research assistance, and financial support over the years. I am first off in-debted to my wonderful parents Pam and Walt Early for all the support they have provided me. I would also like to thank my wife Pamela Early for her depthless patience, love, and encouragement over the many years of work that went into this book.

I would especially like to thank all the institutions that made this book possible through their financial support. I would first like to thank the Center for International Trade and Security at The University of Georgia, which provided me with the initial support for this project. A portion of this project was also researched while I was a Research Fellow with the Belfer Center for Science and International Affairs at Harvard University's John F. Kennedy School of Government from 2008 through 2009. The Belfer Center provided a wonderful intellectual environment for developing a number of the core ideas of this project. I would also like to thank the Dubai School of Government, which hosted me as a Visiting Scholar in 2009, where I gained a lot of first-hand insights into the book's subject matter. My authorship of this book was chiefly made possible by a generous grant from the Smith Richardson Foun-dation as part of its International Security & Foreign Policy Junior Faculty Research Grant Program. I am very grateful to the Smith Richardson Founda-tion for granting me the time and resources I needed for this project. I would not have been able to write this book without the Foundation's support. Lastly, I would like to thank the Rockefeller College of Public Affairs and Policy at the University at Albany, SUNY, for funding my book workshop in the summer of 2013.

I am indebted to a number of individuals who provided me with their feedback on this project as well. At the University of Georgia, I would like to thank Jeffrey Berejikian, Douglas Stinnett, Jaroslav Tir, and Brock Tessman. Special thanks are also due to Gary Bertsch, who opened the door for me to learn about economic statecraft. I would also like to especially thank Matthew Fuhrmann, who has provided me with great advice and feedback throughout this book project. In addition, I would like to thank Navin Bapat, Amanda Carroll, Johannes Karreth, Kristine Kilanski, Rey Koslowski, Cale Horne, Quan Li, Michael Mood, and Patty Strach for the feedback they provided on various aspects of this project. I would also like to sincerely thank Victor Asal, A. Cooper Drury, Sally Friedman, Katja Kleinberg, David Lektzian, Julie Novkov, and David Rousseau for the incredibly useful feedback they provided at my book workshop. Last but not least, I would like to thank all of the current and former government officials and members of the sanctions policy community who provided background and feedback for me on my project. One of the reasons for greater optimism regarding the use of economic sanctions is that there are so many intelligent, motivated individuals in the policy world committed to making sanctions policies more effective.

Finally, I would like to acknowledge the wonderful support I have received from my research assistants in the Department of Political Science at the University at Albany. I would like to thank Nolan Fahrenkopf and Keon Weigold for their excellent editorial support and the supporting research they provided me with during this project. I would like to provide especial thanks, though, to Amira Jadoon for the exceptional assistance she provided in researching the case studies conducted as part of this project. Amira was also instrumental in supporting my efforts to incorporate an explanation of aid-based sanctions busting into my study. I am very grateful to have had her support on this project and all the positive contributions she has made to it.

BUSTED SANCTIONS

1   Introduction

Why Busted Sanctions Lead to Broken Sanctions Policies

THE ISLAMIC REPUBLIC OF IRAN HAS BEEN SUBJECT TO U.S. economic sanctions since 1979, but only in recent years has the U.S. government been really successful in obtaining multilateral support for its efforts to economically isolate Iran. Most notably, in the spring of 2012, the European Union (EU) blocked Iran from employing the Belgium-based SWIFT (Society for Worldwide Interbank Financial Telecommunication) network used by most financial institutions for their international financial transactions. This move, made in concert with aggressive U.S. efforts to isolate Iran's financial system, was designed to make it more difficult for Iran to re-patriate the payments for its fossil fuel exports.[1] Denied access to the interna-tional financial system, Iran turned to using a commodity that had universal value and did not require accessing the international financial system to con-vert: gold. In the case of Turkey, Iran began selling its natural gas to the coun-try in return for Turkish lira that it kept in local bank accounts. Iranians then used these funds to buy gold bullion, the trade of which was not subject to international sanctions. Turkish gold exports to Iran subsequently ballooned in the summer of 2012 and reached $1.8 billion in July. In response to the negative publicity these overt transactions garnered, a less obvious method for delivering the gold to Iran was sought. Dubai, in the United Arab Emirates (UAE), was the perfect middleman through which to launder such transac-tions. Dubai had already served as the locus for sanctions-busting activities on Iran's behalf for the better part of thirty years and had the connections in place to immediately start facilitating the transactions. There was no better venue in the world to carry out such a scheme.

From July to August, Turkish gold exports to the UAE exploded from $7 million to $1.9 billion. The thirty-six tons of gold that Turkey shipped to the UAE in August comprised over 82 percent of Turkish total gold exports that month.[2] Yet how that gold was shipped to the UAE is even more remarkable. Under UAE customs rules, individuals can legally import up to fifty kilograms of gold into the country in a single visit. And so a plan was hatched in which individual couriers—acting on behalf of firms registered in Turkey—would transport small shipments of Turkish gold to the UAE in perfect accordance with the country's laws. Transporting that amount of gold and in shipments that small required couriers to take hundreds of individual trips to Dubai. According to Reuters, most couriers traveled with their gold simply stowed away in their carry-on luggage. As further proof, the story cites the fact that $1.45 billion of Turkey's August gold exports "were shipped through the customs office at Ataturk airport's passenger lounge."[3] Once in the UAE, the gold effectively vanished. With over 8,000 Iranian-owned businesses operating out of Dubai and over 200 ships leaving daily for Iran, almost anything that can be brought into Dubai can be clandestinely shipped out again to Iran. These transactions continued throughout the fall of 2012 and the beginning of 2013—motivating the U.S. government to adopt new sanctions policies targeting entities that trade in precious metals with Iran. Although this legislation curbed Turkey's participation in this "gas for gold" scheme, it certainly won't stop Iran from finding new ways to circumvent the sanctions imposed against it.[4]

This case is fascinating for a number of reasons. First, it is illustrative of the cat-and-mouse game that has evolved between the United States and Iran with respect to the former's sanctions. Iranians have become world-class experts at devising ways of circumventing or undercutting the U.S. and international economic sanctions imposed against it.[5] These skills have significantly contributed to the country's ability to survive U.S. sanctions for the past thirty-plus years. Second, the transactions highlight the critical role that third parties to sanctions disputes can play in undercutting sanctioning efforts. Via their policies, both Turkey and the UAE undercut the effectiveness of the U.S. and EU financial sanctions against Iran. And, finally, the identities of the third parties involved in conducting the sanctions-busting transactions are also intriguing. The UAE has been a close military ally of the United States since 1994, and Turkey is a NATO ally of the United States and most of the EU's members. Their involvement in deliberately undermining their allies' sanctioning efforts against Iran represents an intriguing puzzle in need of an explanation.

The UAE gained international attention for its illicit trade relationship with Iran when it was revealed that the infamous A. Q. Khan proliferation network used Dubai as a central hub for proliferating sensitive nuclear technologies to Iran in the early 2000s.[6] In delving more deeply into the UAE's commercial relationship with Iran, it is clear that the Khan network's activities were not an isolated exception. The UAE had been a leading venue for conducting sanctions-busting trade with Iran since the U.S. government had first sanctioned it. In many ways, Dubai's explosive growth as the Persian Gulf's leading trade hub was linked to its role as Iran's primary entrepôt for circumventing the sanctions imposed against it. When the UAE formally forged a military alliance with the United States in 1994, the UAE's sanctions-busting activities only accelerated further. All the U.S. efforts at making its sanctions against Iran more stringent during the 1990s appeared only to increase the profits reaped by the Emiratis and added little to the pressure felt by the Iranian regime. During this period, American and Iranian firms flocked to Dubai to continue doing business with one another. All this background information became very real for me when I visited Dubai in 2005 and strolled by the scores of dhows docked alongside Dubai's Persian Sea inlet that were stacked high with American products destined for Iran.

There has been surprisingly little research focusing on the causes and consequences of sanctions-busting behavior, especially given its intuitive links to the failure of sanctioning efforts. In observing the states involved in various sanctions-busting cases, there appear to be two distinct profiles for the types of sanctions-busting activities taking place. The first type, as in the UAE–Iran case, appears driven by profit-seeking behavior and relies primarily on the use of international trade. In contrast, the second type of sanctions-busting relationship appears motivated mainly by politics and employs foreign aid. The massive aid packages that the Soviet Union provided to Cuba to undercut the U.S. sanctioning effort against the country during the Cold War exemplify this type of sanctions busting. Although the motives and methods associated with the two types of sanctions busting are different, both appear capable of undercutting the effectiveness of U.S. sanctioning efforts. This book offers the first comprehensive explanation of why both types of sanctions busters emerge and demonstrates the corrosive consequences each one has on the effectiveness of sanctioning efforts.

A clear need exists for a better understanding of how third-party states contribute to the failure of U.S. sanctions policies. The findings of this book should be of interest to students of foreign policy and economic statecraft but also to policy makers charged with the responsibilities of overseeing U.S. economic sanctions policies. Unfortunately, there are no easy solutions to the challenges posed by sanctions busting. Yet the findings from this book and recent reforms in U.S. sanctions policies suggest that U.S. policy makers can become much more effective at addressing the challenges it poses.

U.S. Foreign Policy and Economic Sanctions: A Fatal Attraction?

Since World War II, the United States has played an active leading role in international politics. The United States' enduring foreign policy interests have been in enhancing the country's national security, while advancing U.S. interests abroad and promoting economic prosperity at home.[7] The United States' leadership role in the West during the Cold War, its emergence as the lone superpower following the Cold War's conclusion, and its seat on the UN Security Council have meant that the United States has been politically engaged all over the world. Its foreign policy interests also extend across a range of policy areas, such as economic, environmental, human rights, and international security issues. In the post-WWII era, the United States has been one of only a handful of countries that has possessed both foreign policy interests that extend globally and the capacity to act on them.

With the United States' preponderance of military and economic power, its policy makers have a wide range of policy options available to them with which to pursue American foreign policy interests. U.S. policy makers can pursue policies within the diplomatic, military, or economic realms and employ coercive or incentives-based strategies.[8] In the diplomatic realm, for example, U.S. policy makers can extend foreign governments praise and legitimacy, or, alternatively, they can use public admonishment to tarnish other governments' international reputations. Militarily, U.S. policy makers can offer security guarantees or sell weapons to foreign governments as part of incentives-based strategies, or they can leverage U.S. military power to compel countries into altering their behaviors as part of coercive ones. The final class of policies comprises what David Baldwin refers to as economic statecraft.[9] Such policies seek to influence a target's economic well-being as a means of affecting its behavior. The provision of foreign aid constitutes an incentives-based approach toward using economic statecraft, whereas economic sanctions represent a coercive approach. Although a number of these policy options can often be employed in response to a given foreign policy dilemma, the attendant costs and benefits of each approach affect which option policy makers select.[10]

More than in any other country in the world, economic sanctions have served as the policy instrument of choice for U.S. policy makers. Economic sanctions specifically refer to restrictions that policy makers place on their countries' commerce with foreign states, firms, or individuals to compel a change in their behavior. They tend to be used in response to objectionable foreign behaviors that require a more assertive response than diplomacy alone but in which the use of military force is undesirable. Both of the leading databases that track the global use of economic sanctions indicate that the United States has employed economic sanctions more than any other country in the world—and by a large margin.[11]

A number of reasons exist for why the United States relies so heavily on economic sanctions despite their poor performance. It has long been known in academic and policy circles that economic sanctions have a relatively poor track record of success—achieving their goals only around 23 to 34 percent of the time.[12] Given its preponderance of economic power, though, the United States can more easily afford to absorb the costs of imposing sanctions and can better leverage sanctions in exploiting other countries' dependence on U.S. markets, U.S. capital, and the U.S. financial system. The United States is thus advantaged in using sanctions over most other countries with smaller economies. The United States' active involvement in global politics and its preponderance of power also creates more opportunities for U.S. policy makers to employ the policy. Economic sanctions can serve as an alternative, antecedent, or auxiliary to the use of military force. The high costs associated with using military force abroad can cause sanctions to appear as a low-cost alternative, leading economic sanctions to be used as a frequent substitute for military force when coercive responses are deemed necessary. U.S. policy makers are also thought to rely on economic sanctions for symbolic purposes in response to domestic and international pressure to take action against objectionable behaviors by foreign actors.[13] In such cases, policy makers may deem diplomatic approaches as insufficient, incentives-based approaches as inappropriate, and military approaches as too costly—leaving only sanctions on the table. It also helps that both the president and Congress can impose economic sanctions, and they can do so relatively quickly and with few *up-front* costs. Even with their poor overarching track record of success, U.S. policy makers thus often view economic sanctions as the most expedient, preferable policy option available to them in comparison to the range of alternative options they could employ.[14] Yet, much as the vast bulk of an iceberg sits out of sight below the waterline, many of the costs associated with using economic sanctions are not immediately observable to U.S. policy makers when they decide to employ them. The real costs associated with the use of sanctions tend to be overlooked or ignored.[15]

Not only does the U.S. government frequently employ economic sanctions when they have little chance of succeeding, but U.S. policy makers also remain committed to failed sanctioning efforts for far too long. When the United States has imposed economic sanctions to achieve a political objective, they have failed to achieve their objectives almost 66 percent of the time. On average, failed U.S. sanctioning efforts last almost nine years—with some lingering on for over fifty years.[16] In the case of the U.S. sanctions against Cuba, U.S. policy makers have been trying to use sanctions to bring about the collapse of the Castro regime since 1960. Rather than abandoning their obviously failing strategy, U.S. policy makers have repeatedly doubled down on their sanctioning efforts over the years. Yet whereas the advocates of those policies have long since left office, the Castro regime still rules in Cuba. This is despite the claims by the Cuban government that the U.S. sanctions have cost it roughly $975 billion since they were imposed.[17] Although experts argue that those estimates are inflated, the cost of the U.S. sanctions to its own economy is likely a nontrivial portion of that figure—and that's only with respect to one country.

Failed sanctions costs come at a high price for U.S. businesses and U.S. workers. It was estimated that during the 1990s the U.S. government's sanctions policies cost American businesses approximately $12 to $18 billion a year in lost exports.[18] In one of the only studies of its type, Gary Hufbauer and his coauthors estimated that the U.S. government's sanctions cost the U.S. economy roughly 200,000 jobs in 1995 due to lost export opportunities.[19] By denying American companies the ability to compete with foreign competitors in some markets, the U.S. government's sanctions can hurt their overall competitiveness. Restrictive export control policies on the export of U.S. satellite technology to countries like China, for example, have harmed the U.S. space industry.[20] These policies also can encourage U.S. firms to relocate their business operations abroad to countries that impose far fewer sanctions. For example, Halliburton's decision to move its corporate headquarters to the United Arab Emirates after it endured congressional investigations into its subsidiary's business dealings with Iran appears consistent with these motives.[21] U.S. sanctions can also encourage generally law-abiding companies to engage in smuggling, fraud, and/or money laundering in order to circumvent U.S. sanctions in pursuit of otherwise legitimate, profitable commerce. And whereas a lot of sanctions-busting trade does not technically break any laws, it often requires business enterprises to violate the spirit in which they were imposed. This forces various federal agencies, like the Department of Treasury and the U.S. Bureau of Industry and Security, to engage in costly cat-and-mouse games in enforcing U.S. sanctions policies against the firms whose businesses the sanctions are hurting.[22] If the political objectives for which sanctions are imposed are valid and achievable, these costs may be justifiable; however, at least two-thirds of the time these costs are incurred for naught.

The United States does not bear the costs for its failed sanctions policies alone. A rising body of scholarship has detailed the harsh and often unintended consequences of economic sanctions on their targets. In the case of Iraq, it is estimated that the sanctions imposed against the country after the first Gulf War (1991–2003) contributed to the deaths of hundreds of thousands of innocent civilians within the country.[23] The civilian costs the sanctions inflicted in this case were extreme but otherwise not anomalous. Leaders of sanctioned states, and especially authoritarian ones, have proven adept at insulating themselves from economic sanctions and passing along their burdens to politically disenfranchised communities within their countries.[24] The declines in public health experienced by sanctioned states are a powerful indicator of these effects. Recent studies have also shown that sanctioned governments increase their repressiveness, and their human rights records worsen. These findings suggest that economic sanctions can have devastating impacts on the civilian populations of the countries they target.[25] The human costs of sanctioning efforts can still be high even when they fail to achieve their intended goals.

Economic sanctions' negative effects are not solely limited to their senders and targets but spill over to involve other countries as well. For example, economic sanctions often prove disruptive to their targets' broader network of trade relationships with third-party states. As an unintended consequence, sanctions can thus do a great deal of harm to their targets' trading partners.[26] By encouraging the development of illicit trade and smuggling networks, sanctions can also empower organized criminal enterprises within sanctioned states and their neighbors.[27] These externalities may generate resentment among third-party states that they direct back toward the United States. Yet economic sanctions also create lucrative opportunities for some third-party states to profit from exploiting the sanctions imposed against target states. As such, U.S. sanctions can encourage third-party states to forge closer commercial relationships with its sanctioned adversaries. This can be particularly problematic for the United States when those third-party states are also U.S. allies.[28] Because the primary means the U.S. government has to dissuade countries from exploiting its sanctions are coercive in nature,[29] attempts to make sanctions against a target state more effective often involve angering or even alienating third-party governments. All these factors add to the costs of imposing economic sanctions.

In sum, economic sanctions should not be viewed as a low-cost substitute for the use of military force. In the United States' case, its government's sanctions cost Americans billions of dollars and hundreds of thousands of jobs. Economic sanctions impoverish and often inflict misery on the citizens living in the states against which they are imposed. Sanctioning efforts can also estrange the United States from the countries whose cooperation it needs to make its sanctions successful and drive them to form closer relationships with the state it's sanctioning. These costs accrue irrespective of whether sanctioning efforts succeed or fail. After being told international sanctioning efforts against Iraq (1990–2003) had been linked to the deaths of hundreds of thousands of Iraqi children, then-U.S. Secretary of State Madeline Albright replied that maintaining the sanctions "is a very hard choice, but we think the price is worth it."[30] Although much of Iraq suffered due to the international sanctions imposed against it, Saddam Hussein remained firmly entrenched in power— supported by an extensive sanctions-busting network that his regime had cultivated.[31] Whereas using economic sanctions often involves hard choices, U.S. policy makers have not always made those choices with an accurate understanding of their true costs and the factors that determine their chances of success. Improving U.S. sanctions policies requires not only increasing their success rate but also facilitating better choices concerning when sanctioning efforts are appropriate or should be abandoned.

Explaining the Failure of U.S. Economic Sanctions

Why do economic sanctions fail so frequently? Although a number of different explanations exist for sanctions' poor success rate, the role played by external spoiler states constitutes a significant and still largely unexplained factor responsible for sanctions' failure. By engaging in sanctions-busting behaviors, countries that are not primarily responsible for imposing sanctions against a target state (a.k.a. third-party states) can undermine their effectiveness. Sanctions busters tend to come in two varieties. The first type of sanctions buster engages in extensive commerce on behalf of sanctioned states to exploit the profitable opportunities that U.S. sanctions create—namely through trade. Private, profit-seeking businesses and traders are the principle agents that cultivate these trade-based sanctions-busting relationships, though their governments can adopt policies that protect and encourage such trade. The second type of sanctions buster is driven primarily by politics, comprising governments that seek to undermine the sanctions' effectiveness through providing target states with foreign aid. This type of sanctions busting differs from the trade-based variety in that supporting sanctioned states via foreign aid can be quite costly. As such, aid-based sanctions busters tend to be much rarer. Both types of sanctions busting are driven by different motivations, occur under differing circumstances, and undermine the effectiveness of sanctions in different ways. States targeted with U.S. sanctions can leverage both types of sanctions-busting assistance to hold out against and, ultimately, defeat the U.S. sanctioning efforts imposed against them.

This book offers the first comprehensive explanation of how both aid-based and trade-based sanctions busting influence the effectiveness of sanctioning efforts and why third-party states engage in such behaviors. The sanctions-busting theory developed in the book combines the liberal paradigm's approach toward understanding the role nonstate actors play in shaping their states' foreign policy and international trade behaviors with the more nuanced insights on leader behavior advanced by the literature on political survival.[32] It emphasizes that economic sanctions differently affect and, in turn, can be differently affected by governments' leaders and their constituents. In some cases, the interests of leaders and their constituents may align in favor of supporting sanctions-busting efforts on behalf of a target state, but in other cases they may diverge. These interactions can have surprising results. For example, the sanctions-busting theory developed in this book counterintuitively predicts that the United States' closest military allies will be in one of the best positions to exploit its sanctions for commercial profits. By offering a joint account of why states engage in extensive sanctions busting and how it affects the success of sanctioning efforts, sanctions-busting theory can explain one of the root causes of why U.S. sanctioning efforts so often fail.

Countries sanctioned by the United States can leverage trade-based and aid-based sanctions busting in different ways to defeat sanctioning efforts. Extensive trade-based sanctions busting can help mitigate the adverse economic impact that sanctions have on their targets' economies and constituents. Although trade-based sanctions busters will seek to profitably exploit the commercial opportunities created by U.S. sanctions, they can make adjusting to the sanctions much more affordable for target states than it would otherwise be. Sanctioned states that have extensive trade-based sanctions-busting relationships with third-party states are thus under far less pressure to capitulate to U.S. sanctioning efforts than those without them. The amount of foreign aid made available to the governments of sanctioned states can also influence their ability to resist U.S. sanctioning efforts. Foreign aid surpluses can help target leaders mitigate the economic hardships caused by sanctions and preserve the loyalty of their politically important constituents. Conversely, reductions in the amount of foreign aid provided to sanctioned states can exacerbate the political and economic damages the sanctions inflict and diminish the ability of governments to respond to those grievances. Third-party governments that provide sanctioned states with extensive amounts of foreign assistance can thus undermine the effectiveness of U.S. sanctioning efforts, but states sanctioned by the United States may also be vulnerable to sudden withdrawals of external aid.

For third-party states, the key difference between trade-based and aid-based sanctions busting is that the former can be profitable whereas the latter is necessarily costly. This distinction shapes the factors affecting third-party states' willingness to engage in either type of sanctions busting. Trade-based sanctions busting can benefit a third-party country's commercial constituents and, in some cases, advance its political interests as well. For the most part, though, commercial motivations explain the lion's share of the trade-based sanctions busting that takes place on behalf of target states. By virtue of their preexisting political, commercial, and geographic relationships with target and sender states, engaging in sanctions-busting trade on behalf of target states may be especially lucrative for firms in particular third-party states. In those instances, third-party governments have strong incentives to protect and foster their constituents' trade with targets states even in the absence of foreign policy reasons to do so. Especially when the potential profits from sanctions busting are significant, the commercial interests of third-party states' constituents can readily overwhelm their leaders' foreign policy interests in supporting U.S. sanctioning efforts. The lucrative profits provided by sanctions busting, for example, explain why the governments of some U.S. allies exploit the political cover provided by their alliances to protect their constituents' sanctions-busting activities instead of supporting their ally's sanctioning efforts. Target states, in turn, have significant incentives to focus their sanctions adjustment strategies on forging extensive sanctions-busting relationships with the handful of countries that they can trade with the most profitably. Only the countries that can provide target states with the most cost-effective means of adjusting to the sanctions are thus likely to emerge as extensive trade-based sanctions busters in a given sanctions episode.

Alternatively, third-party states should engage in extensive aid-based sanctions busting in only a relatively narrow set of circumstances. For third-party governments to take on the expense of extensively aiding sanctioned states, they need to have both the resources and the salient political interests, such as an ideological stake in the sanctions dispute's outcome, to make such significant investments in defeating U.S. sanctioning efforts. Due to the costs associated with aid-based sanctions busting, even third-party governments that meet these qualifications should prefer to use a trade-based sanctions-busting approach if that approach is feasible. The presence of a salient political motive, the availability of disposable resources, and the infeasibility of a market-driven, trade-based option should all be jointly necessary for third-party states to engage in extensive aid-based sanctions busting. Even when all three factors are present, though, that may not be enough to cause a third-party government to offer its patronage to a target state. As such, forging aid-based sanctions-busting relationships often require the leaders of target states to actively court the support of potential benefactors. All this suggests that extensive aid-based sanctions busters should be much rarer than trade-based sanctions busters.

My dual accounts of both the causes and consequences of sanctions bust-ing offer new insights into how third-party states influence the success of U.S. economic sanctions. Because the success or failure of the U.S. sanctioning ef-forts often depends on whether the target can obtain sufficient support from third-party sanctions busters, this extends the breadth of sanctions conflicts far beyond the United States and the immediate target of its sanctions. Third-party states serve as one of the primary battlegrounds on which sanction-ing efforts are won or lost, with target leaders actively seeking to form strong sanctions-busting relationships with third-party states and U.S. policy mak-ers seeking to prevent or disrupt such relationships if they can. Despite the United States' preponderance of power, competition for third-party support often tips heavily in favor of target states—as only a handful of sanctions bust-ers can completely undermine a sanctioning effort, and the costs associated with disrupting third-party sanctions busting tend to be disproportionate to the benefits it yields. For even if the United States can sever one third-party state's sanctions-busting support for a target, the target may have many other alternative third parties in line to take that state's place. These insights suggest that it is imperative for U.S. policy makers to understand which third parties are most likely to sanctions-bust, which approach they are likely to use, and what impact their efforts will have on the sanctions' likelihoods of success. Even if U.S. policy makers cannot always stop sanctions busting from taking place, they can better account for its corrosive effects in their decisions to im-pose and maintain sanctions.

Analyzing Sanctions Busting's Causes and Consequences

To evaluate the sanctions-busting theory's ability to explain the role sanctions busting has played in undercutting U.S. sanctions efforts, the book examines U.S. sanctions policies from 1950 to present times.[33] The book employs a bal-anced mixture of quantitative and qualitative analyses. This approach offers insights at both the micro- and macrolevels as to the causes of sanctions bust-ing and the consequences it has on the success of sanctioning efforts.[34] The empirical portions of the book are divided into two sections. The first section seeks to ascertain the impact that aid-based and trade-based sanctions bust-ing have on the efficacy of U.S. sanctioning efforts via a statistical analysis of ninety-six historical cases of U.S. sanctions from 1950 through 2002. The analysis introduces several novel operational measures capable of capturing how much aid-based and trade-based sanctions-busting support a target receives over the course of sanctions episodes. Whereas previous work has relied on a static, dichotomous measure of whether sanctioned states received any external support over the course of a sanctions episode,[35] these new measures are capable of evaluating the distinct and dynamic impacts that trade-based sanctions busting and foreign aid flows have on the success of U.S. sanctioning efforts. This analysis reveals the extent to which sanctions busting actually undercuts U.S. sanctions.

The second, more expansive empirical portion of the book examines why third-party states engage in extensive trade-based and aid-based sanctions busting. The first empirical chapter in this section explores why and how the UAE grew to become Iran's most important trade-based sanctions buster. As the UAE and United States formed a defensive alliance in 1994, this case is particularly useful in exploring why U.S. allies are more likely to become extensive trade-based sanctions busters. The next chapter conducts a statistical analysis of which countries became extensive trade-based sanctions busters in the same ninety-six cases of U.S.-imposed sanctions from the previous paragraph. This analysis broadly tests a number of hypotheses regarding the economic, political, and geographic factors that make third-party states more likely to engage in trade-based sanctions-busting. The last empirical chapter conducts a comparative analysis of the cases in which third-party governments provided extensive sanctions-busting aid to Cuba. Specifically, it examines the patronage that the Soviet Union and China offered to Cuba during the Cold War and the assistance that Venezuela under Hugo Chávez and China have provided it in the post–Cold War era. This chapter also explores the Castro regime's strategies for obtaining sanctions-busting support and why the U.S. government's efforts to prevent third-party sanctions busting were largely ineffective. These chapters draw on the combined strengths of three different methods of analysis to comprehensively analyze why sanctions busting occurs and what form it takes. They also offer policy-relevant insights at multiple levels of analysis.

The Findings in Brief and Their Implications

The findings from the empirical analyses provide strong support for the theory of sanctions busting developed in the book and offer a number of important insights relevant to U.S. sanctions policies. The results from the first statistical analysis demonstrate that sanctions busting has a major detrimental impact on the effectiveness of U.S. sanctions. When target states have the support of trade-based sanctions busters and/or experience surpluses in their foreign aid flows, U.S. sanctioning efforts are far less likely to succeed in their objectives. Even the emergence of a single trade-based sanctions buster can dramatically reduce the likelihood of sanctions being successful. It is important to note that the analysis demonstrates that both aid-based and trade-based sanctions busting exercise strong, independent effects on sanctions outcomes. It also reveals that sanctioning efforts are more likely to succeed when target states experience sharp, sudden reductions in their foreign aid flows. This indicates that the overarching foreign aid flows target states receive can both positively and negatively affect economic sanctions' likelihood of success. Both U.S. and target policy makers can thus manipulate the effectiveness of the U.S. sanctioning efforts by influencing the trade and aid flows that third-party states provide to target states.

Evidence from the UAE–Iran case study and second statistical analysis offer strong support for the sanctions-busting theory's account of why third-party states engage in extensive trade-based sanctions busting. There is overwhelming evidence that the trade-based sanctions-busting relationship that the UAE developed with Iran was driven by commercially motivated actors seeking to profit from the U.S. sanctions against Iran. Sanctions-busting firms and traders took advantage of the UAE's close geographic relationship to Iran, the historically strong commercial ties between Dubai and Iran, and the commercially open, laissez-faire business environment fostered by Dubai. They also exploited the political cover offered by the alliance the UAE government formed with the U.S. government in 1994. These findings illustrate the theory's descriptive account of how and why trade-based sanctions busting takes place. The subsequent statistical chapter further demonstrates that the sanctions-busting theory's predictions about the types of states most likely to become trade-based sanctions busters proved to be remarkably accurate. The analysis indicates that the factors that affect the profitability of sanctions busting are the leading determinants of which third-party states become extensive trade-based sanctions busters. It also provides compelling evidence that U.S. allies are far more likely to become trade-based sanctions busters than are other countries.

The comparative analysis of the Cuban sanctions-busting cases is generally supportive of the sanctions-busting theory's predictions regarding the emergence of aid-based sanctions busters but suggest that a minor revision to the theory is in order. In the cases of the aid-based sanctions busting provided by Cold War China, the Soviet Union, and Venezuela, all three of the necessary conditions identified by the sanctions-busting theory are present. Each country had a salient political motive to defeat the U.S. sanctions and the discretionary resources to invest in the effort, and each lacked a viable trade-based sanctions-busting alternative. The case of post–Cold War China met those first two conditions but deviated in the latter. Instead, it adopted a hybrid strategy of using extensive foreign aid as an augment to its sanctions-busting trade with the country. This suggests that sometimes third-party states may employ sanctions-busting aid in addition to sanctions-busting trade to accomplish their goal of undercutting U.S. sanctioning efforts. The narratives of all four cases also illustrate the active political role Fidel Castro played in recruiting the patronage of the states that aided his country and how he balanced the assistance offered by these states with the use of trade-based sanctions busting as well. Many more states were willing to engage in trade-based sanctions busting on Cuba's behalf than were willing to aid it, but the latter states' support proved essential to Cuba's long-term resistance of the U.S. sanctions.

Together, these findings reveal distinctive profiles for the types of states likely to bust U.S. sanctions using either approach. The United States' democratic, commercially competitive allies with large economies (for example, Great Britain, Canada, and Japan) appear most likely to engage in trade-based sanctions busting, while its wealthy, ideologically motivated adversaries (such as the Soviet Union, China, and Venezuela) appear most likely to become aid-based sanctions busters. U.S. sanctioning efforts are thus commonly besieged on all sides, undercut by friends and foes alike. Yet although the adverse effects of aid-based sanctions busters can be mitigated, the deleterious impact of trade-based sanctions busters rarely can be. As such, it is unfortunate *in this regard* that the United States has so many more friends in the world than adversaries because its closest allies appear to be its sanctions' worst enemies. Overall, the findings indicate that sanctions busting is an endemic and often intractable problem associated with the use of sanctions.

The findings from the analysis offer an array of important insights for policy makers concerning how to better use economic sanctions as an effective tool of economic statecraft. Diagnostically, policy makers can use the empirical models in this book to understand the effects of sanctions-busting trade and foreign aid on their sanctions' likelihood of success. Equipped with this knowledge, policy makers can make more informed decisions about when sanctions can be used most effectively and when it may be best to give up on heavily busted sanctioning efforts. The book's findings can also be used to develop profiles of the types of states that are likely to become extensive sanctions busters. Policy makers can use this knowledge to identify the greatest sanctions-busting threats and focus their efforts at dissuasion accordingly. Lastly, the findings on how the foreign aid flows received by targets affect their ability to resist sanctions provide policy makers with new knowledge on an additional tool they can leverage to improve their sanctions' chances of success. Although many of the challenges posed by sanctions busting may be intractable, policy makers armed with better knowledge about how sanctions busting works and the effects it has should be able to wield economic sanctions far more effectively than those lacking it.

Plan of the Book

The rest of the book proceeds as follows. Chapter 2 provides more in-depth descriptions of sanctions-busting behavior and the profiles of aid-based and trade-based sanctions busters. Chapter 3 presents the sanctions-busting theory's account of how trade-based sanctions busters and foreign aid affect the success of sanctioning efforts and tests it via a statistical analysis. Chapter 4 presents the sanctions-busting theory's explanation of why third-party states choose to engage in trade-based and aid-based sanctions busting. Chapter 5 tests the descriptive accuracy of the theory's explanation of trade-based sanction busting via a process-tracing analysis of how the UAE became Iran's leading trade-based sanctions buster. Employing another statistical analysis, Chapter 6 evaluates the sanctions-busting theory's general ability to explain which states are most likely to become trade-based sanctions busters. Chapter 7 conducts the comparative analysis of the third-party states that became aid-based sanctions busters on Cuba's behalf both during and after the Cold War. The concluding chapter summarizes the combined findings from the analyses and explores their broader theoretical and policy implications.

2   What Are Sanctions Busters?

THIS CHAPTER PROVIDES AN INTRODUCTION TO THE EXISTING
literature on sanctions busting and describes the two leading
types of sanctions-busting activities that third-party states engage in. It begins by discussing how economic sanctions create a demand for third-party
sanctions busting among target states and how existing accounts have sought
to explain its causes and consequences. It then offers a new, more broad-
reaching definition of what constitutes extensive sanctions-busting behaviors
and describes the two archetypical types of sanctions busters that fit that definition: trade-based and aid-based sanctions busters. The chapter discusses the
distinct characteristics associated with both types of sanctions busting and
provides example profiles of states that exemplify the trade-based sanctions-
buster and aid-based sanctions-buster archetypes. As the chapter illustrates,
the characteristics associated with trade-based and aid-based sanctions busting mark them as two distinct phenomena that appear to be driven by different causal motivations and should have differing impacts on the outcomes of
sanctioning efforts.

The Impact of Economic Sanctions
and Demand for Sanctions Busting

Even when the United States imposes unilateral economic sanctions on a
target state, they can have far-reaching political and economic effects that

influence other countries. In conceptualizing sanctions disputes, states fall into one of three categories: the sender state(s) primarily responsible for imposing the sanctions, the target of the sanctions, and the third-party states comprising the rest of the countries in the world.[1] Sanctioning efforts succeed when their targets capitulate to their senders' accompanying demands, and they fail when senders lift the sanctions without fulfilling their objectives. Third-party states can support the senders' sanctioning efforts, offer sanctions-busting support to target states, or respond neutrally. Even third-party states with no preferences as to the sanctions' outcome can be affected by the sanctions' spillover effects or be drawn into the dispute by sender and target governments seeking their support. In theory, the varying ways in which sanctions affect third-party states and how the states respond to them can significantly influence the outcome of sanctions disputes.

When economic sanctions are imposed against a target state, they can have disruptive effects on its firms' network of commercial relationships, weaken their terms of trade, and increase their costs of doing business with foreign trade partners. Adjusting to sanctions tends to be costly for firms in sanctioned states. Sanctions sever otherwise profitable trade relationships and can increase the costs of doing business with other trade partners such that it may no longer be profitable to maintain those business relationships. This inflicts deadweight losses on affected firms and requires them to find ways of circumventing the sanctions, form new business relationships with replacement trade partners, or increase the amount of business they conduct with existing ones. These arrangements are inevitably less profitable than the ones enjoyed by target firms prior to the sanctions. For target governments, the economic pain inflicted on their commercial constituencies is translated into political pressure to either provide compensation for or protection from the sanctions' ill effects or have the sanctions removed. Finding ways of mitigating the damages done by sanctions is thus a common goal that unites governments and most of their commercial constituents.[2]

The extent to which sanctioned states can efficiently and affordably adjust to sanctions by developing alternative trade relationships with third parties heavily influences their ability to resist the sanctions.[3] The immediate, disruptive effects caused by the imposition of sanctions are the most difficult to overcome. Firms are forced to find replacements for their lost trade, respond to new risks and transaction costs involved in doing business, and operate in a new business environment clouded by uncertainty. Third-party firms can take advantage of the target firms' weakened terms of trade, forcing them to pay more for the sanctioned goods they import and paying them less for the sanctioned goods they export.[4] Third-party firms can also profit from helping target and sender firms circumvent sanctions by serving as brokers and/or middlemen in sanctions-busting transactions. So, whereas target states can often replace the trade lost or disrupted by sanctions, that trade is inevitably more costly. Most theories that seriously address this issue assume that the more costly that replacement trade for a target is, the more damage the sanctions will end up inflicting.[5] Target states that are effective at developing less costly replacement trade relationships face fewer economic incentives to capitulate to sanctions than those that are not.

In contrast to sanctions-busting trade, the foreign aid given to sanctioned states tends to be much more subject to governmental control and use. It can come in the form of developmental assistance, concessional loans or trade subsidies, grants, or military assistance. Because foreign aid is not profit driven and is often fungible with other forms of government spending, it can significantly enhance the resources available to governments for responding to the damages sanctions inflict. Although analyses of the Berlin Airlift or the extensive aid the Soviet Union provided to Cuba address how foreign aid can help sustain target states, they do not develop generalizable theories of the phenomenon.[6] And whereas much has been written on the general political and economic effects of foreign aid, no studies appear to have explicitly examined how foreign aid flows affect the success of sanctioning efforts.[7] The foreign aid literature thus suggests that sanctions-busting aid should influence sanctions outcomes in different ways than sanctions-busting trade, but existing accounts have yet to enumerate them.

To the extent that existing works have sought to study the effects of third-party spoiler behavior, they have done so using fairly blunt and conceptually ambiguous means of studying the phenomenon. In their book *Economic Sanctions Reconsidered*, Gary Hufbauer and his coauthors theorized that sanctions imposed against target states that receive significant assistance from a third party should be less effective.[8] They labeled the providers of such assistance as "black knights" and ascribed their motivations as being primarily political. The archetypical case of black knight behavior according to Hufbauer and his colleagues was the massive package of assistance that the Soviet Union provided to Cuba after the United States sanctioned it in 1960. Despite the analogical linkages they drew to such a prominent case, much about their conceptualization of black knight behavior remained ambiguous. For example, Hufbauer and his coauthors did not clarify the specific channels through which black knight assistance flowed.[9] Additionally, the variable they coded to capture the effects of black knight behavior only denoted whether any state provided the target with significant assistance at any point during a sanctions episode. It also did not capture how much assistance was provided, when it was provided, or how many states provided it. Most of the subsequent studies that have used the black knight variable coded by Hufbauer and his coauthors have been unable to find that such assistance actually undermines the success of sanctions.[10] A more recent study by Elena McLean and Taehee Whang analyzes the impact of whether target states' leading presanctions trade partners increase or decrease their trade with the target state over the course of a sanctions regime.[11] They found that if those trade partners decreased their trade with the target, the sanctions were more likely to be successful. Yet they also found no link between the emergence of new leading trade partners during the sanctions (that is, trade-based sanctions busters) and sanctions outcomes. As in the other cases discussed earlier, their study employs fixed measures of trade with sanctioned states that do not vary over time. Given that target states' aid and trade flows can vary significantly over the course of a sanctions episode, there are strong reasons to think these phenomena need to be conceptualized and measured dynamically to capture their true effects.

Slaying the Black Knight? Reconceptualizing Sanctions Busters

Although most of the initial efforts to capture sanctions busting's impact have failed to yield substantive findings, this does not mean that the intuitions of scholars like Hufbauer and his coauthors are incorrect. In a large number of anecdotal cases, third-party states have clearly undercut U.S. sanctioning efforts and contributed to their failure. Rather, the ambivalent empirical track record produced by existing research suggests that more nuanced approaches of identifying sanctions busters and evaluating how their assistance affects sanctions outcomes is necessary. Although the logic of black knight assistance appears to capture the aid-based assistance that third-party governments can provide to target states, it fails to address the role that commercially motivated sanctions busters can play in undermining sanctioning efforts. To accurately capture the role that third-party spoilers can play in undermining sanctioning efforts, a theory of sanctions busting must be able to account for the causes and consequences of both variants.

As a broader alternative to the black knight concept, this book defines sanctions busters as third-party states that respond to the imposition of sanctions by increasing their economic engagement with target states in ways that ameliorate the sanctions' adverse consequences. This definition captures the full spectrum of economic channels between target and third-party states that undermine the effectiveness of economic sanctions, including foreign aid, foreign trade, foreign direct investment (FDI), and foreign remittances. Although new research suggests that FDI and foreign remittances can influence sanctions outcomes,[12] foreign aid and foreign trade appear to be the predominant channels third-party states use to engage in extensive sanctions busting. As such, this book focuses on exploring the causes and consequences of the aid- and trade-based sanctions-buster archetypes. The insights developed with respect to aid-based and trade-based sanctions busting, though, may also cross-apply to the broader range of economic channels that can be used to undercut sanctioning efforts.

The two archetypical forms of sanctions busters that fall under this broad definition employ differing economic channels, are driven by different motivations, and involve differing degrees of active government involvement in their provision. Trade-based sanctions busters are third-party states whose constituents have significantly increased their commerce with sanctioned states to profit from the lucrative commercial opportunities the sanctions have created. Third-party governments can encourage these sanctions-busting relationships by adopting policies that enhance the profitability of trading with target states and by shielding their constituents from sender states' efforts to sever their trade relationships with target partners. Aid-based sanctions busters are governments that have political interests in seeing the sanctioning efforts against a target state defeated, and they use government-sponsored foreign assistance as the primary vehicle for undercutting the sanctions' effectiveness. Nonstate commercial actors are thus the primary agents of trade-based sanctions busting, whereas governments are the primary agents of aid-based sanctions busting. And although the latter type of sanctions busting can be quite costly, the former type can be quite economically profitable for third-party states. Distinct profiles can thus be developed for both types of sanctions buster that can be used to identify when a third party is engaging in such activities.

Profiling Extensive Trade-Based Sanctions Busters

Third-party states that engage in extensive trade-based sanctions busting are primarily defined by the commercial relationships they have with sanctioned states. Trade-based sanctions busters are third-party states that dramatically increase their trade with target states after they have been sanctioned and at high enough levels to mitigate the damages inflicted by the sanctions. Market-based transactions, executed by firms or individuals, should be the primary channel by which trade-based sanctions busting occurs, as opposed to government-negotiated and -executed transactions. Profits are the primary motive for trade-based sanctions busting. The profit-seeking motives of third-party firms will attract them to do business within the third-party states that offer the most profitable venues for trading with target states, whereas the profit-seeking motives of target firms will lead them to seek out the least costly options for adjusting to the sanctions. Although third-party governments may adopt policies that support their constituents' sanctions-busting efforts, they do not play an active role in underwriting or financing the trade with target states in this archetype. Extensive trade-based sanctions busters are thus the third-party states that offer the most profitable business venues for particular sanctioned states, allowing third-party firms to exploit the commercial rents created by the sanctions and providing target firms with a comparatively less costly option for adjusting to the sanctions.

Trade-based sanctions busters can be identified by how their trade flows with target states change during sanctions and their overarching importance to target states as trading partners. For a third party's sanctions busting to have a significant effect, it needs to be a major trading partner of the target state. Preserving status quo trade relationships is not sufficient, though; major trading partners of the target must also significantly increase their trade with target states to ameliorate the sanctions' adverse effects. These two characteristics create a readily observable profile for trade-based sanctions busters that can be tracked via international trade data—at least when such trade does not occur illicitly.

In the case of the U.S. antiapartheid sanctions against South Africa (1985–1991), numerous third-party states appeared to respond by exploiting the commercial opportunities they presented. Figures 2.1 through 2.4 illustrate how the trade flows of Great Britain, Italy, Japan, and West Germany with South Africa, and their proportional shares of South Africa's total trade,

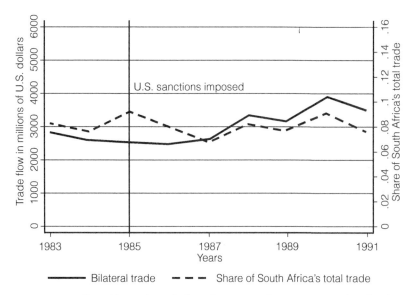

FIGURE 2.1. Great Britain's trade-based sanctions busting on South Africa's behalf.

SOURCE: Barbieri, Keshk, and Pollins 2009.

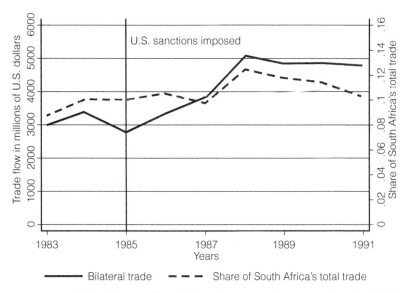

FIGURE 2.2. West Germany's trade-based sanctions busting on South Africa's behalf.

SOURCE: Barbieri et al. 2009.

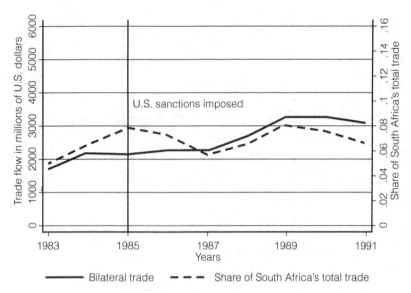

FIGURE 2.3. Italy's trade-based sanctions busting on South Africa's behalf.
SOURCE: Barbieri et al. 2009.

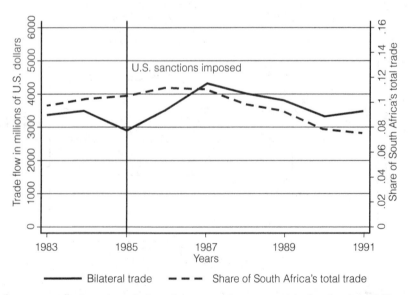

FIGURE 2.4. Japan's trade-based sanctions busting on South Africa's behalf.
SOURCE: Barbieri et al. 2009.

changed following the U.S. sanctions. Each of these countries was flagged as engaging in at least several years of active trade-based sanctions busting on South Africa's behalf by the measure used in the book's subsequent statistical chapters to identify such behavior. The solid lines represent the countries' bilateral trade with South Africa in millions of U.S. dollars, while the dashed lines depict the share of South Africa's total trade they accounted for. As the figures illustrate, all four states constituted major South African trading partners—accounting for at least 5 percent of the country's total trade in each case. Each country experienced significant growth in its bilateral trade with South Africa as well. As the graphs illustrate, West Germany and Japan's trade with South Africa both increased significantly in the immediate aftermath of the U.S. sanctions. British and Italian trade with South Africa significantly picked up only several years after the sanctions had been in place. The increases in the trade they conducted corresponded with declines in the still substantial amounts of trade that West Germany and Japan conducted with South Africa. Interestingly, all four countries also had limited forms of sanctions in place during this period that corresponded with the harsher U.S. sanctions.[13] All of this reinforces the notion that trade-based sanctions busting constitutes a dynamic phenomenon and that the incentives of businesses to capitalize on profitable opportunities do not necessarily align with their home governments' foreign policy prerogatives. Overall, these graphs provide at least suggestive evidence that the U.S. economic sanctions were correlated with increased trade flows between each country and South Africa.

The U.S. and the broader international community's sanctioning efforts are generally thought to have effectively contributed to the South African government's decision to end apartheid.[14] Yet, despite the sanctions' apparent positive contributions, it remains unclear how much more quickly and effectively the sanctioning efforts could have worked absent the sanctions busting that took place on South Africa's behalf. Although target states that receive the support of trade-based sanctions busters may still eventually capitulate to sanctioning efforts, such assistance may aid them in holding out far longer than they otherwise could have. Beyond the issue of success and failure, the impact of sanctions busting on how long sanctions last also represents an important area of inquiry. The next chapter explores the impact the presence of trade-based sanctions busters like the ones flagged in the South African case has on the efficacy of U.S. sanctioning efforts.

Profiling Aid-Based Sanctions Busters

Third-party states that engage in extensive aid-based sanctions busting are countries that employ foreign aid to help a target state resist the sanctions imposed against it. This type of sanctions buster most closely resembles Hufbauer and his coauthors' depiction of third-party states that provide sanctioned countries with black knight assistance. Sanctions-busting foreign aid can be sent through a myriad of channels, including development and/or technical assistance programs, military aid, trade or financial subsidies, or direct grants. Not all third-party states that provide foreign aid to sanctioned countries do so for sanctions-related purposes, but much of the foreign aid given to sanctioned states can potentially contribute to their abilities to hold out against sanctions. As such, the overarching external aid flows that targets receive are what influence their ability to resist sanctioning efforts, not just the singular contributions of extensive aid-based sanctions busters. For third-party states to provide extensive sanctions-busting aid, they must have a significant pool of disposable resources available to task toward that purpose. Contrary to trade-based sanctions busting, aid-based sanctions busting is disbursed primarily through governmental channels or through government-negotiated agreements. Third-party states can primarily be identified as extensive aid-based sanctions busters if their governments dramatically increase the amount of foreign aid they provide to target states during the period they have been sanctioned. The governments of such countries tend to publically acknowledge their patronage of target states and sometimes even publicize the spoiler role they are playing to gain international recognition for it.[15]

In the case of the U.S. sanctioning effort against North Korea (from 1950 up through the present), North Korea has been the beneficiary of extensive aid from both the Soviet Union and the People's Republic of China over the course of the sanctions. By the late 1980s, North Korea had grown extremely dependent on Soviet support, and the Soviet Union's collapse had a devastating impact on North Korea's economy and basic ability to even feed its own citizens. After the Soviet Union's collapse, China emerged as North Korea's primary patron. Although China's trade relationship with North Korea has fluctuated significantly over the past two decades, it has consistently been a leading source of food aid and broader foreign assistance for the North Korean regime.[16] China's patronage has been crucial to sustaining North Korea's economically isolated regime. According to Jaewoo Choo, "If Chinese aid did not make up the majority of [North Korea's economic] deficiencies, given that there is no other consistent and willing provider of aid, the North Korean economy and perhaps the life of the nation, would have earlier come to an end."[17] From 1996 to 2005, China is estimated to have provided North Korea with anywhere between 40,000 and 510,00 tons of food aid per year—averaging 195,000 tons per year over that period and often stepping in to fill food shortages that no other countries were willing to fill.[18] Absent China's critical support, the North Korean regime would likely have collapsed during the economic crisis and deadly famine it experienced during the latter part of the 1990s.

The assistance that China has provided to North Korea has not just been limited to food aid. The Chinese government has also been a critical source of fuel and fertilizer for North Korea and is estimated to have provided it with over 70 percent of its oil imports in some years.[19] More broadly, the Chinese government has subsidized the significant trade deficits that North Korea has run with China.[20] During North Korea's economic crisis in the latter part of the 1990s, for example, the Chinese government extended North Korea special "friendship prices" in its trade with the country.[21] Since 2000, North Korea's reliance on trade with China has grown significantly—with China emerging as its largest trading partner by a large margin. Although a significant portion of that upswing in Chinese trade with North Korea has been conducted on a for-profit basis, the Chinese government is still thought to subsidize some part of those transactions. China has also offered North Korea assistance through funding the construction of factories and other infrastructure within North Korea, which coincided with other direct investments that China began making in North Korea.[22] Economists Stephen Haggard and Marcus Noland estimate that, from 1990 through 2005, China provided North Korea with overarching aid flows that fluctuated between $100 and $200 million a year. Given the lack of transparency surrounding Chinese aid, however, their analysis suggests that those aid flows could actually run much higher.[23]

The overarching economic dependence of North Korea on China has only grown stronger in recent years. From 2005 through 2008, China accounted for approximately 31 to 40 percent of North Korea's total trade. The string of nuclear and rocket tests North Korea conducted starting in 2008 and the militarized disputes it had with South Korea in 2010 served to further isolate the country, as it was subjected to more international sanctions and lost a significant degree of its support from Western donors. Thus, in 2012, China accounted for a staggering 84 percent of North Korea's external trade.[24] China also dramatically increased the food aid it was offering to North Korea, continuing its long-standing approach of stepping in with additional aid to stave off significant domestic instability within the country.[25]

The motivations of China's support for North Korea have largely been political, even if commercial considerations became more salient as North Korea became increasingly dependent on China for its external trade. The Chinese government shares an ideological affinity with North Korea, given their shared commitment to communist-oriented ideologies. It also has an abiding interest in preserving the stability of North Korea's regime. China's leaders want to avoid a disastrous collapse of the country that could cause substantial humanitarian and refugee crises and lead to a potentially unified, pro-Western Korean Peninsula. It also does not want to be dragged into a potential war if North Korea's escalatory saber rattling leads to a full-blown conflict with South Korea, Japan, and/or the United States. Although Chinese leaders have shown signs of increasing frustration at North Korea's nuclear policies and bellicose diplomacy, China has not indicated a public willingness to withdraw its patronage of the country.[26] The political costs of letting North Korea succumb to the U.S. and international sanctioning efforts imposed against it thus outweigh the considerable economic costs of continuing to sustain North Korea. Since the end of the Cold War, China has served as North Korea's indispensable patron, and it is difficult to imagine how its regime could continue to endure U.S. and international sanctions in the absence of China's sanctions-busting support.

As this vignette of aid-based sanctions busting illustrates, the costs of offering substantial assistance to a sanctioned state can be considerable and mount over time. Very few third-party states, even those that are sympathetic, can often afford to offer target states substantial support and sustain those flows over time. North Korea's utter dependence on China makes it an extreme example of how sanctions busting can undercut the effectiveness of sanctioning efforts. That level of dependence is rare and often unsustainable for third-party patrons over the long run. Yet this extreme case perfectly illustrates the critical role that aid-based sanctions busters can play in undermining sanctioning efforts that would otherwise likely be successful. Explaining what motivates aid-based sanctions busting and the role that foreign aid plays in undercutting sanctioning efforts are thus of critical importance.

Conclusion

Past works on sanctions busters' causes and effects have tended to overlook the important distinctions between third-party states that undercut sanctioning primarily with their trade versus those that do so via foreign aid. Both types of sanctions busters have distinct profiles, though, suggesting that the reasons why third-party states engage in either type of extensive sanctions busting and the impact of those activities are quite different from one another. The profiles for aid-based and trade-based sanctions busters described in this chapter represent idealized archetypes, and not all third-party states will perfectly fit into one category or the other. Foreign aid and foreign trade can serve as substitutes for one another but can also enhance each other's effectiveness. As such, there is no a priori reason to think that third-party states must make a mutually exclusive choice between extensive aid-based versus trade-based sanctions busting. Yet I argue that, most of the time, extensive sanctions busters will tend to be associated with one archetypical behavior or the other in sanctions busting on a target state's behalf. The distinct profiles of aid-based and trade-based sanctions busters also suggest that the assistance they provide to target states will have differing effects on their ability to resist and defeat sanctioning efforts. In developing an explanation for both the causes and consequences of aid-based and trade-based sanctions busting, the next section begins by seeking to explain their consequences in order to obtain additional insights as to why third-party states would want to engage in either behavior.

3 Assessing the Consequences of Sanctions Busting

THE LITERATURE ON ECONOMIC SANCTIONS HAS IDENTIFIED a wide variety of factors that influence whether sanctions succeed or fail.[1] A lot of focus has been given to factors such as the political relationship between the target and sender states, the type of governments they possess, the target's economic conditions, and the goal(s) of the sanctions. For the most part, policy makers have little control over these factors and the ways in which they influence the success of sanctioning efforts. In contrast, the type of sanctions policy makers impose, their stringency, their duration, and whether other states and international organizations participate in sanctioning efforts are factors that policy makers wield some control over.[2] Another factor that policy makers can potentially influence is the amount of international cooperation their sanctioning efforts receive from third-party countries, but obtaining such cooperation has been shown to often be difficult and quite costly.[3] Far less attention has been paid, however, to the cooperative support that target states receive in defeating sanctions. This chapter explains how the sanctions-busting assistance provided via trade and foreign aid affects the success of sanctioning efforts and evaluates its substantive impact. As the analysis in this chapter reveals, the amount of sanctions busting that takes place on behalf of a target state is a major determinant of whether sanctions are successful.

Broadly speaking, the sanctions-busting theory is nested within the liberal paradigm's general assumptions about the role played by societal actors in affecting their states' political and economic behavior.[4] The theory draws distinctions between the leaders of governments and the constituencies they represent. Survival-oriented leaders must seek to balance their states' foreign policy interests and the interests of the constituencies that keep them in power domestically.[5] As states' commercial constituencies (that is, firms and individual businesspeople) are the primary constituency affected by sanctions, they have incentives to lobby their leaders for policies that are favorable to their interests. This perspective views governmental policies as emerging from an amalgamation of leaders' preferences, their constituents' preferences, and their states' positions within the international system. The ability of commercial constituencies to influence their states' policies on sanctions issues will thus be moderated by their leaders, governing institutions, and the broader distribution of preferences within their states. At the individual and firm levels, commercial actors may also have incentives to pursue their economic interests at the expense of their host governments' foreign policy interests.[6] As such, commercial constituencies, in addition to government leaders, play influential roles in determining how target, third-party, and sender states respond to economic sanctions.

Drawing distinctions between states' governments and their constituencies is important because economic sanctions impose different sets of costs (and benefits) on governments' leaders than they impose on their constituents.[7] Whereas the leaders of target and sender states are the only ones who can ultimately determine whether sanctions succeed or fail, states' commercial constituencies directly bear the highest costs for their imposition and shape how the sanctions affect the international trade flows of affected states. The interests of the leaders of sender, target, and third-party governments often do not align directly with the preferences of their commercial constituencies in responding to sanctions. Understanding that these conflicts of interest between governments and their constituents exist is crucial to understanding the behaviors of all the states involved in or affected by sanctions disputes.

This chapter focuses on explaining how and why third-party sanctions busting influences the outcomes of sanctions disputes between the United States and the countries it sanctions. It explains the impact sanctions have on the governments and constituents of target states and why the availability of sanctions-busting assistance undermines the effectiveness of U.S. sanctioning efforts. According to the sanctions-busting theory developed in this chapter, both trade-based and aid-based sanctions busting play distinctive roles in affecting whether target governments resist sanctions or capitulate to them. This chapter also lays the theoretical foundations for subsequently understanding why third-party states engage in either trade-based or aid-based sanctions busting based on the consequences they have.

Busting Sanctions via Trade and Foreign Aid

When a sender imposes economic sanctions against a target state, both parties face uncertainty over what the potential outcome will be. The extent of each party's resolve remains private information, and the costs each party faces in allowing the sanctions to persist can be difficult to judge.[8] Over time, however, the leaders of both parties can gain additional information about the extent of each other's resolve and the associated costs and potential benefits each state has in allowing the sanctions to continue.[9] Assuming that the primary goal of leaders of target states is to stay in power, they will resist sanctioning efforts if conceding to them jeopardizes their political survival and concede to them when costs of resistance threaten their survival even further.[10] If a target's leaders perceive that their current (and potentially future) costs of continuing to resist sanctions outweigh the costs of acquiescing to their sender's demands, they should thus capitulate to them. Similarly, a sender state's leaders should give up their sanctioning efforts if they perceive their chances of success and attendant benefits are outweighed by the prospective costs of maintaining the sanctions. If neither party views the prospective costs of allowing the sanctions to persist as less than the costs of terminating them, then the sanctions will continue in a mutually hurting stalemate. Sender and target leaders will regularly update their costs–benefits analyses of allowing the sanctions to persist based on new information about their opponents' likelihoods of capitulating and the costs associated with allowing the sanctions' persistence.

The extent to which economic sanctions prove costly to both parties will influence their decisions to allow the sanctions to persist or terminate in failure or success. Focusing on the perspective of target states, sanctions inflict commercial damages on their constituents while they do political harm to their leaders and sap governmental resources. Economic sanctions affect their targets' commercial constituencies in a number of ways. Foremost, they disrupt otherwise profitable trade relationships between parties in the target and sender states. This forces target firms to find alternative trade partners, find costly ways of circumventing the sanctions, or experience deadweight losses. Trade sanctions also force target firms to accept diminished terms of trade with the rest of the world in which they are forced to pay more for imports and receive less for their exports.[11] They also experience up-front transaction costs in searching for new trade partners, negotiating new contracts, and ensuring that those new contracts are enforced under conditions wrought with uncertainty.[12] The latter cost can be particularly expensive, as the sender states' sanctions create additional risks of punishment for firms doing business with partners in sanctioned states. The costs these factors impose can extend far beyond the actual sectors being sanctioned and raise the overall cost of doing business within target states. Lastly, economic sanctions can disrupt the broader trade networks and business relationships that target firms participate in with partners from third-party states.[13] The greater the commercial damages the sanctions inflict, the greater the political pressure leaders will be placed under to find ways of mitigating the sanctions' ill effects or ending them altogether.

Beyond just political pressure placed on target states' leaders by the constituencies that are hurt by the sanctions, sanctions can weaken governments. Economic sanctions can diminish the resources available to governments by reducing their customs and tax revenues. Economic sanctions directed toward restricting target governments' access to military or strategic technologies can also disadvantage or weaken them militarily as well as economically. Economic sanctions can also place new strains or make new demands for governmental resources as the affected populations seek redress or compensation for the damages the sanctions do to them. Target leaders thus face the political dissatisfaction of their constituents with diminished resources to be able to meet those demands, potentially jeopardizing their hold on power. As a number of works have shown, however, the leaders of authoritarian regimes are advantaged over those in democratic states in their ability to influence which constituents suffer the most.[14] They can use the state apparatus to shield or provide compensation to their supporters much more effectively than democratic leaders to preserve their base of domestic political support. Even given the incentives of leaders to manipulate the costs imposed by sanctions in self-serving ways, most of the time, target states' leaders and their firms are united in seeking ways to mitigate the negative impact of sanctions on their economies and, ultimately, having them lifted. Obtaining foreign aid or forging strong trade relationships with sanctions busters can help accomplish both goals. Although receiving sanctions-busting assistance from third parties is not the only strategy that target leaders can pursue to help them resist the sanctions imposed against their governments, it may be the most effective.

Undermining Economic Sanctions through Sanctions-Busting Trade

Economic sanctions do harm to both the states that impose them and their targets. Given the United States' preponderance of economic strength over the past sixty years, its sanctions tend to do greater proportional damage to its targets' economies than to its own. Yet just because U.S. sanctions do greater damage to their target's economies does not mean those costs will necessarily be sufficient to convince their target to capitulate. Numerous factors can influence whether the net costs of the sanctions experienced by the targets of U.S. sanctions are greater or less than the gross costs they could be thought to initially inflict. It is the extent of these real economic costs experienced by target states that translates into political pressure on their leaders to capitulate to them. These real costs affect the extent to which sanctions sap their target's governmental resources. For U.S. policy makers, weighing the real costs that their sanctions impose against a target and their perceived chance of success versus the costs the United States bears in maintaining them should heavily influence their decisions to maintain the sanctions or give them up.

To illustrate this point, let's consider a hypothetical example in which the United States has imposed an embargo on $75 million worth of an agricultural product from Nicaragua. The actual damage the embargo would inflict on the Nicaraguan economy would depend on its firms' ability to find alternative destinations for their surplus sanctioned products, the diminished prices they are apt to receive for them, and the transaction costs involved in finding and negotiating those new contracts. Nicaraguan businesses would also face greater transaction costs due to the uncertainty the U.S. sanctions create, as they could be a precursor to harsher unilateral sanctions, multilateral sanctions, or even military action.[15] The U.S. government also has a track record of imposing extraterritorial sanctions on firms and individuals that deliberately violate its sanctions, adding to the risks associated with doing business with Nicaragua.[16] Let's compare two ideal type cases in which the U.S.-imposed embargo would impose minimal versus maximal levels of economic damage on Nicaragua.

In the first case, let's assume that Nicaragua has a number of existing trade partners that could readily absorb the surplus of the embargoed product it possessed, some of whom it possesses close political ties with. In such a scenario, Nicaraguan businesses would have extensive preexisting commercial ties with trade partners in those states that they could turn to in selling the surplus products. Those extensive commercial ties would also make it politically costly for those third-party governments to join the U.S. sanctioning efforts if pressured to do so. This would reduce the uncertainty for both the target and third-party firms of the risks associated with undermining the U.S. sanctions. One of Nicaragua's military allies might also offer to provide its firms with subsidies for buying Nicaraguan products in a show of solidarity with its beleaguered ally. Given these circumstances, Nicaraguan businesses might be able to sell their sanctioned agricultural products for only slightly lower than market prices and with few additional transaction costs. The longer the sanctions persist, the better the deals that Nicaraguan businesses could find and negotiate and the stronger the sanctions-busting relationships with third parties they could develop. The *real* net costs imposed by the U.S. sanctions would thus be much lower than the $75 million per year they might appear to impose on paper.

In the second case, let's assume instead that Nicaragua does not have any significant trade partners that are either *able* or *willing* to expeditiously step in and purchase the agricultural products sanctioned by the U.S. government. At least initially, those products could be left to spoil in storage as exporters frantically searched for new buyers. This would drive them, in turn, to sell their products at heavily discounted rates. In the long run, the difficulties and costs associated with finding alternative buyers could dramatically depress the sanctioned Nicaraguan agricultural sector. It could drive down owners' earnings and laborers' wages and employment opportunities and discourage new investment in the affected agricultural sectors. Aggrieved parties would place political pressure on their government to help them and foment political discontent if it was unable to do so. The Nicaraguan government, already suffering from revenues lost because of the sanctions, would subsequently be burdened with increased demands for its even scarcer resources. Across the board, Nicaraguan businesses would also pay a premium for the sanctions-imposed risks associated with doing business with them. Adjusting to the sanctions in such a case might require a structural shift in the Nicaraguan economy, not just a shift in its trade partners. The net costs of the sanctions in this case could hypothetically run far greater than the $75 million they represent on paper and have an enduring, negative impact on the Nicaraguan economy even after they are lifted.

Comparing the two scenarios, which were based on the exact same set of sanctions imposed by the U.S. government, it is clear that the Nicaraguan government would have far fewer incentives to capitulate in the first case. Assuming that the costs to the U.S. economy remain relatively constant across both the scenarios presented, U.S. policy makers would also then have far fewer incentives to remain committed to their sanctions in the first scenario compared to this second one—once they learned which situation Nicaragua was facing. The ability and willingness of third-party states to bust the U.S. sanctions can thus have a major impact on the real costs the sanctions impose on their target and their likelihoods of success. In particular, the scenarios illustrate that having the support of extensive sanctions busters can play a major role in helping target states mitigate the costs that sanctions impose.

To elaborate further, there are a number of interrelated politically and commercially based reasons to expect that trade-based sanctions busters have a salient impact on the success of sanctioning efforts. Third-party states engage in extensive sanctions-busting trade when they dramatically increase their trade with a target state after it has been sanctioned and in high enough absolute levels to mitigate the damages the sanctions inflict. For firms in target states, concentrating their sanctions adjustment strategies on a small number of states with which they possess relatively strong commercial linkages poses a number of advantages. First, redirecting their trade to preexisting trade partners allows target firms to minimize the search, contracting, and enforcement costs involved in replacing the trade disrupted by the sanctions. The transaction costs involved in finding and developing new business relationships, especially under the cloud of uncertainty created by the sanctions, can otherwise be very expensive—especially if target firms are forced to seek out business with trade partners in previously unfamiliar states. Second, there are gains in efficiency that target firms can obtain from concentrating their efforts to replace their trade via partners in a small number of states. If third-party states already have extensive logistical connections with targets, it will be easier and less costly to absorb additional sanctions-busting trade than to establish new connections. Firms willing and able to specialize in helping the target circumvent sanctions can establish themselves in such states. They can benefit from each other's knowledge, leverage economies of scale that come from drawing on a common logistical support infrastructure, and find safety in being one of many firms undermining the sanctioning efforts. As the sanctions-busting reputations of certain third-party states grow, firms from other third parties might be attracted to shift their business activities to those states. Over time, target firms will concentrate their business on the sanctions-busting partners in third-party countries that provide the most cost-effective means of adjusting to the sanctions. These factors tend to drive sanctions busting toward concentrating among the target's trade partners via which sanctions-busting trade can be conducted most profitably.

For the leaders of target states, having one or more third-party states sanctions-bust on their behalf can dramatically reduce the costs of resisting sanctions. If the affected commercial constituencies can readily adjust to the disruptions and costs sanctions impose, they will associate less discontent with the sanctions and they will make fewer demands on their governments for assistance. If the economic damage of the sanctions is minimized, the budgetary impact of lost customs and trade revenue on target governments will also be minimized. The latter will not always be true, however, depending on the degree to which target firms turn toward the use of black and gray markets to circumvent the sanctions. As authors like Peter Andreas have highlighted, economic sanctions can facilitate the development of transnational criminal networks and governmental corruption to exploit the profitable smuggling opportunities created by sanctions.[17] Yet, if target firms develop ostensibly legitimate sanctions-busting trade relationships with nonparticipant third parties, less trade should be driven to these illicit channels. Possessing the support of extensive sanctions busters thus provides leaders with confidence they can hold out against the demands of sender countries without crippling their economies or destabilizing their grip on power.

The emergence of trade-based sanctions busters on behalf of a target state should alter the perceptions of sender leaders about their sanctions' likelihoods of being successful. If the real costs imposed on target states are minimized by the emergence of one or more sanctions busters, they should know that the incentives that target leaders have to capitulate to their sanctions should be diminished. Especially if the costs borne by sender states in imposing their sanctions are high, this should diminish the incentives that sender states have to maintain their sanctions. As previously noted, the United States is fairly exceptional in that any given set of sanctions it imposes on a target is likely to impose only minimal damage on its overarching economy. Due to

U.S. policy makers' willingness to sanction a multitude of countries at any given time, though, these costs add up in the aggregate. As such, U.S. sanctions should end in failure more often than success when target states receive the assistance of extensive sanctions busters:

> *Sanctions-Busting Trade Hypothesis:* The more third-party states that engage in extensive trade-based sanctions busting on a target state's behalf, the less likely it becomes that the sanctions will be successful.

Affecting Economic Sanctions via Foreign Aid

Whereas sanctions-busting trade has the most direct impact on the commercial constituencies affected by sanctions, foreign aid most strongly affects the governments of target states. Foreign aid flows directly influence the resources available to the leaders of target states that can allow them to assist their adversely affected constituents or compensate for the loss of governmental resources. It has been shown that governments that are recipients of foreign aid can be sensitive to unexpected volatility in the amount they receive,[18] and this should be especially true for sanctioned states. Due to the fungibility of foreign aid, windfall increases in the amount of foreign aid received by states can be used by leaders to compensate their constituents and maintain the loyalty of their supporters in the wake of sanctions. Acquiring increased foreign aid can also positively influence the reputations of leaders, as they can use it to show that they have the support of the international community in spite of the sanctions imposed against their regimes. In contrast, reductions in the amount of foreign aid given to sanctioned governments can exacerbate the damages that the sanctions inflict on their countries. Aid reductions can reduce the already depleted resources available to governments and impose even greater hardships on countries' citizens. This can increase the practical and political pressure on the leaders of target states to concede to the sanctions, especially the extent to which leaders' constituents link the sanctions issue to reductions in foreign aid that their countries are receiving. The foreign aid flows targets receive thus affect their efforts to resist sanctions differently than the ways that sanctions-busting trade influences those efforts.

Target governments can potentially benefit from the foreign aid provided by any third parties, not just those that provide them with extensive support. So rather than solely focusing on the aid flows provided by extensive aid-based sanctions busters, it makes sense to theorize about the trends in the overarching amount of aid targets obtain from the international community. It should be understood, though, that the aid flows provided to target states by aid-based sanctions busters often comprise a substantial portion of the total aid a target receives. Their behavior thus exercises a disproportionately large effect on the aggregate trends in the aid flows directed toward sanctioned states.

The literature on foreign aid remains rather divided on how foreign aid affects the economies, societies, and governments of recipient states. One significant vein of the literature argues that foreign aid can positively contribute to countries' economic growth and development, while another vein argues that foreign aid's overarching effects tend to be negative. Overall, though, the balance of evidence suggests that foreign aid tends to have positive effects on recipients' economies.[19] Where portions of both the foreign aid and sanctions literature converge is in focusing on how survival-focused leaders respond to international stimuli that either destabilize or strengthen their grips on power.[20] There appears to be a consensus that leaders will generally seek to use the foreign aid their governments receive to improve their own domestic grip on political power—to the extent that their political institutions allow them to do so. To varying degrees in authoritarian and democratic states, leaders can use the foreign aid they receive to benefit the political coalition of supporters that keeps them in power. Yet even if aid resources are not used directly for those purposes, Kosack and Tobin point out that most of the foreign aid that states receive is budgetarily fungible.[21] This means that even when foreign aid funds specific projects or services, it frees up the government's resources so that they can be spent elsewhere. In the short term, then, leaders of governments with access to foreign aid have higher levels of resources than they otherwise would—though no guarantee exists that they will be used wisely or to the general population's long-term benefit. At the same time, leaders who lose foreign aid may face significant budgetary shortfalls that can disrupt their ability to govern effectively.[22] Generally speaking, then, fluctuations in the amount of foreign aid states receive can serve as a boon or a bane for their governments depending on whether they involve positive or negative changes in the aid flows they receive. This premise offers a foundation for explaining how changes in the foreign aid flows target states receive can influence sanctions outcomes.

Even more than other recipients of foreign aid, sanctioned states are highly sensitive to changes in the foreign aid flows they receive. Significant foreign aid reductions, or "aid shocks," have highly detrimental effects on aid recipients' economies. They introduce uncertainty into the budget-making process and force recipient governments to deal with unexpected shortfalls. According to research conducted by Homi Kharas, experiencing an aid shock can cause a recipient state to experience an average deadweight loss upward of 1.9 percent of its gross domestic product (GDP).[23] The deleterious effects of economic sanctions on an aid recipient's economy and government can only exacerbate the damages inflicted by sudden aid withdrawals. Reductions in foreign aid should thus magnify the problems posed by scarce governmental resources, increased constituent demands for governmental assistance, and political discontent within their countries. Given that governments rely on foreign aid as a budgetarily fungible resource,[24] if those aid resources are suddenly withdrawn, governments must still find a way to cover their expected expenditures. Reliance on foreign aid may have committed leaders to providing far more extensive governmental programs, subsidies, or rewards to constituents than their governments have the independent capacity to fund. Once a government's constituents have adjusted to a particular level of governmental spending made possible by foreign aid, this sets the baseline expectations for what benefits the constituents expect to receive.[25] If their governments can no longer pay for the benefits that foreign aid once provided, leaders will have to cut those programs or other governmental spending lest they face fiscal insolvency. Such reductions would be apt to raise the ire of their constituents. The additional economic hardship and political costs associated with foreign aid reductions should thus increase the attractiveness of conceding to sanctions to lift the burdens they are similarly inflicting.

Politically, the citizens of sanctioned states may hold their leaders accountable for whether the amount of foreign aid their countries receive declines or rises. Resisting the sanctions can become a prominent domestic political issue, on which leaders stake their political reputations. If the sanctions become highly politicized internationally, a leader's ability to convince other countries to take its side will likely be important. The amount of foreign aid a target state receives is one measure of whether the international community supports it or the sender state more. A decline in foreign aid could signal to a target state's constituents that its leaders are losing the international political fight regarding the sanctions issue. Although the extent to which leaders' constituents will tie reductions in their foreign aid to the sanctions issue is subject to variation, that linkage may intensify the domestic political pressure on leaders to acquiesce to the sanctions.

Conversely, sanctioned states receiving an influx of additional foreign aid should be able to mitigate the damage caused by the sanctions. New foreign aid can be used to make up governmental resource deficits caused by the sanctions, either directly or indirectly. Leaders can also direct foreign aid toward politically important constituencies to ease the hardships sanctions impose on them. For example, the North Korean government has made it notoriously difficult for international aid providers, such as the World Food Programme, to track whether the substantial amount of food assistance they provide actually reaches its intended recipients.[26] In 2005, Noland and Haggard offered conservative estimates that approximately 10 to 30 percent of the food aid given to North Korea was subject to diversion.[27] Surveys of North Korean refugees have further suggested that a substantial portion of the North Korean population has never received access to international food aid and that, among those aware of the program, the vast majority of those interviewed thought that the North Korean military establishment was the primary recipient of such aid.[28] The food aid that North Korea received from the international community also freed up a substantial pool of resources that the regime had previously spent on food imports. From 1999 through 2005, over 90 percent of the food imported into North Korea was supplied via foreign aid as opposed to commercial purchase.[29] International food assistance has thus allowed the North Korean regime to ensure the welfare of its loyal military supporters while freeing up its budget to pursue other prerogatives that have helped it survive the sanctions imposed against it. This suggests that, even in the case of foreign aid given chiefly for humanitarian purposes, recipient governments can exploit such aid as part of their sanctions resistance efforts.

For the leaders of target states, foreign aid increases are analogous to windfall gains that can be used to preserve their political power and resist sanctioning efforts.[30] Even though countries' foreign aid inflows tend to be significantly smaller than their international trade flows, dollar-for-dollar aid can be much more useful for mitigating the commercial and political damages inflicted by sanctions. Indeed, Amanda Licht finds evidence that donors are more likely to provide foreign aid to distressed regimes for the purpose of helping their leaders maintain their grip on power.[31] Thus, it could be expected that donors that increase their foreign aid to countries *after* they have been sanctioned would be tolerant of having recipient leaders use that aid in politically self-serving ways. Foreign aid increases thus strengthen leaders' abilities to resist the sanctions imposed against their countries.

Similar to how experiencing the loss of foreign aid can hurt leaders' reputations during sanctions, increasing the amount of foreign aid their countries receive can enhance their domestic reputations. Leaders who increase the foreign aid their countries receive can use that achievement to demonstrate their effectiveness at standing firm against the sanctions. Courting specific donors to provide foreign aid can be a high-profile endeavor for the leaders of target states. It serves as a way for leaders to demonstrate to their citizens that they are actively doing something to counter the sanctions. By obtaining significant aid surpluses, target leaders can also discourage sender leaders about their sanctions' prospects for success. So beyond just the practical value that foreign aid windfalls can provide, they can help foster the perception that target leaders are succeeding in their sanctions resistance efforts.

All these factors suggest that the success of sanctioning efforts is linked to the volatility of the foreign aid flows that target states receive. When a target state receives greater than expected levels of foreign aid, its leaders' domestic political position should be strengthened and they should be less likely to capitulate to sanctions. Cognizant of their sanctions' diminished chances of success and of the international opposition to their sanctioning efforts that the aid increases signal, U.S. policy makers should be more likely to abandon their sanctions when targets receive substantial foreign aid increases. Conversely, reductions in the amount of foreign aid received by target states should exacerbate economic damages inflicted by the sanctions and increase the political pressure on target leaders to capitulate to them. Observing the hardships experienced by target leaders, U.S. policy makers should remain committed to their sanctioning efforts. This gives rise to the following hypothesis concerning the effects of foreign aid on sanctions success:

> *Foreign Aid Hypothesis:* When the amount of foreign aid target states receive in
> a given year increases, the sanctions imposed against them are less likely to be
> successful, and when the amount of foreign aid target states receive in a given
> year declines, they are more likely to be successful.

Assessing the Impact of Sanctions-Busting Trade and Aid

This section evaluates the impact of third-party sanctions busting on the success and failure of U.S. economic sanctions. The analysis explores the effects of sanctions-busting trade and foreign aid on the outcome of ninety-six episodes of U.S.-imposed sanctions from 1950 through 2002. This set of cases, which is drawn from the Hufbauer and his coauthors' data set, focuses on the politically motivated economic sanctions that the U.S. government has imposed on sixty-three different target states.[32] It represents a sample of sanctions episodes from both during and after the Cold War, which ensures that structural factors alone are not driving the results. To analyze the factors correlated with sanctions outcomes, this chapter employs a competing risks analysis capable of assessing the variables that influence the likelihoods of sanctions persisting in a stalemate or ending in success or failure within a given year.[33] The approach models sanctions episodes as events that unfold over time and that are influenced by dynamic factors. It provides the means to assess, on a yearly basis, which factors influenced the decisions made by U.S. and target policy makers to either maintain the sanctions or terminate them. This analysis can test whether extensive sanctions busting and foreign aid volatility are both linked to the outcomes of U.S. sanctioning efforts.

Modeling the Success and Failure of Economic Sanctions

Sanctions disputes can be viewed as ongoing processes in which targets and senders regularly evaluate whether allowing the sanctions to persist is in their interests.[34] For the competing risks analysis, sanctions episodes are broken down into yearly observations for which one of three categorical outcomes exist: The sanctions persist in a stalemate, the sanctions terminate in failure, or the sanctions terminate in success. Observations for individual sanctions episodes are coded as stalemates on a yearly basis until the year in which they terminate in success or failure, after which the terminated episodes exit the data set. Data from Hufbauer and his coauthors are used to code whether sanctions episodes ended in success or failure. Their approach measures the extent to which senders' sanctions achieved the goals for which they were imposed and the contributions that the sanctions made to those efforts. For a sanctions episode to be coded as at least partially successful, the sanctions must have obtained a moderately successful policy result when they were terminated and the sanctions had to have played a partially decisive role in obtaining that positive outcome.[35] The *Sanctions Outcome* dependent variable used in the analysis codes yearly observations in which sanctions persist as *Stalemate*, observations in which U.S. sanctions terminate in at least a partial success as *Success*, and observations in which sanctions otherwise terminate as *Failure*. This allows for the comparative likelihoods of each yearly outcome to be analyzed over time.

Because both the level of sanctions-busting trade and foreign aid fluctuate over the course of a sanctions regime, both are coded as dynamically changing variables. Extensive trade-based sanctions busters are third-party states that respond to sanctions by significantly increasing their trade with the target state and in high enough absolute levels to substitute for the trade losses entailed by the sanctions. To operationalize this variable, a data set of third-party trade with target states was compiled for each year in which the United States had sanctions in place against a target state for each of the ninety-six sanctions episodes. Yearly data on target states' imports from and exports to third-party states in millions of current-year U.S. dollars were obtained from the *Correlates of War Bilateral Trade* data set.[36] Observations in which third parties' exports to or imports from the target increased by more than 5 percent relative to the previous year were then identified. Next, the yearly observations in which a target's bilateral trade with a third party constituted at least 5 percent of a target's total yearly trade were also flagged. Using these indicators, a new variable was created to flag those observation years in which a target state experienced at least a 5 percent spike in its imports or exports with a third-party trade partner that also accounted for at least 5 percent of its overall trade. All subsequent years in which a third party's imports and/or exports with a target continued to grow relative to the previous year and its share of the target's trade remained above 5 percent were also flagged to denote that the sanctions-busting behavior persisted. These procedures create a dynamic variable (*Trade-Based Sanctions Busting*) that indicates which third parties engaged in extensive sanctions-busting on behalf of a target during any given year U.S. sanctions were in place.

Whereas the *Trade-Based Sanctions Busting* variable will be the subject of Chapter 6's analysis, an aggregate measure of the total sanctions busting conducted on a target's behalf is needed for the current analysis. The variable *Trade-Based Busters* is coded as the three-year running average of the total number of third-party states engaging in trade-based sanctions busting on a target's behalf to denote the cumulative, near-term effects of the support target states receive from trade-based sanctions busters. This variable provides a measure of the total amount of sanctions-busting assistance a target has recently received, which can influence the target and sender states' decisions of whether to concede or allow the sanctions dispute to persist. *Trade-Based Busters* should have a negative effect on the likelihood of sanctions terminating in success.[37]

To test the hypothesis concerning the effects of foreign aid volatility, a dynamic measure of how the foreign aid inflows target states receive change on a yearly basis is needed. While Official Development Assistance (ODA) does not capture all of the types of assistance third-party states can provide to targets (such as military assistance), it is the broadest measure of foreign aid for which global historical data are available. Generally, though, ODA is recognized as a fairly representative measure of the foreign aid inflows states receive.[38] Target states' foreign aid inflows are coded using a net measure of the total amount of ODA they receive in a given year, minus the interest they paid on concessional loans and the cancellation of non-ODA loans.[39] This approach best reflects the actual foreign aid flows received by target states and prevents the occurrence of large, one-off debt cancellations from skewing the measure.[40] The variable Δ *Aid Flow* is coded as the difference in current-year dollars of the net aid target states receive during a given year of analysis relative to the previous one. According to Kharas, measuring the differences in aid flows is the best method of capturing the effects of foreign aid volatility.[41] Δ *Aid Flow* should have a negative effect on the likelihood of sanctions terminating in success.

In addition to the main independent variables, a number of additional variables could also influence sanctions outcomes. It could be expected that economic sanctions will be less effective against countries with better-developed economies. To account for the level of economic development within target states (*Target Economic Development*), a logarithmically transformed version of the target's GDP per capita value is included within the model. To account for the regime type of the target, a dummy variable (*Target Democracy*) is included to denote whether the target is a democracy. Following a general practice, data from the *Polity IV* Project is used to identify the degree to which countries' formal political institutions are democratic.[42] Because the United States is always coded as a democracy in the period analyzed, *Target Democracy* accounts for the effects of a target state's regime type when it is being sanctioned by a democracy.

Several other political variables could also potentially affect the outcomes of sanctioning efforts. As alliance relationships between sender and target states have previously been shown to influence sanctions outcomes, the model includes a dichotomous variable that denotes whether the United States possessed a defense pact (*U.S. Defense Pact*) with the target in a given year during the sanctions.[43] Beyond just the military relationships that exist between the

United States and the targets of its sanctions, their prior political relationship could also shape the likelihood of sanctions being successful. To account for this factor, the model employs Hufbauer and his coauthors' three-point ordinal *Prior Relations* variable, in which a 1 denotes antagonistic relationship, a 2 denotes a neutral relationship, and a 3 denotes a congenial relationship.[44] Especially as this study focuses exclusively on U.S. economic sanctions, it is important to control for the structural effects of system polarity. One might expect that, in becoming the world's lone superpower following the Cold War's conclusion, the U.S. economic sanctions might have become more effective. It is also notable that the United States' use of economic sanctions also increased dramatically during the 1990s.[45] The variable *Post–Cold War* codes the years prior to and including 1991 as 0s and as 1s in the following years.

Lastly, the model controls for the characteristics of the sanctions employed by the United States using variables that denote the amount of international cooperation the United States received in imposing them, whether the sanctioning effort received the support of an international organization, and the salience of the goals sought by the sanctions. *U.S. Cooperation* is a four-point ordinal variable, coded with a 1 denoting that the U.S. efforts received no international support and a 4 denoting that they received extensive international cooperation.[46] *IO Support* is coded dichotomously to denote whether an international organization supported the sanctioning efforts against the target. To account for how salient a goal the United States seeks to achieve with its sanctions, Hufbauer and his coauthors' *Modest Goal* dummy variable is employed. It distinguishes between the instances in which the United States sought to obtain modest policy changes from the target with its sanctions, as opposed to pursuing more challenging objectives.[47] U.S. sanctions should be more likely to be effective when they seek more limited policy changes. Although various other explanatory factors exist, this core set of variables should control for most of the potentially confounding factors that could influence the hypotheses being tested.[48]

Analyzing the Results

This section presents the results from the statistical analysis on how sanctions busting affects the outcomes of U.S. sanctioning efforts. Table 3.1 depicts the results of models run using a multinomial logit estimator with standard errors clustered by individual sanctions episodes.[49] The main analysis focuses on the impact that trade-based sanctions busters and foreign aid flows have on the comparative likelihood that sanctions will terminate in success or failure. In addition, the effects that sanctions busting has on duration of sanctioning efforts are also discussed. To control for temporal dependence, a count variable (*Time*) for the number of years that sanctions have been in place during a particular sanctions episode and the variable's squared (*Time²*) and cubed (*Time³*) values are included in the analyses.[50] To demonstrate the findings' robustness across various specifications, results of five different models are depicted in Table 3.1. Models 1 and 2 show the results for the *Trade-Based*

TABLE 3.1. Analysis of U.S. economic sanctions outcomes; comparing the likelihoods of termination in success versus failure.

	Model 1	Model 2	Model 3	Model 4	Model 5
Trade-Based Busters	−0.240*	−0.353**			−0.422***
	(0.123)	(0.158)			(0.164)
Δ Foreign Aid			−0.022***	−0.017*	−0.018**
			(0.007)	(0.009)	(0.009)
Target Economic Development		−1.002**		−1.001**	−1.019**
		(0.397)		(0.418)	(0.412)
Target Democracy		−0.375		−0.105	−0.166
		(0.669)		(0.691)	(0.669)
U.S. Defense Pact		0.195		0.358	0.211
		(0.677)		(0.731)	(0.724)
Modest Goal		1.580**		1.414**	1.368**
		(0.624)		(0.683)	(0.653)
Prior Relations		1.426***		1.251**	1.238**
		(0.452)		(0.505)	(0.502)
U.S. Cooperation		−0.214		−0.089	−0.113
		(0.386)		(0.407)	(0.419)
IO Support		0.560		0.880	0.777
		(0.757)		(0.797)	(0.791)
Post-Cold War		−0.494		−0.619	−0.594
		(0.772)		(0.815)	(0.815)
Time	−0.078	−0.044	−0.064	0.274	0.428
	(0.182)	(0.782)	(0.179)	(0.793)	(0.829)
Time²	0.002	0.078	0.004	0.027	0.014
	(0.013)	(0.149)	(0.013)	(0.147)	(0.153)
Time³	−0.000	−0.007	−0.000	−0.004	−0.004
	(0.000)	(0.008)	(0.000)	(0.008)	(0.008)
Constant	0.396	3.921	−0.472	2.405	3.649
	(0.629)	(3.295)	(0.507)	(3.593)	(3.608)
Prob. χ²	0.000	0.000	0.000	0.000	0.000
Observations	840	787	813	760	760

Clustered standard errors are included below the variable coefficients in parentheses. Asterisks (*, **, and ***) denote statistical significance at the 90 percent, 95 percent, and 99 percent confidence levels using one-tailed tests.

Busters both excluding and including the control variables, whereas Models 3 and 4 do the same for Δ *Foreign Aid*. Model 5 depicts the results of running the analysis with *Trade-Based Busters*, Δ *Foreign Aid*, and the full set of controls.

The results depicted in Table 3.1 can be interpreted as follows. Coefficients are reported for the variables used in each model along with their clustered standard errors below in parentheses. Positive coefficients indicate that an increase in the variable's value makes sanctioning efforts more likely to terminate in success than failure in a given year, whereas negative results indicate the opposite effect. The coefficients that have statistically significant effects on how sanctioning efforts terminate are identified with asterisks. The results pertaining to *Trade-Based Busters* and Δ *Foreign Aid* in all five models are consistent with the sanctions-busting theory's hypotheses concerning their impact on the success and failure of sanctioning efforts.[51]

Looking first at the impact of trade-based sanctions busting on sanctions outcomes, the *Trade-Based Busters* variable exercises a negative and statistically significant effect on the likelihood of sanctions terminating in success as opposed to failure in a given year. It is important to note that *Trade-Based Busters* retains its statistical significance when Δ *Foreign Aid* is included in Model 5. This indicates that the amount of sanctions-busting trade a target receives exercises effects on sanctions outcomes that are distinct from those of foreign aid. Substantively, having the support of trade-based sanctions busters also has a significant impact on sanctioning efforts' likelihoods of success or failure. Under a scenario in which the amount of foreign aid a target receives does not change,[52] the predicted probability of economic sanctions terminating in failure in a given year increases by roughly 7 percent for every one-unit increase in *Trade-Based Busters*. Trade-based sanctions busters have an even more dramatic effect on the likelihood of achieving success in a given year. Comparing a scenario in which a target has one trade-based sanctions buster versus one in which the target has none, the likelihood of the sanctions succeeding in that given year is 30 percent lower if the target has the support of just that single sanctions buster. Making the comparison using three trade-based sanctions busters instead of just one, the predicted probability of success is 66 percent lower than if the target received no sanctions-busting support. The presence of trade-based sanctions busters thus modestly increases the likelihood of sanctions failing in a given year, but their presence has a

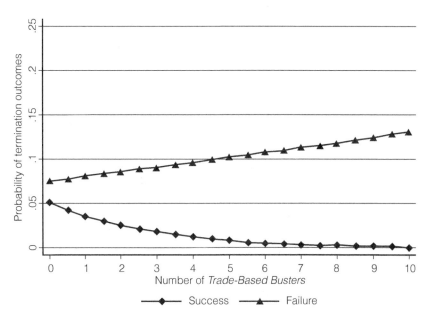

FIGURE 3.1. The marginal effects of *Trade-Based Busters* on the probabilities of success and failure.

potent, negative effect on the sanctioning efforts' likelihood of succeeding. Figure 3.1 provides a clear graphical illustration of these trends. Although the absolute levels of change in the predicted probabilities of success and failure may appear low, it is valuable to remember that these probabilities relate to the likelihood of success or failure in a given year. Over time, the corrosive effects of trade-based sanctions busters can make sanctioning efforts significantly more likely to end in failure than they otherwise would. The results thus support the hypothesis that the presence of extensive sanctions busters has a negative impact on their effectiveness.

Turning now to Δ *Foreign Aid*, it exercises negative and statistically significant effects on the likelihood of sanctions ending in success versus failure across all the models in which it is included.[53] This indicates that the sanctions imposed against target states become more likely to fail when they receive windfall foreign aid surpluses in a given year. Conversely, sanctioning efforts are more likely to succeed when targets experience sharp declines in the amount of foreign aid they receive. Figure 3.2 illustrates the substantive effects of Δ *Foreign Aid* on the predicted probabilities of sanctions terminating

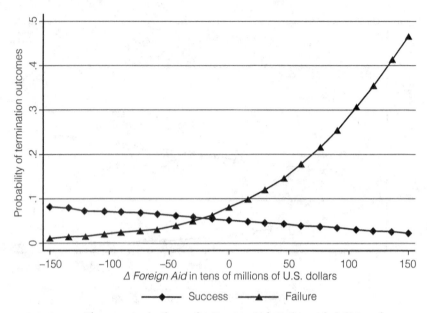

FIGURE 3.2. The marginal effects of Δ *Foreign Aid* on the probabilities of success and failure.

in success or failure.[54] The graph shows that Δ *Foreign Aid* has the more salient impact on the likelihood of sanctions failing, especially as the amount of
surplus aid received by target increases. A one-standard-deviation increase in
Δ *Foreign Aid* relative to 0 (approximately $230 million) leads to a 41 percent
increased likelihood of the sanctions failing in a given year. Conversely, a one-
standard-deviation reduction in Δ *Foreign Aid* relative to 0 diminishes the
likelihood of sanctions failing by 30 percent. Examining the effects of Δ *Foreign Aid* on a sanctioning effort's chances of success instead, a one-standard-
deviation increase in the variable relative to 0 causes the sanctions' likelihood
of succeeding in a given year to decline by 9 percent. A one-standard deviation reduction in Δ *Foreign Aid* relative to 0 has the reverse effect, increasing
the likelihood of the sanctions succeeding in a given year by 9 percent. So,
whereas Δ *Foreign Aid* has a rather linear effect on the likelihood of sanctions succeeding, its effects on sanctions failure grow magnitudes stronger
the greater the foreign aid surpluses that target states receive. Overall, these
findings offer strong support for the second hypothesis. They suggest, however, that restricting the foreign aid received by sanctioned states plays a

larger role in preventing the sanctions' failure than necessarily in achieving their success.

These findings indicate that the amount of external support target states receive from third parties profoundly affects the outcomes of sanctioning efforts. The amounts of sanctions-busting trade and foreign aid that sanctioned states obtain can each play distinct roles in shaping whether sanctions succeed or fail. Target states seeking to resist and defeat the sanctions imposed against them can rely on one or both methods as part of their strategies. Their combined effects are greater than the effects of either one in isolation. By increasing both *Trade-Based Busters* and Δ *Foreign Aid* by one standard deviation above 0 in a typical scenario, the predicted probability of the sanctions ending in success during that year would decline by 48 percent and their likelihood of failure would rise by 55 percent. It is also important to note that changes in *Trade-Based Busters* and Δ *Foreign Aid* can offset one another. As such, target states that respond to foreign aid cuts by forming additional sanctions-busting trade relationships may not be at greater risk of capitulating. Both types of external support can be employed in a complementary fashion to defeat sanctioning efforts, but target state leaders can rely exclusively on one or the other if need be. Sanctions-busting trade and aid are not perfect substitutes for one another, however.

Beyond just their impact on the comparative likelihoods of success versus failure, the competing risks model also sheds light on how *Trade-Based Busters* and Δ *Foreign Aid* affect sanctions' likelihoods of persisting in stalemate. In additional results yielded by Model 5, *Trade-Based Busters* is also shown to exercise a negative and statistically significant effect on the likelihood of sanctions terminating in success as opposed to persisting in a stalemate. The variable does not, however, significantly affect the likelihood of sanctions failing as opposed to persisting. This indicates that, the more trade-based sanctions busters a target has supporting it, the more likely sanctions are to persist unsuccessfully. Assuming that sanctions have been in place for three years, shifting *Trade-Based Busters* from 0 to 3 increases the likelihood of sanctions persisting in a stalemate by 2 percent. In contrast, Δ *Foreign Aid* has a positive and statistically significant effect on sanctions terminating in failure compared to persisting in stalemate but does not significantly impact sanctions' likelihoods of success versus stalemate. Assuming that sanctions have been in place for three years, a one-standard-deviation increase in Δ *Foreign Aid* relative to 0 reduces the likelihood of sanctions continuing to persist in a

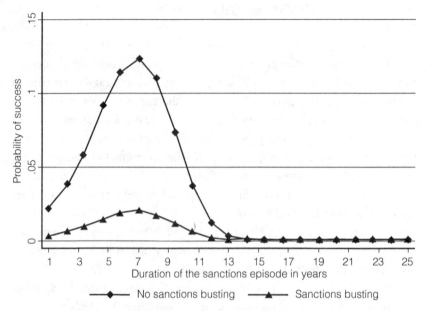

FIGURE 3.3. Sanctions busting's impact on the likelihood of success over time.

stalemate by 3 percent. This means that foreign aid increases exercise a potent effect on sanctions' likelihood of failing, reducing both the comparative chances of sanctions terminating in success and persisting in a stalemate.

The substantive effects of sanctions busting on sanctioning efforts' likelihoods of succeeding or failing over time can best be illustrated graphically. In Figures 3.3 and 3.4, the same otherwise typical scenarios as presented earlier are used to illustrate the differences in likely termination outcomes between a case in which a target receives no sanctions-busting support versus one in which it receives a fixed, moderate amount of both aid-based and trade-based sanctions-busting support. Figure 3.3 indicates that U.S. sanctioning efforts are substantially more likely to achieve success over the first thirteen years they are in place if the target receives no sanctions-busting support. The substantial gap between the two nonbusting and moderate sanctions-busting cases illustrates the strong negative effects that *Trade-Based Busters* exercises on sanctioning efforts' likelihoods of success. After about thirteen years, however, the marginal impact that sanctions busting has on sanctions' chances of succeeding diminishes to negligible levels. This reflects that, overall, sanctions

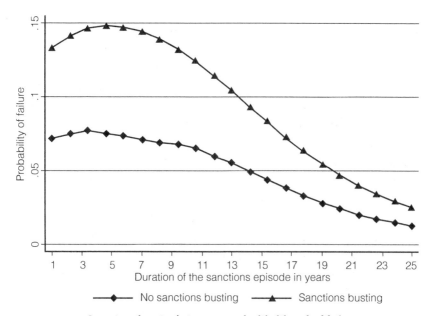

FIGURE 3.4. Sanctions busting's impact on the likelihood of failure over time.

become far less likely to succeed after they have persisted for long periods of time because their targets have effectively adjusted to them.[55]

The effects of sanctions busting on sanctioning efforts' likelihood of failure over time are illustrated in Figure 3.4. As the graph reveals, the case in which the target receives moderate amounts of sanctions-busting aid and trade is significantly more likely to fail even over the course of very long sanctions episodes. The gap between the two scenarios in this case reflects the stronger effects that Δ *Foreign Aid* exercises on sanctioning efforts' likelihood of failing. Although the substantive significance Δ *Foreign Aid* also diminishes the longer sanctions persist, its effects still remain fairly significant even after the sanctions have been in place for twenty-five years.

Substantively, these analyses indicate the external support that the targets of U.S. economic sanctions receive plays a significant role in undercutting their effectiveness. The evidence suggests that trade-based sanctions busters and foreign aid surpluses considerably reduce the likelihood of sanctions succeeding in a given year although they modestly increase their likelihood of failing. Sanctions-busting trade and foreign aid surpluses thus prevent

U.S. sanctions from succeeding and contribute to their eventual failure. This means that busted sanctioning efforts are more likely to linger in costly, unproductive stalemates before U.S. policy makers finally give up on them in most cases. It does suggest, however, that U.S. sanctions can be made somewhat more effective by restricting the amount of foreign aid targets receive.

For the leaders of target states, a clear imperative exists to obtain as much external support as they can in response to being sanctioned. They can do this by either cultivating stronger commercial relationships with existing trade partners or seeking to acquire the patronage of foreign governments or the international community. The findings indicate that the most effective strategies for resisting economic sanctions entail a combination of acquiring increasingly generous foreign aid packages and encouraging multiple states to become trade-based sanctions busters on their behalf. The leaders of target states will often prefer receiving foreign aid over sanctions-busting trade because it provides them with the greatest flexibility in shaping their responses to sanctions. To obtain the foreign assistance they seek, target leaders will be constrained by their countries' commercial attractiveness as a foreign trade partner in seeking to encourage the emergence of extensive sanctions busters. They will be similarly constrained by their international reputations and portfolio of political relationships in seeking to acquire new sources of foreign aid. And lastly, target leaders must also often compete with the sender government(s) in influencing whether third parties adopt policies that support or undercut the sanctioning efforts. Explaining why some countries choose to sanctions-bust on target states' behalves while others do not—and which methods they use—is thus central to understanding the strategies target leaders can and should pursue in responding to sanctions.

Lastly, the results from Table 3.1 indicate several other factors that affect the outcomes of U.S. sanctioning efforts. First, the results indicate that U.S. sanctions are much more successful when they are imposed in pursuit of modest policy goals. *Modest Goal* has positive and statistically significant effects across all the models in which it is included. This finding is rather intuitive: Sanctions imposed to drive the leaders of target states out of power or end the military adventurism of foreign governments seek concessions that may be too great to make acquiescing to them acceptable. In those cases, leaders will tend to bear the costs of sanctions—even if they are extremely costly. Secondly, the results also indicate that U.S. sanctions will tend to be more effective against friends than foes. *Prior Relations* has a positive and statistically significant effect across all three models it is included in. This indicates that the U.S. government tends to be more successful in sanctioning states with which it has positive relationships compared to adversaries. Because adversaries potentially have more to lose vis-à-vis the United States by acquiescing to its sanctions, it makes sense that they would strive harder to resist them. Lastly, the findings indicated that the higher the level of economic development within a target state, the less likely that U.S. sanctions will be successful against it. The variable *Target Economic Development* has robust, negative effects on the likelihood of sanctions terminating in success compared to failure across all three models. This suggests that U.S. sanctions are much less effective against wealthier countries than when used against less-developed states. No other factors included in the models were statistically significant.

Conclusion

This chapter has argued that the amount and type of foreign assistance that target states receive from third parties can heavily influence economic sanctions' success. Economic sanctions work by inflicting salient enough costs on their targets that acquiescing to the sanctioner's demands becomes a more attractive option for target leaders than resisting them. Trade-based sanctions busters and increasingly generous foreign aid packages can help target states mitigate the aggregate harms they experience as a result of being sanctioned. Whereas sanctions-busting trade directly alleviates the economic damages sanctions inflict on a target's commercial constituencies, foreign aid surpluses provide the leaders of target governments with discretionary resources in alleviating the economic damages and attendant political fallout from sanctions. Both methods of sanctions busting can be used individually or used in conjunction with one another to help target states resist the sanctions imposed against them.

The findings from the statistical analyses reveal that the number of states that engage in extensive sanctions-busting trade on a target state's behalf and the volatility in the foreign aid flows they receive profoundly affect sanctions outcomes. The more states that sanctions-bust on a target's behalf, the less likely it becomes that sanctions will end in success and the more likely it becomes that they will end in failure. For U.S. policy makers, this means that preventing the emergence of trade-based sanctions busters is crucial to allowing their sanctions to have any meaningful chance of success. With respect to the provision of foreign aid, target states that receive significant influxes of foreign aid become much less likely to capitulate to sanctions and sender states become much more likely to abandon their sanctioning efforts when targets experience dramatic increases in their foreign aid flows. When target states face significant foreign aid reductions, though, their likelihood of acquiescing to sanctions increases and the senders' likelihood of abandoning them declines. This suggests that U.S. policy makers can forestall their sanctions' failure by preventing target states from receiving large influxes of new aid and contribute to their sanctions' success by cutting target states off from existing aid flows. This chapter has been agnostic as to sources of the foreign aid that targets receive, but the rest of the book focuses on explaining why third-party states occasionally provide targets with extensive amounts of foreign aid.

Although this chapter has shown that limiting the amount of external support target states receive is a critical determinant of whether sanctioning efforts succeed, the findings thus far offer little indication for how that can be accomplished. To respond to the challenges posed by sanctions busting, a clearer understanding of why third-party states sanctions-bust via trade and aid is needed. By understanding the motives that drive third-party sanctions busting, senders can then develop strategies to prevent it, disrupt it, or make it too costly to engage in. At the same time, this knowledge cuts both ways. Target states can use it to optimize their strategies for leveraging sanctions-busting assistance to help them defeat economic sanctions. Because the survival of regimes like those in Iraq, Iran, and North Korea has depended on their ability to circumvent the sanctions imposed against them, it could be expected that they are already privy to a great deal of practical knowledge on the subject and that sender governments are the ones behind the learning curve. The next four chapters explore the reasons why third-party states engage in sanctions busting via trade and foreign aid and how, from a practical perspective, those relationships between target and third-party states operate.

4 For Profits or Politics?

Why Third Parties Sanctions-Bust via Trade and Aid

THIS CHAPTER EXTENDS THE PREVIOUSLY DEVELOPED sanctions-busting theory to explain why only a limited number of states engage in extensive sanctions busting and which approach they use.[1] Whereas commercial motivations play a dominant role in motivating sanctions-busting trade, political and ideological factors largely motivate the provision of foreign aid. It is theorized that the latter option is also used only if employing sanctions-busting trade is not a viable option. Given a choice between assisting target states via profitable trade versus costly aid, even politically motivated third-party governments should prefer to use a trade-based approach. As such, instances in which third-party governments bankroll robust efforts to assist target states in defeating sanctions are relatively rare in comparison to trade-based sanctions busting.

For third-party states, the interplay between how economic sanctions affect their governments and their constituents influences whether they sanctions-bust and which approach they employ. When third-party leaders have a political interest in undercutting the effectiveness of sanctioning efforts against a target state, that can enhance their constituents' incentives to engage in trade-based sanctions busting on the target's behalf. At the same time, the profitability of sanctions-busting trade for a third-party state's constituents also influences whether its government can effectively use trade to assist a target state or whether it must instead employ foreign aid. Thus, it is necessary to understand both whether target governments have a political interest in sanctions busting on a target state's behalf and the extent of their constituencies' ability to do so via market-based trade. These factors help determine which third-party states engage in extensive sanctions-busting trade on a target state's behalf and, more rarely, which ones might offer the target their patronage via foreign aid.

This chapter proceeds by first explaining the various ways that sanctions disputes between target and sender states can spill over to affect third-party states. This serves as the foundation for developing an overarching account of what motivates third parties to sanctions-bust via trade or aid. The extension of the sanctions-busting theory developed in this chapter provides a cohesive explanation of why certain third parties undermine sanctioning efforts and the factors that affect its general prevalence during sanctioning efforts. By gaining a better understanding of what motivates the various types of sanctions-busting behavior, actionable insights can be gleaned that can be used to address the challenges that it poses to the success of sanctioning efforts.

How Economic Sanctions Affect Third Parties

Economic sanctions can have profound political and economic effects on third-party states. Target and sender governments, for example, may seek to actively influence the policies that third-party governments adopt, rewarding or punishing them for their responses. From a commercial perspective, economic sanctions can have broadly disruptive effects on the foreign trade that targets conduct with third parties. These disruptive effects and the transaction costs they impose can serve to make the trade relationships that some third parties have with the target more profitable and others less profitable. Market forces will drive firms to respond to the new commercial environment created by the sanctions by shifting their business to or growing their business in those third-party states from which sanctions-busting trade with target states can be conducted the most profitably. Third-party states are subject to these broad economic consequences of sanctions even if their governments take no active role in supporting one side or the other. They are affected differently by the sanctions imposed against a target state, though, depending on a combination of political and economic factors.

Focusing first on the foreign policy pressures that sanctions place on third-party governments, both target and sender governments have incentives to seek third-party support during sanctions disputes. As the previous chapter demonstrates, the leaders of target governments possess significant incentives to seek third-party support in defeating the sanctions imposed against them. In most cases, targets end up paying at least some political or economic costs for the sanctions-busting support they receive from third parties. In some cases, though, leaders of target governments can leverage their relationships with friendly third-party states to obtain sanctions-busting assistance either as a gesture of goodwill or by framing the sanctions' defeat as a matter of common interest. Target governments can also use the economic and/or political clout they possess over third parties to compel their sanctions-busting assistance. For example, the apartheid regime in South Africa forced its land-locked neighbors, Botswana and Zimbabwe, to engage in sanctions-busting trade on its behalf despite their governments' support for the sanctions. It did so by threatening to restrict those countries' access to vital South African ports that linked their economies to the rest of the world.[2] Lastly, target leaders can exploit third-party governments' interests in having the sanctions fail. If both the target and third-party states share a common military or ideological rivalry with the sender, that could help motivate third parties to sanctions-bust on their behalf. To the extent that target leaders expend their political energies on obtaining third-party assistance, their efforts should focus on those states most capable of and amenable to providing them with sanctions-busting support.

Though previous findings have been mixed on whether having multilateral support for sanctioning efforts makes them more successful,[3] sender governments still frequently seek to obtain international cooperation for their sanctions. Sender governments may seek the limited cooperation of a few key states or the cooperation of entire international organizations.[4] Because imposing economic sanctions can be politically and economically costly for third-party governments, sender governments will often face significant challenges in convincing them to participate. In terms of the recruitment strategies open to senders, inducement-laden approaches tend to be more costly than coercive ones because they involve definitive payments to third parties. Coercive strategies that rely on threats and arm twisting may incur few actual costs if the sender does not have to follow through on them. As such, coercive strategies that make the perceived costs of not participating more painful than doing so are often the only cost-effective way of convincing third-party governments to participate. Indeed, Lisa Martin demonstrates that the use of coercion is central to sender governments' ability to obtain multilateral support for their sanctions.[5] Given that the participation of any third-party state will—at best—only marginally improve the sanctions' likelihood of success, the costs entailed in recruiting such participation often outweigh the potential benefits achieved by it. In general, sender states will avoid incurring greater costs in recruiting the participation of third parties than they expect to gain from such cooperation. This suggests that senders employ coercion selectively, using it only when its benefits outweigh its costs.[6] Yet, even when the costs of compelling third parties to participate in sanctioning efforts is too expensive, sender governments may still have incentives to use coercive measures to disincentivize extensive sanctions busting by nonparticipants.

Although sender governments may apply pressure to third-party governments to abide by their sanctions, the pressure applied by sender firms may actually be just the opposite. Because the sanctions imposed by sender governments disrupt the profitable trade relationships their firms had with target trade partners, those firms may want to maintain those ties. Because firms are almost entirely motivated by the pursuit of profits, they tend to have a divergent set of interests from those of their governments when they impose sanctions. In response, sender firms may directly violate their governments' sanctions if they perceive their chances of being caught and/or the severity of punishments as acceptable given the benefits of sanctions busting.[7] Alternatively, they may seek to violate the spirit of the sanctions by working with partners in third-party states to facilitate sanctions-busting transactions or shifting their business to third-party venues where such trade is not illegal. Sender governments can make such behavior illegal, but in many cases they do not. Thus, sender firms sometimes work at cross-purposes with their governments' sanctions policies, and this can influence third-party trade with target states.

Economic sanctions can inflict costly disruptions on third-party states' commerce and create additional transaction costs on the business their firms conduct with target states,[8] but they can also create lucrative sanctions-busting opportunities for those states well-situated to exploit those opportunities. The economic sanctions imposed against target states disrupt or prevent their senders' firms from engaging in otherwise profitable trade with partners in the target state. The initial disruptions that are caused by the sanctions can ripple out to directly affect third parties' trade with the target state or other third parties and sender states.[9] For example, if a product manufactured in a target state relies on precursors from both sender and third-party states, the sanctions imposed by the sender government may block the target manufacturer's ability to build that product. Until the target manufacturer is able to find an alternative source for the lost sender imports, it may not need to purchase the third parties' precursor products. If alternatives for those products are unavailable or too expensive because of the sanctions, the manufacturer may discontinue its relationship with its other third-party suppliers. Economic sanctions can also cause logistical disruptions in third parties' trade networks, as transactions that involved items being transported to, from, or through target states may no longer be viable. This can increase the "trade costs" associated with transactions that involve target firms, decreasing or even eliminating their profitability.[10] The extent to which these disruptions affect any given third-party states' trade will vary, depending in large part on the extent of their commercial ties with both the sender and target states.

Beyond these factors, economic sanctions impose an additional set of transaction costs on trading with firms from target states. As previously discussed, these costs arise from the additional uncertainty created by the sanctions regarding the future risk of additional sanctions or military action and the potential to be punished by sender governments via extraterritorial sanctions.[11] These additional risks may vary across various third-party states, as their governments may have differing sets of incentives to potentially join in sanctioning efforts and abilities to protect their firms from retaliation by sender governments. Lastly, firms can potentially face reputation costs if they continue to do business with target states even if their host governments do not prevent it. For example, many international companies were pressured to stop doing business with partners in South Africa as part of the sanctions campaign to depose its apartheid regime. Depending on the extent of these sanctions-imposed transaction costs, firms in certain third parties may no longer find it profitable to do business with the target state.

Yet even as sanctions can impose broad disruptions on third-party commerce, they can also create lucrative opportunities that some third parties can exploit by sanctions busting. The economic sanctions imposed against target states can diminish their targets' terms of trade, contracting the markets available for the products they export or import.[12] With less demand for their exports, target firms will have to sell their products for reduced prices. Depending on the international availability of substitutes for the products previously imported from the sender, target firms will also likely have to pay higher prices for those alternatives. Third-party firms can obtain premiums for the business they do with target states based on the extent the sanctions have reduced their terms of trade and the sanctions-imposed transaction costs that exist for such transactions. This creates significant advantages for firms operating out of third-party states for which the additional transaction costs imposed by the sanctions remain minimal—allowing them to profit by exploiting the target's reduced terms of trade and the higher transaction costs target firms must pay in doing business with other partners. On the whole, economic sanctions will tend to make trading with target states more costly for the vast majority of states while potentially more profitable for the states able to capitalize on the opportunities they create.

Third-party states can obtain a mixture of costs and benefits in the political and commercial realms depending on how they respond to the sanctions. Third-party governments often have relationships with sender and target governments that may incentivize them to support either the sender's sanctioning efforts or the target state's efforts to resist them. By sanctions-busting on a target state's behalf, a third-party government may create political tensions vis-à-vis the sender state while strengthening its relations with the target. Conversely, third-party governments can improve their relationships with sender governments by cooperating with their sanctioning efforts and harm their relationships with target governments by doing so. By exploiting profitable sanctions-busting opportunities, third-party governments may strengthen their existing economies, attract new international business, and satisfy the constituencies to which they are politically beholden. If third-party governments instead join in the sanctioning efforts or block their constituents from sanctions busting, they may face extensive opportunity costs and create significant domestic political dissatisfaction. All of this suggests that the willingness of third-party states to sanctions-bust on behalf of target states will be affected by their governments' interests in seeing the sanctions succeed or fail, their governments' relationships with those of the target and sender states, and how the sanctions affect the profitability of their trade with the target.

Why Third Parties Sanctions-Bust via Foreign Trade and Foreign Aid

Explaining why some states sanctions-bust using foreign trade whereas others do it via foreign aid requires accounting for both the political and economic factors that affect third-party states' incentives to sanctions-bust. Trade-based sanctions busting can enrich third-party constituents and provide political benefits to their leaders, whereas aid-based sanctions busting drains governmental resources and offers leaders fewer domestic political returns.[13] The pursuit of profits rather than political objectives thus explains the majority of the sanctions-busting trade that takes place on behalf of target states. Even when third-party governments have political incentives to support a target's efforts to resist sanctions, they will generally seek to do so via sanctions-busting trade to the extent that method is viable. Only if sanctions-busting via trade is not a viable option and third-party governments possess salient political interests in having the sanctioning efforts fail will they resort to foreign aid intensive sanctions-busting strategies. In contrast, the commercial interests that third-party firms have in sanctions busting can swamp the political disincentives that their governments have to prevent such trade. Extensive trade-based sanctions-busting relationships are most likely to emerge when the interests of both third-party governments and their commercial constituencies align in support of sanctions busting on a target's behalf. All of this suggests that the conditions under which third parties will sanctions-bust via foreign aid are more limited than those under which they will sanctions-bust via foreign trade.

In any given sanctions episode, only a handful of states are apt to respond to a target getting sanctioned by extensively sanctions busting on its behalf. They will be states that either have a salient commercial interest in sanctions busting on a target's behalf and/or a salient political interest in doing so and, of those states, the majority will sanctions-bust via trade. Figure 4.1 provides a parsimonious depiction of the motivations that drive third parties to sanctions-bust. The three key determinations that influence if and how third-party states sanctions-bust are the following: (1) whether they have a political interest in undercutting the sanctions against the target; (2) whether trade-based sanctions-busting on behalf of the target is profitable; and (3) whether third-party governments have the resources to offer extensive foreign aid to target states. As the figure illustrates, third parties are most likely to sanctions-bust via trade when doing so is profitable and unlikely to do so otherwise. Third-party governments with interests in supporting a target's effort to resist the sanctions can enhance the profitability of their firms' trade with the target by signaling their unwillingness to participate in sanctioning efforts or even by subsidizing such trade. As such, an alignment of

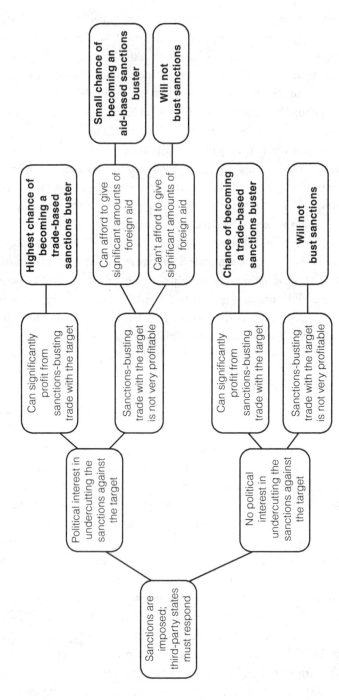

FIGURE 4.1. Causal map of the determinants of third-party sanctions-busting behavior. The expected outcomes are indicated in **bold** text.

interests between a third-party state's government and commercial sector in sanction busting leads to the highest probability of an extensive sanctions-busting trade relationship emerging. Only if trading is not profitable will third-party governments consider aid-based sanctions busting. Given the cost of aid-intensive strategies, third-party governments should employ them if they possess a salient interest in defeating the sanctions, a viable trade-based option does not exist, and they can actually afford to provide the target with extensive assistance. This type of aid should thus be relatively rare and occur mainly in highly politicized sanctions disputes. Absent either salient political or commercial interests in sanctions busting, third-party states will be highly unlikely to engage in it.

Explaining Extensive Sanctions Busting via Foreign Trade

High levels of profitability are generally required for extensive sanctions-busting trade relationships to develop between third-party and target states. Political factors primarily influence the emergence of extensive sanctions-busting trade relationships by affecting how profitable it is for third-party firms to trade with target states. In some cases, the interests of third-party firms in exploiting the profitable sanctions-busting opportunities vis-à-vis a target state can trump a third-party government's foreign policy interests in supporting the senders' sanctioning efforts. The third-party states most likely to engage in extensive sanctions-busting trade with target states are those that can forge the most mutually profitable trade relationships with them under the conditions created by the sanctions. It is important to note that the states that had the most profitable trade relationships with a target prior to the sanctions' imposition may not be the same as the states best positioned to profit from trading with the target during the sanctions. If the sanctions-busting theory is correct, the factors most strongly associated with becoming an extensive trade-based sanctions buster should relate to those that affect the profitability of their trade.

Already within international relations, the liberal paradigm has been used to explain how political and economic factors affect the distribution of international trade flows. Its emphasis on individual actors as the agents that conduct trade and their sensitivity to governmental policies provide a solid foundation for developing theories that can account for the joint roles that economic and political factors play in shaping international trade flows. For example, past works have invoked the theory to explain how profit-driven firms determine their states' international trade flows and how states' trade flows are affected by political conflict.[14] This perspective views the distribution of international trade flows as the product of the commercial opportunities available to firms and their capacity to take advantage of them. Firms' capabilities, the political and commercial environments in which they operate, and the costs entailed in carrying out transactions all affect their choice of international trade partners. The extent to which transaction costs affect firms' ability to engage in commercial transactions depends heavily on the degree that uncertainty and imperfect information obfuscates their choices.

Firms' responses to the high-risk/high-reward opportunities created by sanctions are especially affected by these considerations. Driven by the pursuit of profits and "under the constraint of uncertainty, rational firms continuously formulate and update their expectations of future returns and adjust trade accordingly."[15] Sanctions-busting firms will thus gravitate to those third-party venues possessing constellations of political, commercial, and geographic factors that make trade with the target comparatively more profitable. Firms already in third parties from which sanctions-busting trade with a target is profitable have incentives to increase the amount of trade they conduct with target partners. Firms operating out of third-party states from which doing business with target states is more costly have incentives to shift their business to more profitable third-party venues. On the other hand, firms in target states will seek out the most profitable trade arrangements available to them, forcing potential sanctions busters to compete for their business. Whereas identifying the most profitable replacement trade partners may be difficult for target firms immediately after the imposition of sanctions, over time their business will gravitate toward the most profitable third-party trading partners.

This perspective also provides insight into how firms pursue their interests vis-à-vis governments. Firms have incentives to lobby governments to adopt favorable trade policies when the benefits of doing so outweigh the costs of forsaking their trade or shifting their business to alternative venues. Though governments are responsible for pursing their countries' diplomatic interests, their leaders must often maintain the domestic political support of their countries' commercial constituencies that possess salient interests in trade-related issues. In some cases, the interests of firms will be congruent with those of their governments, but the existence of divergent interests may not stop them from lobbying for myopically favorable trade policies.[16] This implies that states' more diffuse security interests are vulnerable to the concentrated interests of profit-driven firms when it comes to setting policies toward sanctioned states.[17] Firms may also violate their governments' policies by continuing to trade with sanctioned states when such trade is profitable and the potential costs of punishment are low.[18] In other words, firms will seek to maximize their profits even if their actions come "at the expense of the diplomatic preferences of the[ir] home state."[19]

Whether third-party states engage in extensive trade-based sanctions busting on a target's behalf is determined by the extent their commercial constituents can profit from trading with the target and their governments' interests in encouraging or discouraging the trade. If the interests of a third-party state's leaders align with those of its commercial constituents in terms of their desire to sanctions-bust on a target's behalf, supportive governmental policies can help foster the creation of an extensive sanctions-busting relationship. Conversely, though, third-party governments will find it difficult to restrict their commercial constituents from sanctions busting if it is highly profitable for them. Third-party firms, in such cases, will have strong incentives to protect their profitable trade opportunities from government interference. Self-interested firms will pressure their host governments to refrain from joining in the sanctioning efforts and to protect them from retaliatory measures by sender governments. When a third-party government's constituents have a salient commercial interest in extensively sanctions busting on a target's behalf, its leaders will *tend* to privilege their constituents' commercial interests over the foreign policy interests their states might have in supporting the sanctioning effort.[20] This is because the concentrated domestic political pressure third-party firms can place on their governments will, for the most part, outweigh the foreign policy costs entailed in allowing it. Generally speaking, then, the third-party states most likely to engage in extensive trade-based sanctions busting are those that offer the most profitable venue for trading with a target, given the constellation of political, economic, and geographic factors that affect the costs of trading with the target. A number of hypotheses can be generated to test this explanation of trade-based sanctions busting's observable implications.

Commercially Oriented Hypotheses

The ability of a third-party state to capitalize on the economic opportunities created by sanctions can be heavily influenced by its economic profile.

In responding to U.S.-imposed sanctions, the states best equipped to provide substitute markets to targets are apt to be ones with large, well-developed economies. States with large domestic markets will be more capable of absorbing the target's surplus imports and provide target firms with a wider variety of potential trade partners than third-party states with small markets. At the same time, countries with large economies are apt to produce a larger range of export-available products that could serve as substitutes for U.S. products. This provides significant advantages for target firms seeking to find new trade partners, as concentrating their trade-adjustment efforts reduces the search, contracting, and enforcement costs involved in developing new trade relationships. It also allows target firms to benefit from logistical efficiencies if all their new trade partners are located in a single large market. Given that target states benefit the most from developing a small number of extensive sanctions-busting relationships, their governments and firms have incentives to cultivate sanctions-busting ties with third-party states that can provide as much market access as possible to efficiently adjust to the sanctions. As such, third-party states with large economies should be much more likely to become extensive sanctions busters than third parties with smaller sized economies:

> *Third-Party Economic Size Hypothesis:* The larger the economy of a third-party state is, the more likely it will be to engage in extensive sanctions-busting trade with target states.

Another economic factor that can influence the profitability of third-party venues is the extent of their preexisting involvement in international trade. States that engage in extensive amounts of international trade tend to possess better-developed logistical infrastructures (for example, ports, roads, and railway networks) and be more intertwined in commercial and transshipping networks.[21] Possessing well-developed transportation infrastructures, extensive commercial networks, and marketplaces with logistical and brokerage sectors creates better environments for taking advantage of sanctions-busting opportunities. These attributes can attract firms interested in sanctions busting on behalf of a target state both by direct and indirect means. If target firms are exporting or importing products directly to or from the third party, the third-party state's possession of an expansive logistical infrastructure and heavy engagement in trade can make those transactions less costly and harder for sender authorities to track. Third-party states that are major trade hubs or that possess significant trade relationships with sender states can also serve as active diversion points or middlemen for sanctions-busting transactions. Firms in third-party states can import the sanctioned products denied to target states and then resell them to target firms, helping both the firms from sender states and target states hide the transaction from sender state governments. Alternatively, target firms can export their products to the third-party states that, in turn, can resell them to the sender with their true point of origin concealed. Commercially active third-party states can thus serve as ideal venues for exploiting sanctions-busting opportunities, especially for transactions involving firms from sender states.

To illustrate this logic, let's compare two countries that possess very different levels of engagement in international commerce, Singapore and Tajikistan. Singapore may have a very small domestic economy, but it also serves as a major global shipping hub for East–West trade. Because Singapore possesses one of the world's busiest ports, products from all over the world flow through it and in incredibly high volumes. Target firms seeking to acquire sanctioned U.S. products should have a much easier time finding and acquiring those products from a third-party venue like Singapore than from a more commercially isolated venue. The sheer volume of the transactions taking place in Singapore also makes identifying diversions of U.S. products more difficult for U.S. authorities. Conversely, target firms would have a much more difficult time finding what they desire in Tajikistan, as it engages in far less international trade and is more isolated from global trade networks. As it is a mountainous, landlocked country, the costs of getting products to and from the country are also much higher. Comparatively, then, Singapore should constitute a much more attractive sanctions-busting venue than Tajikistan in most cases. On the basis of this logic, third-party states that possess economies that are heavily involved in international trade should generally be more attractive sanctions-busting venues:

> *Third-Party Commercial Openness Hypothesis:* The more commercially open a third-party state's economy is, the more likely it will be to engage in extensive sanctions-busting trade with target states.

For firms within targets and third parties, the extent of a third party's commercial dependence on the target positively influences its attractiveness as a sanctions-busting venue. Third-party states that conduct a lot of trade with a target state will have sizeable commercial constituencies with vested interests in protecting their trade relationships with target partners. These constituencies have significant incentives to lobby against their governments' participation in sanctioning efforts, raising the commercial *and* political costs of cooperating with senders' sanctioning efforts. The higher the costs third-party governments must bear to participate in sanctions, the greater the effort senders must invest to obtain their cooperation. Because inducement-laden strategies are so resource intensive, sender governments rely largely on coercion to obtain cooperation from recalcitrant third parties.[22] Convincing third-party states to disrupt their highly profitable trade with target states thus requires the use of a great deal of targeted, coercive pressure. Yet the use of threats, diplomatic arm twisting, and punishments can also damage sender governments' broader political relationships with the third parties whose cooperation they seek. This means that even if a sender government has the ability to compel a third party to join its sanctions, the costs of using that strategy may be too high. As the amount of coercion necessary to obtain a third-party government's cooperation rise, the aggregate costs associated with its use quickly outstrip the potential benefits it provides. In the absence of significant political interests in seeing sanctioning efforts succeed or intense external pressure to participate, most third-party governments will refrain from joining in sanctioning efforts if their states are heavily dependent on trade with a sanctions target.

Recognizing the incentives and constraints that exist for third-party and sender governments, firms interested in sanctions-busting on a target state's behalf will gravitate to those third-party states that possess extensive commercial ties with the target state. Within such venues, the risks that future trade will be disrupted due to governmental participation in sanctioning efforts are significantly reduced. The transaction costs involved in finding new trading partners also provide target firms with incentives to focus on their existing network of trading partners rather than seeking out new ones. It is far less costly for target firms to simply redirect their disrupted trade to existing business partners than it is to find new ones. This is also true for third-party firms that already do business in target states, as they are in prime position to exploit whatever sanctions-busting opportunities arise. Aggregating the implications of these firm-level incentives to the state level, this suggests that target states tend to redirect their sanctions-disrupted trade toward those third-party states that they already possess strong trade relationships with, encouraging those relationships to grow even stronger. The extent to which a third party depends on trade with a target thus influences its attractiveness as a sanctions-busting venue and provides for greater firm-level sanctions-busting opportunities. This makes third-party states that have extensive pre-existing commercial ties with target states much more likely to boost their trade with them after they have been sanctioned than third parties lacking such ties:

> *Third-Party Commercial Dependence Hypothesis:* The greater a third-party state's level of commercial dependence on trade with a target state is, the more likely it will be to engage in extensive sanctions-busting trade on its behalf.

Alliance Politics and Regime-Type Hypotheses

In addition to the more economically oriented factors, there are a number of important political factors that can affect the profitability of sanctions busting on a target state's behalf. The alliance relationships that third-party governments possess with the governments of sender and target states can heavily affect their likelihood of sanctions busting in important and surprising ways. Intuitively, it could be expected that the allies of sender states should be more likely to cooperate with sanctioning efforts, whereas allies of target states should be more likely to cooperate in sanctions-busting efforts to defeat the sanctions. Yet although the political interests created by a third-party government's alliance ties with target states may complement its firms' interests in sanctions busting, alliance ties to sender governments may place third-party governments' political interests in supporting their allies' sanctions in conflict with their constituents' interests in busting them. Strong commercial incentives to sanctions-bust on a target's behalf can often outweigh third-party governments' concerns about undercutting their allies' sanctioning efforts. Moreover, sender governments face greater constraints in using coercion to prevent their opportunistic allies from sanctions busting than they do in coercing other third parties. Sender firms are also advantaged in using their host government's allies to circumvent sanctions restrictions as opposed to other states. As such, third-party allies of both target and sender states should be more likely to engage in extensive sanctions busting than other states.

In general, states form military alliances as a means of improving their national security and ability to pursue their national interests. The formation of formal alliances provides information about the degree of commitment that exists between potential military partners to aid one another once a conflict is initiated. Defense pacts, in particular, have been shown to exercise a potent deterrent effect on foreign aggression.[23] Yet although such treaties can be effective deterrents, they do not actually guarantee that the promised assistance will be provided if invoked. Indeed, Brett Ashley Leeds and her coauthors find that alliance partners tend to renege on their commitments about 25 percent of the time.[24] This raises two conceptually important points. The first is that alliance partners do not always share congruent security and foreign policy interests, especially in nonmilitary-related areas. Secondly, the quality of intra-alliance relations may affect the likelihood of states abiding by their alliance commitments. As such, the management of intra-alliance relations on issues where divergent interests exist has salient implications for the well-being of alliances.

Managing alliance relationships can be a complicated affair. As Glenn Snyder writes, "Allies bargain with each other to settle immediate disagreements, often about how to deal with an opponent, but they also seek to preserve the long-term health of their relationship, and their own interests within it, apart from specific conflicts with an adversary."[25] From this perspective, the management of intra-alliance relationships extends far beyond crisis situations or the immediate decision to fulfill alliance commitments. This implies that allies should not take their partners' willingness to cooperate on peripheral issues for granted and avoid alienating them with their policies. Alliances can also create unrealistic expectations that partners' cooperation should extend beyond immediate obligations of alliance agreements, which can further complicate the task of managing intra-alliance relationships.[26] So although both the sender and the target states may expect assistance from their third-party allies, these expectations may be misplaced.

Another important insight to emerge from this body of research is that not all types of military alliances exercise the same effects on states' trade and security. Defense pacts represent the strongest form of alliance commitment that states can make to one another and are the most effective at deterring military aggression.[27] Andrew Long has further shown that defense pacts constitute the only form of alliance relationship that exerts a positive effect on partner states' bilateral trade.[28] Given the demonstrated strength of their effects, the theory focuses on explaining how defense pact alliances influence the trade relationships of third parties and sanctioned states.

For a target's defense pact allies, both commercial and political incentives exist to aid the target after it has been sanctioned. The sender's sanctions can weaken the economies of target states, destabilize their regimes, disrupt their participation in trade networks, and cut them off from strategically important goods that could weaken their military strength. These effects can have negative consequences on third parties' security, as declines in the target's relative power can weaken the alliance blocs of which the target is a member. Given the sanctions' consequences, allies of the target should at the very least refrain from participating in the sender's sanctions. By offering direct aid or adopting policies to encourage private sector trade with the target, third-party governments can take active measures to help mitigate the damage done to their allies by sanctions. At the firm level, companies should prefer trading to and from the target's allies because there is less of a risk of those states joining the sanctions regime. The trade-promoting policies adopted by allied governments may also attract foreign firms interested in trading with the target. For the defense pact partners of target states, the foreign policy interests of their governments should be mostly congruent with those of their firms. The incentive structures of both firms and governments, then, should work in conjunction to increase trade between a sanctioned state and its defense pact allies:

> *Target-Third Party Defense Pact Hypothesis:* A third-party state will be more likely to engage in trade-based sanctions busting on behalf of a target state if their governments possess a defense pact with one another.

When a third-party state has a defense pact alliance with a sender, the alliance's effects are apt to create conflicts of interest between governmental foreign policy prerogatives and the interests of its commercial constituencies. Firms interested in pursuing the profitable opportunities created by the sender's sanctions will pressure their governments not to join in the sanctioning effort irrespective of the foreign policy benefits. As such, third-party governments may face strong domestic opposition to participating in their allies' sanctions. Moreover, third-party allies of the sender many not share the sender's specific interests in achieving the policy goals sought by its economic sanctions. For example, most U.S. allies have had little at stake security-wise with respect to the American sanctions against Cuba—even during the Cold War. The strength of the commercial constituencies favoring trade with the target and the commercial linkages between the target and third party affect how costly it is for third-party governments to participate in the sender's sanctions. The larger the commercial incentives for sanctions busting are, the stronger the domestic pressure on third-party governments to allow or even protect its firms' freedom to sanctions-bust will be.

For senders, the task of recruiting the participation of allied states is made more difficult by the limitations that alliance considerations place on the tactics they can use. There are diplomatic costs involved in using coercion against allied states that do not exist for using it against nonallied states. Senders are sensitive to the damage that coercing the participation of their allies can have on the well-being of their alliance relations. To compel their allies' participation, senders may have to employ unpopular coercive measures, such as extraterritorial sanctions. These arm-twisting methods can breed resentment among allies and potentially contribute to intra-alliance rifts. Because the expected marginal contribution of most third-party states' participation to the likelihood of a sanctions regime being successful is apt to be low, the diplomatic costs of using coercion will often outstrip the benefits. This suggests that senders have far more limited options in compelling their allies' cooperation than they do other states, and they will be less willing to escalate disputes with their allies over the sanctions issue.

Evidence of this constraint is apparent in the most frequently analyzed case of multilateral sanctions failure: the U.S.-backed gas pipeline sanctions against the Soviet Union in 1981–1982.[29] In the episode, the United States was responding to a Soviet-supported crackdown in Poland with sanctions directed against Poland and a planned transcontinental pipeline that would transport natural gas from Siberia to Western Europe. President Ronald Reagan made the imposition of multilateral sanctions against the Soviet pipeline a high-profile foreign policy prerogative vis-à-vis the United States' NATO allies and Japan. Initial European recalcitrance to support the U.S. proposed sanctions led the United States to impose unilateral sanctions against the Soviet Union in December 1981. President Reagan also threatened to impose extraterritorial sanctions against individual European firms involved in pipeline-related commerce.[30] In the summer of 1982, a number of NATO allies, including Great Britain, France, West Germany, and Italy, came out in public opposition to the U.S. attempts to coerce their cooperation in the sanctioning effort. The French and British governments actually ordered their firms to fulfill their contractual obligations with the Soviet Union, despite the threatened retaliation they faced from the U.S. government if they did so.[31] Although President Reagan initially followed through with his threat to impose extraterritorial sanctions against the offending firms, he backed down after being confronted by the united opposition of the U.S. alliance partners and the looming threat of a highly divisive intra-alliance trade war. Unwilling to escalate the dispute any further, President Reagan ended the crisis by unilaterally suspending the U.S. extraterritorial sanctions against its allies—having failed to achieve the concessions he had sought with them.[32]

The episode is instructive in that it demonstrates the willingness of a sender state's allies to oppose its sanctions and champion their firms' commercial interests with respect to the target. This is especially notable in that the Western European states were highly dependent on their alliance relationships with the United States for their own security. Calculating that the United States did not view the sanctions as important enough to warrant disrupting its alliance relationships over, European leaders stood up to their senior alliance partner in refusing to participate. In addition, the Soviet Union was also able to wield leverage over its European trade partners because the issue concerned its supply of natural gas to those states. These countries' dependence on foreign energy supplies magnified their commercial dependence on the Soviet Union and the gas pipeline it was constructing to service their markets.[33] As such, the decisions of countries like France and West Germany to break with their ally to support its adversary were shaped by both the interests of their domestic constituencies and their broader foreign policy interests. Via its high-profile back-down, the United States signaled to firms that they could continue to sanctions-bust on the Soviet Union's behalf with impunity.

As a last effect, a sender's alliance relationships can affect its firms' choices of where to redirect or relocate their business if they seek to continue trading with the target. Savvy sender firms realize that their governments are less capable of punishing their allies or their businesses for allowing sanctions-busting trade. For example, the United States has repeatedly waived provisions to impose extraterritorial sanctions against firms that violate its sanctions when they did business in allied states. For sender firms, this makes relocating their business operations to allied states less risky than transferring their business to nonallies. Conducting their sanctions-busting business through their home states' allies may also generate less negative publicity for such firms' business dealings. For example, U.S. firms relocating to France to continue doing business with Iraq during the sanctioning efforts imposed against it would face less scrutiny than those relocating to Syria to do the same thing. Because defense pact partners tend to trade more heavily with one another,[34] sender firms can likely draw on more extensive commercial networks in third-party allies that can be used to trade with target states. They may also find it less costly to relocate their business activities to such countries. This can partially account for the increase in trade that the sender's allies may experience after the imposition of sanctions.

In focusing on those states with the greatest likelihood of become extensive trade-based sanctions busters, this constellation of factors suggests that third parties possessing defense pact alliances with sender states will be more likely to do so than third parties without them. The fact that sender governments face far greater constraints in using the harsh coercive methods necessary to discourage sanctions-busting against allies makes such states more attractive sanctions-busting venues for firms. Sender firms also enjoy a number of advantages in redirecting or relocating their business to the third-party allies of their host governments. Counterintuitively, then, defense pact allies of sender states should be far more likely to become trade-based sanctions busters than nonallied states:

> *Sender–Third Party Defense Pact Hypothesis:* A third-party state will be more likely to engage in trade-based sanctions busting on behalf of a target state if its government possesses a defense pact with the sender government.

The type of regimes that target and third-party states possess may also affect whether they develop sanctions-busting relationships, as liberal democratic states' relationships tend to be more stable, transparent, and less prone to conflict. More generally according to liberal theory, "private actors will be drawn to partner choices that minimize political risk that could disturb long-run relations. This implies that trade relationships are most likely to prosper under conditions where diplomatic conflict is least likely to pose a serious threat."[35] This should be especially true for target firms that have already had their trade relationships with the initial senders disrupted by sanctions and have significant incentives not to repeat that experience. Additionally, the development of extensive trade ties between firms in democratic third-party and target states can build powerful constituencies that could lobby to prevent third-party governments from joining in sanctioning efforts. This is broadly consistent with similar liberal arguments that have been offered to explain the democratic peace theory. Whereas the extent to which democratic peace theory applies to economic sanctions has produced mixed findings, the liberal logic appears as if it should apply in these particular circumstances.[36] As such, the transparency and stability created by the presence of jointly democratic institutions within the target and third-party states should make extensive sanctions-busting relationships more likely to emerge between such states:

Target–Third Party Democratic Regimes Hypothesis: If target and third-party states both possess democratic regimes, they are more likely to form extensive trade-based sanctions-busting relationships than if neither possesses them.

Geographic Hypotheses

Finally, a third party's geography can provide it with advantages and disadvantages in trading with sanctioned states. The distance between two states and whether they share a border are relational characteristics that can affect the profitability of their trade and the methods by which it takes place. The general finding within the literature on international trade is that distance has a negative effect on two countries' bilateral trade, although a shared border has a positive effect.[37] The farther a third party is from a target state, the more difficult it may be for the commercial transactions to take place by virtue of the sender's aggressiveness in recruiting third-party participants and seeking to disrupt the target's transportation networks. It should also be easier for the target's regional trading partners to divert their trade flows to the target, as they are likely to have close commercial, social, and infrastructural linkages with one another.[38] In examining third-party trade with apartheid South Africa during the 1980s, William Kaempfer and Martin Ross found that third parties that were geographically proximate to South Africa traded more with it than did third parties that were further away—irrespective of their political support for the sanctions.[39] As such, there are strong reasons to expect that third-party states that are proximate to target states will be advantaged in sanctions busting on their behalves:

Target–Third Party Distance Hypothesis: The farther apart a third party is from a target state, the less likely it will be to engage in extensive trade-based sanctions busting on the target's behalf.

The consequences of sharing a border with a sanctioned state on a third-party state's likelihood of extensively sanctions-busting are more complicated. For individuals and firms, engaging in illicit trade entails greater risks than legitimate trade. Under some circumstances, however, it is more profitable to trade illicitly when legitimate trade is prohibited or raises the risk of external retaliation. As Peter Andreas has shown, sanctions regimes can facilitate the development of transnational criminal networks to service the commercial needs of sanctioned states.[40] These networks thrive in conducting cross-border smuggling from the target's regional neighbors. Border countries represent the ideal points from which to engage in illicit transactions because the trade is purely bilateral—preventing both the sender and the broader international community from monitoring or policing the commerce. Especially in cases in which a sender state is actively seeking to punish sanctions-busting firms or a sanctions regime has broad multilateral support, it may be cheaper to engage in illicit or clandestine trade with the target than in legitimate trade. This expectation conforms to the theoretical account, as individuals and firms are employing the most cost-effective means of achieving their desired commercial transactions. Third-party governments might be complicit in this trade or just unwilling to invest the resources in stopping it.[41] During the UN sanctions imposed against Iraq after the first Persian Gulf War, for example, illicit trade with Jordan, Syria, and Turkey served as key sources of income that helped Saddam Hussein's regime weather the sanctions.[42] Thus, although it could be expected that the target's contiguous neighbors are the most likely states to have their trade with the target increase after sanctions are imposed, a large proportion of that trade may be conducted illicitly.

The practical issue this raises is that the legitimate trade flows of states bordering sanctioned countries are likely to suffer from an underreporting bias of the true value of the bilateral trade being conducted. Few data exist on the scope and size of illicit trade flows with sanctioned countries, however, and especially not in a cross-sectional time-series format amenable to statistical analysis.[43] Limiting the sanctions-busting theory's predictions to observed levels of bilateral trade, it could be expected that the offsetting effects of illicit trade would, in general, cause bordering states' legitimate trade flows with sanctioned states to remain neutral or decline after sanctions are imposed. As such, the third parties bordering a target state are less likely to sanctions-bust extensively on its behalf via legitimate trade flows. Instead, such states are more likely to employ illicit channels to conduct their sanctions busting:

> *Target–Third Party Shared Border Hypothesis:* If a third party shares a border with a target state, it will be less likely to engage in extensive trade-based sanctions busting on its behalf via legitimate, officially recorded trade.

The enumerated hypotheses provide a broad test of the sanctions-busting theory's account of trade-based sanctions busting. They capture the primary commercial, political, and geographic factors that should influence which third-party states will become extensive trade-based sanctions busters and under what conditions. They also highlight the novel and unexpected insights offered by the sanctions-busting theory regarding the effects of alliances and illicit trade.

Explaining Extensive Sanctions Busting via Foreign Aid

Although most sanctions busting takes place via commercially driven trade, a small but significant portion of it takes place via the provision of foreign aid. Within this book, it is theorized that third parties provide extensive amounts of foreign aid under three primary conditions: (1) They have a politically salient interest in preventing the success of the sanctions imposed against a target; (2) developing an extensive sanctions-busting relationship based primarily on trade is infeasible; and (3) the third-party governments can afford to provide target states with extensive aid packages. All three factors are hypothesized as being jointly necessary for a third-party government to engage in extensive aid-based sanctions busting on a target's behalf. Even when all these circumstances align, a sender government may still refrain from offering a target state extensive assistance. Target leaders must often play an active role in soliciting the aid of potential patrons, which also helps explain the rarity of this situation. The rest of this section offers a more detailed explanation of the particular circumstances under which third-party governments are most likely to provide target states with extensive sanctions-busting aid.

Using a narrow definition of what constitutes aid-based sanctions-busting presents numerous challenges, as there are a myriad of channels by which third-party governments can aid target governments. Evidencing such challenges, Hufbauer and his coauthors intentionally left vague their criteria for identifying when target states had received significant amounts of black knight assistance over the course of a sanctions episode.[44] The challenge grows even harder if one seeks to identify the specific third-party states providing the assistance to the target. Third-party governments, for example, can provide target states with ODA, other forms of bilateral financial and economic aid, humanitarian aid, and military aid. Foreign aid can also entail providing a recipient state with resources, such as food or fuel, at highly concessional prices. Whereas the impact of changes in the ODA inflows received by target states were assessed in Chapter 3, ODA captures only a proportion of the full scope of foreign aid that targets can receive.[45] Third-party governments may also have incentives to hide how much foreign aid they actually give to a target state. Third-party governments thus possess a range of aid-based options to assist target states and can employ whichever one best suits their circumstances. The impact of the aid a third party provides to a target can be as much influenced by how it is channeled as it is by the quantity in which it is given.

Extensive sanctions-busting aid is the act of providing a target state with a significant, sustained increase in foreign aid for the purpose of helping it offset the costs and/or consequences of the sanctions imposed against it. Similar to the impact sanctions busting via trade has, sanctions busting via foreign aid has near-term rather than permanent effects on the efficacy of sanctioning efforts against a target state. The interests of third-party governments in supporting a target state and the means at their disposal to do so can change over the course of a sanctions episode. Some third-party governments may provide targets with one-time aid packages in response to critical needs, whereas others may be willing to sustain longer-term aid packages. Given the potential costs of extensively supporting sanctioned states, sustaining high levels of foreign assistance to target states will be difficult for most third-party governments. As a result, it is far riskier for target governments to be critically dependent on the foreign aid patronage of one or two third parties than it is to rely on a similarly small number of sanctions-busting trade partners. Whereas the latter have vested commercial interests in maintaining the sanctions-busting relationships, continuing to support the target can be a costly drain on the resources of aid-based sanctions busters. The patronage a target receives is best viewed as a dynamic phenomenon that can change from year to year depending on third-party governments' ability and willingness to continue providing their aid.

The broader literature on foreign aid suggests that governments provide foreign aid both altruistically and for political and strategic benefits.[46] The extent to which individual governments provide such aid for either purpose is known to vary. For example, Sweden has a reputation as being a highly altruistic donor whereas the People's Republic of China (PRC) has a reputation of using its foreign aid chiefly as a political tool.[47] In general, more states appear to use their foreign aid for political purposes than for chiefly altruistic ones. The sanctions imposed against a target can potentially affect the motives that donors have to provide aid to target states for both altruistic and political purposes. As previously noted, economic sanctions can devastate their targets' economies, degrade their public health, erode their democratic institutions, and even cause full-blown humanitarian crises. Altruistic third-party governments could respond to any one of these situations by increasing the amount of foreign aid they give to target governments to help them alleviate those harms. Whereas politically motivated donors might also provide aid to help address those problems, their concern is likely to be focused on providing a target government's leaders with resources that will help them maintain power and the political will to continue resisting the sanctions. In comparing which set of motives is more apt to drive a third-party government to provide extensive patronage to a target, salient political or strategic motives appear far more likely to drive third-party governments to invest significant resources in aiding a sanctioned state.

Two political motives tend to drive third-party governments to provide sanctioned states with significant amounts of foreign aid. The first motive relates to whether a third party's leaders view the sanctions dispute within the context of a rivalry with the sender government. In such cases, the sanctioning effort against a target can become a proxy dispute between third-party and sender governments. Competition over the outcome of the sanctions can serve to demonstrate the superiority of either side without involving a direct conflict between the two. Pursuing such proxy conflicts may fit into the broader strategies that third-party governments possess vis-à-vis sender governments that extend beyond the context of the particular sanctions episodes. However, the important condition that must be met for third-party governments is that they view the issues at stake with regard to the sanctions' outcome as worth making significant investments in aiding the target state. If defeating the sanctioning efforts offers third-party governments broader political benefits, this should increase the incentives they have to offer the target extensive assistance. For third-party leaders, such benefits might come from demonstrating their resolve in countering a sender state's more aggressive foreign policy prerogatives. It might also come from demonstrating to international audiences that they can successfully challenge and defeat the sender government in a dispute.[48] Being able to contextualize the patronage of sanctioned states within an ongoing rivalry can also help third-party leaders gain domestic support for the policy. Notably, the circumstances already described are most likely to emerge out of great power competition between sender and third-party governments.

The second salient motivation that can drive third-party governments to provide a target with extensive patronage is to support an ideologically friendly state. Such states may be allies, but they do not necessarily need to be. If third-party governments view the sanctions imposed against a target as threatening their core values or the mandates of their core ideology, they will have stronger political incentives to assist the target. This extends beyond seeking to help keep a friendly leader in power or helping to maintain the strength of an alliance partner. Rather, it stems from a third party's leaders viewing a target's capitulation to a sender's sanctions as jeopardizing their core international values or goals. Just as rivalries can help justify aiding a sanctioned state, linking the sender–target sanctions dispute to a broader ideological conflict can help convince third-party policy makers and their constituents that supporting the target is in their interests. When both rivalry-based and ideological motivations exist for a third party to see the sanctions against a target defeated, their leaders will have the greatest imperative to offer their states' patronage to the target state.

Several historical examples appear to suggest that ideology and rivalries play a crucial role in motivating the provision of costly sanctions-busting assistance. For example, the generous support the United States provided to Israel after the Arab League boycott imposed against it in 1948 was, and has continued to be, couched largely in ideological terms.[49] Supporters of the American aid given to Israel argue that the United States has a moral obligation to support the Middle East's only Western-style democracy—despite the foreign policy and economic costs involved. The sanctions-busting aid given to the Marxist Sandinista government in Nicaragua in the early 1980s also appears to have been driven by a combination of ideological and rivalry-based motives. "Within a few weeks" of the U.S. government's reimposition of sanctions against Nicaragua in 1981, "the USSR had offered to provide Nicaragua with 20,000 tons of wheat . . . Libya had offered a $100 million loan, and Cuba agreed to provide $64 million in technical aid."[50] For the small, still-developing Nicaraguan state, these were substantial quantities of assistance. In all three cases, the third-party governments that offered Nicaragua extensive foreign aid packages had rivalries or ongoing ideological disputes with the United States.

Although the political imperatives provide the motivation for third-party governments to sanctions-bust, two other key factors determine whether doing so via foreign aid is necessary and feasible. Sanctions busting via foreign aid is a second-best option for third-party government due to its considerable costs. Even third-party governments that are highly motivated to assist a target state should prefer to use trade when that mechanism is feasible. For example, one could expect that the apartheid regime in South Africa would have viewed the broad international sanctions imposed against the minority-ruled Rhodesian government in the 1960s as a core threat to its values and system of governance. Yet the South African government showed little generosity in how it chose to support its neighbor's regime because it was in a position to use commercial means to sanctions-bust on the state's behalf. The South African government realized that it could help the Rhodesian government and enrich its constituents by sanctions-busting via trade rather than foreign aid. As Jesmond Blumenfeld observes, "South Africa extracted its full pound of flesh for bailing Rhodesia out of its trade and transport problems" created by the international sanctions imposed against it.[51] By adopting a trade-based sanctions-busting strategy, the South African government was able to achieve its political objectives in sustaining the Rhodesian regime but in a way that profited itself and its citizens.

Yet, such win-win solutions are not always possible. In some cases, the sanctions imposed against target states can be so disruptive and crippling that target firms cannot readily afford adjusting to them. When economic sanctions have such devastating effects, target states may not be able to use market-based trade to redress the damages the sanctions inflict on their economies. If third-party governments want to support a target in those cases, they will have to provide the target with foreign aid or extensively subsidized trade instead. Alternatively, a target state may be able to afford international trade, but it might not be possible to conduct it profitably with particular third-party states. If a third party is geographically distant from the target or its economy does not produce, consume, or traffic in the type of products the target needs to import or export, it may not be possible to develop a commercially viable sanctions-busting relationship.

In response, third-party governments may heavily subsidize their trade with the target to make it commercially viable. Rather than being surplus generating, these trade relationships can be quite costly for third-party governments to maintain. Such arrangements often take the form of government-negotiated trade agreements that establish subsidized, nonmarket-based terms of trade between the third-party and target states. The higher the level of subsidization these arrangements entail, the more they can be associated with outright forms of foreign aid. For third-party governments, labeling such deals as "trade agreements" may make them more palatable to their constituents than identifying the transactions as pure foreign aid. These arrangements

partially blur the conceptual distinctions between sanctions-busting strategies based chiefly on foreign aid versus foreign trade. Yet the fact that such
arrangements are costly rather than profitable for third-party governments
helps establish why the provision of heavily subsidized trade should be catego-
rized as primarily an aid-based strategy rather than a trade-based one.

The last key factor that determines whether a third-party government will
provide its patronage to a target state is its ability to afford the provision of
such aid. Because providing extensive foreign aid to a target can be very costly,
not all third-party governments can afford to provide it. This limiting condition once again favors great powers as being the type of third parties most
likely to offer target states their patronage, but that is not always the case.
Wealthy states, such as Saudi Arabia, can also draw on their expansive governmental budgets to fund sanctions-busting efforts. For example, the Saudi
government allegedly provided the Muslim forces of the Bosnian government
with $300 million worth of military assistance in the mid-1990s in spite of the
UN-imposed arms embargo imposed against it.[52] Even for powerful states,
the long-run drain of providing extensive foreign aid to a target state can limit
how long it can be sustained. The availability of disposable resources within
third-party governments thus greatly constrains the use of foreign aid-based
sanctions-busting strategies, whereas it is not an impediment to the emergence of sanctions-busting trade relationships.

In the case of China's sanctions-busting relationship with North Korea
discussed in Chapter 2, it is important to note that China established its aid-
based sanctions-busting relationship with North Korea long before it grew
to become the country's dominant trading partner. The growth of China's
sanctions-busting trade relationship with North Korea was closely linked to
the aid it was providing the country. Chinese subsidies helped promote North
Korea's increasing reliance on trade with the country. As North Korea grew
increasingly isolated from the external sources of aid and trade on which it relied, its overarching economic dependence on China grew increasingly larger.
For China, the costs of sustaining North Korea via foreign aid alone would
have likely been unsustainable in the long run. The growth and increasing
openness of China's economy also better equipped Chinese firms to engage in
trade-based sanctions busting than they had been in the 1990s. China's shift
from a sanctions-busting relationship primarily based on aid to one primarily
based on trade is consistent with the sanctions-busting theory's overarching
predictions, even if its continued involvement in aid-based sanctions-busting

blurs the crisp distinctions the theory draws between states' reasons for engaging in one versus the other.

The theoretical account also appears to provide a powerful explanation for one of the highest-profile sanctions-busting efforts ever undertaken: the Berlin Airlift.[53] Following World War II's conclusion, control over the city of Berlin was split among Great Britain, France, the United States, and the Soviet Union, despite the city's location deep within the Soviet-occupied zone of East Germany. In 1948, the Soviet Union blockaded the land routes to Berlin to pressure the Allies to back down from their efforts to create a unified West German state. In response, the United States and—to a lesser extent—Great Britain initiated an ambitious air campaign to supply West Berlin to prevent its capitulation. Over the course of the airlift, the United States made over 190,000 deliveries of food, fuel, and miscellaneous cargo.[54] The city's 2 million beleaguered inhabitants were in no position to pay for this massive airlift on their own, as their economy had still not recovered from the war and they were completely isolated from the outside world.[55] Instead, the citizens of West Berlin could endure the blockade imposed against their city only with a massive amount of foreign assistance.

For the United States, carrying out the massive air campaign to supply Berlin during the blockade was an incredibly costly venture. Beyond the strategic costs involved in devoting squadrons of military aircraft to the airlift, the campaign is estimated to have cost over $200 million (roughly $1.9 billion in current dollars).[56] The principal factors that drove the U.S. government to invest so heavily in preserving the freedom of its recently vanquished enemy appear to have been its emerging rivalry with the Soviet Union and its efforts to combat the international spread of communism. Conducting the airlift on Berlin's behalf served to signal U.S. resolve to defend Allied-controlled Europe against Soviet aggression and its commitment to preserving the democratic systems of Western Europe.[57] Given the isolation and economic circumstances of Berlin, using market-based trade to sanctions-bust on the city's behalf was not possible. The city simply could not afford to sustain itself during the blockade. Although historical accounts indicate that U.S. President Harry Truman and his advisors did not fully weigh the potential financial cost of the Berlin Airlift before the decision was made to initiate the campaign, the United States was one of the few countries that could afford such massive expenditures.[58] Absent U.S. participation in the sanctions-busting effort, it is unlikely the British could have or would have sought to sustain

Berlin on their own. In broad strokes, this prominent case appears consistent with the sanctions-busting theory's explanation of why third-party governments engage in aid-based sanctions busting:

> *Sanctions Busting via Foreign Aid Hypothesis:* Third-party governments will engage in aid-based sanctions busting on behalf of a target only if the following three necessary conditions are met: (1) They have a salient political interest in the sanctions' failure; (2) a sanctions-busting relationship based on market-driven trade is infeasible; and (3) their governments can afford to provide the target with extensive aid.

Plan for Evaluating the Hypotheses

Given the differing natures of aid-based and trade-based sanctions-busting behavior, differing methodological approaches are best suited to evaluate each one. Whereas the factors driving third-party states to engage in sanctions-busting trade tend to constitute broadly discernible characteristics and relationships of third-party states, the factors driving third-party states to engage in aid-based sanctions busting are much more circumstantial. The comparative rarity of extensive sanctions busting via foreign aid and the difficulties involved in creating a universal operational measure to capture its occurrence also create a differing set of research design challenges in studying it.

To test the hypotheses concerning why third-party states engage in extensive sanctions-busting trade, the following section pairs a process-tracing case study of the phenomenon along with a statistical analysis of the general factors correlated with trade-based sanctions busting. The detailed process-tracing case study of the UAE's emergence as Iran's leading trade-based sanctions-busting partner provides the means with which to assess the sanctions-busting theory's descriptive accuracy. The subsequent statistical analysis tests the theory's general utility in explaining which third-party states engaged in extensive trade-based sanctions busting during U.S. sanctions episodes from 1950 through 2002. Together, these empirical analyses provide complementary tests of the sanctions-busting theory's explanation of why and how trade-based sanctions busters emerge.

To evaluate the sanctions-busting theory's explanation of why third-party states become aid-based sanctions busters, a different methodological approach is required due to the rarity of the phenomenon. Furthermore, testing the theory's arguments related to aid-based sanctions busting requires a fairly detailed understanding of third-party states' capabilities, foreign policy preferences, and relationships with the target and sender states. As such, a "structured, focused comparison" of the factors that caused third-party governments to engage in aid-based sanctions busting in a small number of cases offers the best option for evaluating the theory's aid-based sanctions-busting hypothesis.[59] Given the historical significance of the aid the Soviet Union provided to Cuba and the case's role in defining black knight behavior, reevaluating that case along with the other major cases of aid-based sanctions busting on Cuba's behalf can help demonstrate both the sanctions-busting theory's descriptive accuracy and its substantive significance. By examining a number of different cases within the Cuban sanctions episode, it is also possible to explore the Castro regime's general strategies for leveraging sanctions-busting support in resisting the U.S. sanctions and why the U.S. government's efforts at preventing sanctions busting have largely failed.

Together, these three empirical chapters should provide the sanctions-busting theory with a broad test of its descriptive accuracy and predictions. The chapters should also produce a myriad of policy-relevant insights that are related to or extend from the theory. The aggregate insights that can be drawn from these chapters and their implications for policy makers will be explored in more depth within the conclusion.

5   Sanctions Busting for Profits

How the United Arab Emirates Busted
the U.S. Sanctions against Iran

THIS CHAPTER EXPLORES WHAT HAS DRIVEN THE UNITED ARAB Emirates (UAE) to actively sanctions-bust on Iran's behalf for the past three decades. It seeks to establish the descriptive accuracy of the sanctions-busting theory by showing that the sanctions-busting trade relationship that emerged between the UAE and Iran was mainly driven by profits instead of politics. The U.S. government has had sustained sanctions in place against the Islamic Republic of Iran since 1979, though their intensity and scope have varied widely over that period. The U.S. government has used its sanctions to pursue a myriad of goals. These motivations most notably include convincing the Iranian government to stop supporting terrorist groups and to abandon its efforts to acquire a full nuclear fuel cycle that would allow it to produce nuclear weapons. The U.S. government has also sought to use its sanctions to destabilize Iran's ruling regime and encourage the emergence of a more democratic form of government within the country. Though the U.S. sanctions have taken on many forms and have periodically been strengthened, they have been notably unsuccessful in achieving the goals for which they were imposed. A key reason why the sanctions against Iran have failed has been Iran's success in developing numerous trade-based sanctions-busting relationships—the most important of which has been with the UAE.

This case is important to understand for a number of reasons. At first glance, the UAE constitutes a curious candidate for becoming a leading trade-based sanctions buster. In the 1980s, the UAE was a small, oil- and gas-rich state in the Persian Gulf with little domestic industry and whose greatest security threat was Iran. In recent years, U.S. policy makers have focused a lot of attention on figuring out ways to stem the tide of sanctions-busting trade occurring via the UAE. In particular, U.S. policy makers found the amount of strategically sensitive goods, including nuclear technologies, being sold to Iran via the UAE particularly disturbing. Yet over the period analyzed in this chapter, the sanctions busting conducted by the UAE was acknowledged but mostly ignored by the U.S. government. This, too, is puzzling. Finally, the case offers valuable analytical leverage in that the UAE signed a defense accord with the United States partway through the period analyzed. As such, it provides somewhat of a natural experiment on the effects that sender–third party defense pacts have on third-party sanctions busting. This case thus offers significant leverage in evaluating the sanctions-busting theory and may yield a number of salient policy-relevant insights.

The chapter begins with an overview of the U.S. sanctioning effort against Iran from 1979 through 2005. To isolate the effects of the defensive pact signed between the UAE and United States in 1994, the narrative is divided into two case periods, 1979 through 1994 and 1995 through 2005. This allows for a before-and-after comparison of the sanctions busting conducted by the UAE with respect to the alliance.[1] Given its probabilistic nature, not every one of the sanctions-busting theory's hypotheses will be supported by this single case.[2] On the balance, however, the evidence should demonstrate that the reasons why the UAE sanctions-busted—and the methods it employed—are consistent with those of the overarching theoretical account. The analysis also provides insights into aspects of the theory related to firm-level behavior, the role played by illicit trade, and the specific policy response of target, sender, and third-party governments that cannot be captured via a statistical method of analysis.

This chapter's analytical narrative provides clear evidence that regional businesses and traders, U.S. firms, and multinational corporations (MNCs) flocked to the UAE to sanctions-bust on Iran's behalf. The UAE's proximity to Iran, its historically strong commercial ties to the country, and the emergence of Dubai as a major shipping and commercial hub all served to make the country an attractive sanctions-busting venue. As the analysis also reveals, the amount of sanctions busting conducted by the UAE skyrocketed after its government signed a defense accord with the United States in 1994. Consistent with the sanctions-busting theory's predictions, U.S. firms actively exploited the opportunities offered by UAE to circumvent the U.S. government's sanctions against Iran. Another striking aspect of this case is the major role Dubai played in the A. Q. Khan proliferation network's efforts to export nuclear-related items and technologies to Iran.[3] The UAE appears to have played a significant role in undermining the U.S. government's efforts to stymie the progress of Iran's nuclear program. Understanding why and how the UAE emerged as such an effective sanctions buster offers important insights into why the U.S. sanctions imposed against Iran since the mid-1980s have largely failed to achieve their goals.

The U.S. Sanctions against Iran from 1979 through 2005

Since 1979, the U.S. sanctions against Iran have served to define the two countries' commercial relationship. The first round of American sanctions against Iran occurred from 1979 to 1981, serving as retaliation for the hostage taking of U.S. embassy personnel during the Islamic Revolution. The sanctions included a ban on the importation of Iranian oil, a ban on weapons exports, and the freezing of all assets controlled or owned by the Iranian government in the United States. All told, the United States froze roughly $12 billion of Iranian assets.[4] These initial sanctions were reinforced by a complete ban on imports and exports from Iran in April 1980. President Jimmy Carter had some success in gaining international support for the American sanctions. France, Great Britain, West Germany, Italy, Japan, and Switzerland all agreed to impose limited financial sanctions against Iran and ban military exports to the country.[5] The American financial and trade sanctions lasted until the United States and Iran arrived at a negotiated settlement for the release of the American hostages in January 1981, which also entailed the unfreezing of most Iranian assets.[6] The United States kept its arms embargo against the Iranian regime in place, however. This first round of sanctions forced Iran to diversify its commercial portfolio and to begin the process of seeking out new, more reliable trade partners.[7]

The second distinct period of American sanctions lasted from 1984 to early 1995 and involved the imposition of sanctions for nonproliferation and antiterrorism purposes. Due to its support of Hezbollah in connection to the 1983 bombing of the American marine barracks in Beruit, Iran was placed on the U.S. State Department's list of state sponsors of terrorism in January 1984. This designation entailed a complete ban on the export of military goods to Iran and stringent restrictions on the sale of dual-use goods to the country. These export control restrictions were further strengthened under the auspices of the Export Administration Act. President Ronald Reagan made the American sanctions even more potent in 1987 (via Executive Order [E.O.] 12,613) by placing an embargo on the direct import of all Iranian goods and restricting fourteen other categories of exports.[8] This measure did not extend, however, to transactions conducted by American firms taking place outside of the United States and therefore did not forbid American firms from buying Iranian crude oil for sale to third-party markets. They also allowed for the import of "Iranian-origin raw materials or components" as long as they had been substantially modified by third-party countries.[9]

The third and most extensive phase of sanctions began in May of 1995 after President Bill Clinton issued Executive Order 12,959. This executive order imposed a complete ban on all imports and exports between the United States and Iran. The order also prohibited U.S. firms from investing in Iran and from buying Iranian crude oil. Preceding this full trade ban, President Clinton had issued an executive order in March 1995 (E.O. 12,957) that prohibited U.S. investment in Iran's energy sector. In 1996, Congress passed the Iran–Libya Sanctions Act (ILSA), which imposed sanctions on foreign firms that invested more than $20 million in Iran's energy sector in a year's time span.[10] According to Arthur Downey, who testified against the ILSA in congressional hearings:

> [The] ILSA was born out of frustration that our [American] allies and friends were unwilling to restrict investment into Iran's petroleum sector—as the United States did in 1995. In the U.S. view, Iran's economy was fragile, but development of its gas and oil capacity would provide strength to Iran and give it the ability to acquire weapons of mass destruction and the will to continue to engage in terrorist acts. The Act forced non-U.S. companies to choose between the United States and Iran.[11]

The ILSA had the effect of invoking the ire of not only foreign firms but also their governments.[12] Yet the U.S. government had little stomach to follow through with the stringent implementation of the measure, preferring instead to offer waivers to foreign firms in return for agreements with their governments to impose tougher strategic export controls against Iran.[13]

In August 1997, President Clinton passed another executive order specifically addressing the problem of sanctions busting.[14] Executive Order 13,059 explicitly forbade U.S. citizens from engaging in both direct and *indirect* trade with Iran. The order created criminal culpability for individuals who exported American products to third-party states with the "knowledge or reason to know that . . . such goods, technology, or services are intended specifically for supply, transshipment, or re-exportation, directly or indirectly, to Iran or the Government of Iran."[15] This legislation specifically targets sanctions-busting transactions that used third-party states as middlemen to obscure the point of origin or final destination of sanctioned products. E.O. 13,059 was designed to prevent U.S. companies from simply laundering their transactions through third-party states to circumvent restrictions on trading with Iran. In 2000, Congress passed the Sanctions Reform and Export Enhancement Act of 2000, which eased U.S. export sanctions on the sale of food and medicine to states charged with supporting terrorism (for example, Iran, Libya, and Cuba).[16] Also in 2000, the Clinton administration initiated a partial lift in the American embargo against Iranian imports. The new regulations made it legal once again to import carpets, dried fruits, grains, pistachios, and caviar from Iran, which constituted some of the country's largest exports.[17]

At the same time, the U.S. sanctions were relaxed in some areas, increasing concerns regarding Iran's interest in acquiring nuclear weapons, which led Congress to pass the Iran Nonproliferation Act of 2000. The law provided the executive branch with the authority "to take punitive action against individuals or organizations known to be providing material aid to weapons of mass destruction programs in Iran."[18] This law empowered the U.S. government to take action against foreign firms and traders that violated its nonproliferation sanctions against Iran. It thus authorized the executive branch to globally police all sanctions-busting trade that involved designated sensitive items, not just those transactions that involved U.S. firms and citizens. These sanctions constituted only one part of a much broader diplomatic effort on the part of the U.S. government to prevent foreign countries from supplying Iran with nuclear materials and technologies during this period. After information emerged about Iran's clandestine nuclear program in October 2003, the United States launched an active campaign to persuade the UN Security

Council to impose broad multilateral sanctions against Iran to compel it to come clean about its nuclear program and cease its construction of a full nuclear fuel cycle.

The Effects of the U.S. Sanctions on Iran, 1979–2005

When the United States first imposed sanctions against the Iranian government in 1979, Iran had an exceptionally high degree of commercial dependence on the United States. Proportionally, bilateral trade with the United States comprised almost 20 percent of Iran's total trade in the years leading up to the Islamic Revolution.[19] As Figure 5.1 shows, American imports from Iran peaked at just over $4.7 billion dollars in 1978, with its exports going to Iran figuring about $1.5 billion. By 1981, American imports from Iran had fallen to 1.4 percent of their 1978 total, while American exports to the country declined to 20 percent of their past value. A number of experts credit the American sanctions—including the freezes on Iranian assets—for giving the United States a strong bargaining chip in negotiating the release the American hostages held in Iran.[20] Given that Iran's military and oil sectors were largely provisioned with American equipment and relied on American spare parts, "Iran was . . . uniquely vulnerable to American sanctions."[21] Given the

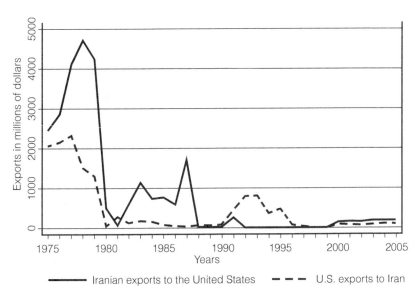

FIGURE 5.1. Bilateral trade between the United States and Iran, 1975–2005.
SOURCE: Barbieri et al. 2009.

domestic and international turmoil created by the revolution and the extent of Iran's prior dependence on trade with the United States, the country was not able to adjust to the U.S. sanctions imposed against it. Thus, the initial round of U.S. sanctions was successful in large part due to the extensive commercial costs the United States was able to inflict on the Iranian economy.[22]

The effectiveness of the subsequent round of sanctions designed to punish the Iranian regime for its support of terrorism and check its military power is not as easy to evaluate. As Figure 5.1 shows, American trade with Iran recovered somewhat over the period of 1982–1987 before plummeting after President Reagan issued Executive Order 12,613. Some scholars argue that the American sanctions did not hurt importation of Iranian crude oil until the 1987 ban on its direct importation, though the nonoil U.S. imports from Iran remained negligible during this period.[23] Although denying Iran arms and re-placement parts for its American-made military hardware during its war with Iraq (1980–1988) hindered its military strength, the sanctions ultimately did not convince the Iranian government to give up its support of terrorism. The goals of the American sanctions against Iran became more expansive during the early 1990s. The U.S. government sought to use its sanctions to discourage the Iranian regime from developing a nuclear program capable of produc-ing nuclear weapons and to support regime change within the country. De-spite the harsh restrictions on Iranian imports during the 1990s, demand for American products in Iran did lead to a brief resurgent period of American exports to the country.

The American goals of hamstringing the Iranian regime's military and domestic political power led to the strengthening of U.S. sanctions against Iran in 1995 and 1996. Executive Order 12,959 severed nearly all the *direct* bilateral trade between the two countries over the next several years. It has been estimated that the total sanctions-related costs incurred by Iran from 1996 through 2001 ranged from roughly $950 million to $1.5 billion per year.[24] Trade between the United States and Iran recovered to a limited extent after the passage of the Sanctions Reform and Export Enhancement Act of 2000 loosened some of those restrictions—even after Iran was named a part of President George W. Bush's "axis of evil" in 2002.

There is a general consensus that, excepting the period from 1979 through 1981, the costs imposed upon by the U.S. sanctions against Iran through the mid-2000s caused only minor damage to Iran's economy, with most of its losses occurring through higher financial costs, mark-ups on trade with

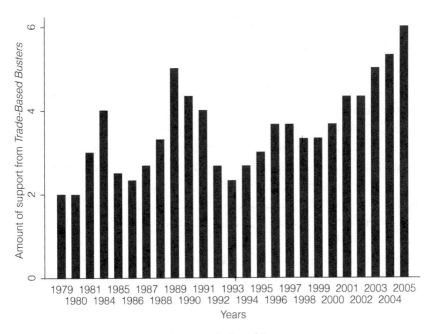

FIGURE 5.2. Iranian support from *Trade-Based Busters*, 1979–2005.

third parties, and spoiled opportunities to develop its oil sector.[25] As Figure 5.2 illustrates, using the *Trade-Based Busters* variable, Iran had the support of numerous trade-based sanctions busters over the course of this period. Whereas the focus of this chapter is on the UAE as Iran's leading trade-based sanctions buster, it is only one of a number of countries to have profited from extensively sanctions-busting on Iran's behalf. Consistent with the sanctions-busting theory's expectations about the deleterious impact of sanctions busting, the U.S. sanctions largely failed to make significant progress toward achieving their objectives. From 1995 through 2005, conservative elements within Iran retrenched their control over the Iranian government, Iran continued to strongly support the terrorist activities of organizations like Hezbollah, and Iran made substantial headway in the development of its nuclear program. Although U.S. efforts certainly impeded the progress of the Iranian nuclear program, they did not make the costs of pursuing the program sufficiently high to force the Iranian government to abandon its efforts, nor did they prevent the regime from receiving substantial third-party assistance for its programs.

The UAE's Sanctions Busting on
Iran's Behalf from 1979–1994

This section describes the UAE's emergence as a leading trade-based sanctions buster on Iran's behalf. It discusses how the U.S. sanctions imposed against Iran caused the UAE to increase both its legitimate and illicit trade with Iran due to the lucrative commercial opportunities they created. During this period, the Islamic Revolution in Iran and the Iran–Iraq War created an environment in the Persian Gulf in which black and gray markets could flourish. A significant proportion of the UAE's sanctions busting on Iran's behalf thus involved smuggling and unreported trade. As Figure 5.3 illustrates, official trade statistics show that bilateral trade between the UAE and Iran markedly increased following the initial U.S. round of sanctions from 1979 through 1981 and the sanctions it imposed in 1984. Although the trend lines are not consistently positive, they appear supportive of the notion that a portion of the trade flows that were lost to Iran because of the U.S. sanctions were diverted to and/or through the UAE. Increases in both legitimate and illegitimate trade in response to Iran being sanctioned would count as evidence of an extensive trade-based sanctions-busting relationship. As such, the trends

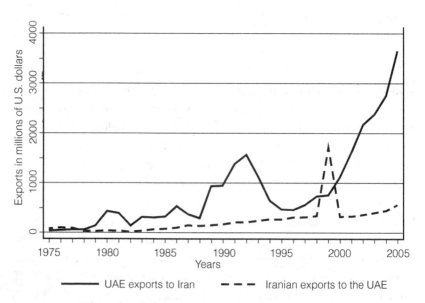

FIGURE 5.3. Bilateral trade between the UAE and Iran, 1975–2005.
SOURCE: Barbieri et al. 2009.

associated with both forms of trade are discussed to the extent that the evidence allows.

As already noted, the UAE was not the only country to take advantage of the commercial opportunities created in Iran by the U.S. sanctions from 1979 through 1994. Australia, for example, experienced a threefold increase in its exports to Iran following the imposition of American trade sanctions in 1980, supplanting the United States as Iran's largest provider of agricultural products.[26] Figure 5.4 depicts the exports that Iran received from four of its other leading trading partners during the American sanctions.[27] This list includes Italy, Japan, the Netherlands, and the United Kingdom, which all had large, open economies and alliance relationships with the United States. Interestingly, Figure 5.3 and Figure 5.4 show that Italy, Japan, and the UAE all experienced substantial growth in their exports to Iran from 1988 to 1992. Askari and his coauthors attribute this sharp peak in Iranian imports to the "pent-up demand" for foreign products following the conclusion of the Iran–Iraq War.[28] This spike in the demand for imports in Iran followed just after the imposition of more stringent American sanctions in 1987, forcing Iranians to seek alternative third-party trading partners. Yet strong demand for

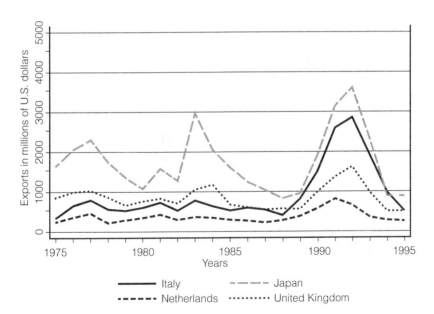

FIGURE 5.4. Other leading exporters to Iran, 1975–1995.
SOURCE: Barbieri et al. 2009.

American products still existed in Iran during this period—even if it could not be met by direct means.[29] Third-party states with strong commercial ties to the United States thus had significant opportunities to serve as middlemen in exporting American-made products to Iran. Financed on foreign credit, Iran's import boom was not sustainable. After going $23 billion into debt and falling behind on its loan repayments in 1993, Iran was forced to sharply curb its imports from 1993 through 1995.[30] It is important to note that this sharp decline occurred before the ILSA was imposed, eliminating the United States' use of extraterritorial sanctions as a proximate cause for the decline.

Emirati Sanctions Busting on Iran's Behalf, 1979–1981

The series of harsh sanctions imposed against Iran from November 1979 through April 1980 completely severed Iran's commerce with what had been its largest trading partner. This left a gaping void in its economy's ability to fulfill consumers' demands for American-made consumer goods, machinery, spare parts, armaments, and foodstuffs. In the aftermath of the sanctions' imposition, Dubai emerged as one of the Iranian merchants' leading venues for acquiring sanctioned American goods and their foreign equivalents. Even before the United States imposed its complete ban on trade with Iran in April of 1980, the UAE's American imports jumped from $100 million in January to $400 million of that year, with much of the difference being reexported to Iran.[31] This immediate spike in trade flows being redirected through Dubai is significant because it shows that such diversions began before the Iran–Iraq War started. Importantly, this suggests that the UAE's trade with Iran was not being conducted as a politically motivated relief effort to aid the beleaguered Iranian state. Indeed, quite the contrary was the case. During the first two years of the Iran–Iraq War, the UAE's federal government actually provided Iraq with $1.5 billion worth of wartime aid.[32] This suggests that the UAE's interests in increasing its trade with Iran were largely commercially driven.

The Emirati port city of Dubai, which was already a transshipment hub of some notoriety and hosted a large merchant community with historical ties to Iran, was well situated to take advantage of commercial opportunities the U.S. sanctions created vis-à-vis Iran. Of especial importance in those efforts were the fleets of small trading vessels (known as "dhows") at the disposal of traders in Iran and Dubai. Specific figures on how much trade was redirected from Dubai to Iran during this period are not available, nor are precise

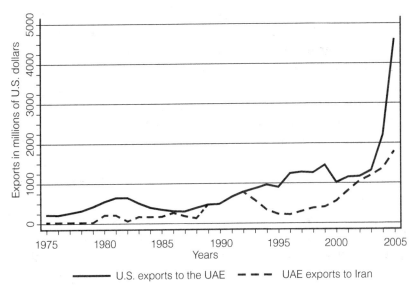

FIGURE 5.5. Comparing U.S. exports to the UAE with UAE exports to Iran, 1975–2005.
SOURCE: Barbieri et al. 2009.

data on the types of products being traded. Figure 5.5, which compares U.S. exports to the UAE and the UAE's exports to Iran, reveals corresponding increases in both during this initial round of sanctions. It is also notable that the quantity of U.S. exports received by the UAE markedly supersedes its recorded exports to Iran. Most of those surpluses were likely reexported to Iran via unreported trade. Indeed, much of the export trade between Dubai and Iran involved smuggling during this period because sanctions-busting traders sought to avoid paying customs duties on the products they sold to Iran or because the products they were exporting had been prohibited by Iran's Revolutionary Government. Recognizing that lost tax revenues from smuggling posed a large problem for its weak regime, the Iranian government responded by forbidding private importers from bringing goods into the country in 1980. Instead, it mandated the use of state-run import offices. The Iranian government was much too weak to enforce this policy, however, and such restrictions were often easily evaded by smugglers.[33] Although trading with Iran was perfectly legal in Dubai, the Iranian government created additional incentives for sanctions-busting traders to keep their transactions off the books.

The Iranian regime reversed its position on smuggling once the war with Iraq began. After the war's outbreak and the effective closure of Iran's northern ports, foreign traders began dropping off their goods destined for Iran in Dubai because they feared to make direct deliveries to the country. Within two months of the conflict's outbreak, Iranian agents developed an informally organized system of coordinating the reexport of undelivered cargo, relying on Dubai's fleet of small dhow traders.[34] Even for those traders in Dubai motivated by their cultural and social linkages to Iran, the profits entailed in smuggling products to Iran were still significant.[35] By October 1980, the *Wall Street Journal* reported that smugglers operating out of Dubai were transporting roughly 15,000 tons a day of "essential commodities" to Iran with the Ayatollah Khomeini's tacit approval.[36] Thus, the outbreak of war intensified the amount of smuggling that was already going on between Dubai and Iran, some of which entailed busting American sanctions, and some of which did not. It is important to note that Dubai's avid role in sanctions busting preceded its subsequently larger role in wartime smuggling, and American goods constituted a large part of what Iran needed to sustain its wartime activities.

Emirati traders reportedly smuggled a wide variety of American goods into Iran, ranging from frozen pizzas to essential spare parts.[37] In May of 1980, one observer noted that sanctions-busting traders from Dubai could "undersell the competition by 25% and still make a big profit with many types of merchandise."[38] As time went on, many of the transactions involved bartering due to a lack of hard currency in Iran. While the Emirati government had officially barred arms sales to both combatants, Dubai's free trade policies were conducive to such transactions. As one port official put it, "The success of Dubai was built on its reputation as a place that helps merchants . . . We only inspect cargo here if we are suspicious. In fact, most of these containers going out on barges and virtually all of the cargo on the dhows is hardly ever seen."[39] Given such policies, almost anything could have been transited through Dubai to Iran. This suggests that despite the substantial pressure the U.S. government sought to place on the Iranian government and the public support for the sanctioning effort, many firms—including American ones— were unwilling to support the U.S. government's efforts to commercially isolate Iran.

Another telling indicator of the effect that American sanctions had on the UAE's trade with Iran is what happened after the United States ended its sanctions in January 1981. The end of the American sanctions marked the resumption of direct trade between U.S. companies with Iran and an end to the boom times in Dubai. Due to the Iranians' desire to cut out the middleman in their transactions, shortages in the Iranian government's currency reserves, and the overabundance of foreign traders that had descended on Dubai in the wake of the sanctions, the sanctions-busting bubble in Dubai burst.[40] In the last six months of 1981, Dubai's reexports to Iran declined by 46 percent relative to their 1980 levels.[41] In the wake of this economic bust, the Abu Dhabi–led federal government issued a new round of protectionist measures from 1982 to 1984 meant to restrict the ability of foreigners to own businesses in the UAE and foreign firms to do business in the country. Designed to protect indigenous firms from foreign competition, these laws were antithetical to Dubai's free port model and threatened to undermine exactly that which had made the emirate an attractive venue for foreign firms and investors.[42] Indeed, it was in response to these measures that Dubai's Sheikh Rashid was driven to create Dubai's system of free trade zones to preserve his emirate's free port status.[43]

These events are important because they signal that wartime profiteering alone was not sufficient to maintain the extensive reexportation sector that had developed after the United States first sanctioned Iran. If Dubai's business prospects had remained as strong as they had been during the sanctions, then it is unlikely there would have been such an extreme protectionist backlash on the part of the UAE's federal government. The dramatic influx of foreign firms into Dubai also supports the sanctions-busting theory's contention that third-party firms will flock to those venues offering the best prospects for profitable sanctions busting. When the sanctions disappeared, so too did the businesses created to exploit them. The commercial downturn that occurred following the repeal of the American sanctions demonstrates just how much Dubai's commerce had been affected by them.

Emirati Sanctions Busting on Iran's Behalf, 1984–1988

From January 1981 through January 1984, the United States did not have any sanctions in place against Iran beyond the arms embargo it had imposed in 1979. The legitimate and illicit commercial networks built up between Dubai and Iran during this first round of sanctions continued to persist during this period because of the war with Iraq but saw less use.[44] The sanctions and export controls imposed by the U.S. government against Iran in 1984 focused on denying the Iranian regime a broader set of strategic and military goods that extended beyond those items included in the 1979 arms embargo. Though these new restrictions substantively strengthened the American sanctions against Iran, their narrow focus limited their general effects on third-party trade.

As R. T. Naylor details, the Iranian regime actively pursued weapons and spare parts for its American-made military hardware on the black market throughout this period.[45] Naylor's account illustrates how sanctions busters dealing in low-volume/high-value goods, like small arms, can profitably employ more circuitous routes in carrying out their transactions. The sensitive nature of such transactions increases the value of the discretion and/ or opacity provided by particular third-party venues above the logistical advantages they offer. Though Dubai continued to offer an attractive venue for conducting such transactions, a wider array of third-party venues, such as Singapore and South Africa, also constituted attractive sources for acquiring illicit armaments.

Unlike other venues, the UAE also had officially prohibited the sale of arms to Iran, though it did not have any restrictions in place on the sale of dual-use goods or spare parts. Given the sensitivity of these types of transfers, such transactions would have almost always been kept under the table and, hence, would not have been included in official trade statistics. As Figure 5.5 indicates, American exports to the UAE fell steadily from 1981 through 1986. This suggests that Dubai was not being used as a large-scale diversion point for significant amounts of sanctioned American goods during this period.

Although the trade flows might not have been as high, numerous accounts suggest that Dubai was still used to transship and/or smuggle sanctioned goods into Iran. In one case uncovered by the U.S. government in 1985, an American export company run by expatriate Iranians shipped over $1.7 million worth of spare parts for military vehicles to Iran via Dubai. Using a common scheme, the sanctions violators claimed that the parts were being sent to a falsified end user in Dubai, when really their ultimate destination was Iran. Procurement agents from the Iranian government supposedly even published a "wish list" of the types of American spare parts that were needed.[46] In another example of Dubai being used as an illicit transshipment point, *The Times* of London ran a story that quoted an arms broker's account of how Egyptian small arms were being transshipped to Iran via Dubai.[47] These stories offer anecdotal evidence that suggest Dubai was still being used as a sanctions-busting venue during this period. Though the volume of diverted trade flows may have declined, Dubai was still playing a crucial role in helping Iran obtain strategically important goods to which it could not otherwise gain access.

From 1986 through 1988, the United States became increasingly involved in attempting to safeguard shipping in the Persian Gulf as the so-called Tanker War between Iraq and Iran intensified. This led to heightened hostilities between the United States and Iran and numerous militarized disputes. In 1987, growing concern in the Reagan administration over the amount of American trade occurring with Iran led to the imposition of a full ban on all direct Iranian imports and new sanctions on fourteen categories of exports. Though the strengthening of American sanctions provided greater incentives for sanctions busting, the intensification of the fighting in the Gulf made trading with Iran significantly more dangerous.

Due to the expense of insuring large cargo ships, an increasing amount of the trade conducted during this period relied on the use of dhows. Such trade was quite dangerous. In traversing the gulf, dhows risked being blown up by Iranian mines that had been sown along the waterways and risked being shot at by Iranian, Iraqi, and American warships.[48] The intensification of the fighting in the Gulf had two observable effects: It led to the decline of legitimate trade between the UAE and Iran (Figure 5.3) and increased the amount of smuggling that occurred between the two states. Reportedly, an average of fifteen to twenty dhows per day departed from Dubai for Iran in 1987—hauling an estimated 3 to 4 million tons worth of cargo a year.[49] In one sign of the conflict's effects, Dubai's reexports rose 18 percent in 1987 to over $1.4 billion, with Iran serving as those goods' leading destination.[50] With conflict raging around it and stringent American sanctions back in place, Dubai was once again attracting a lot of business as Iran's leading entrepôt.

In the fall of 1988, the Iran–Iraq War finally came to an end. The war's conclusion led to wild overspeculation in Dubai about the prospects for "a profitable peace."[51] Coming off eight years of war, the Iranian regime had little money to spend on anything other than essential products.[52] Furthermore, firms in other countries also began to feel as if trading directly with Iran was once again safe. This left speculative merchants in Dubai with vast surpluses of goods they had bought to reexport to Iran and nowhere else to send them. By October 1988, the dhow traffic with Iran in Dubai had come to "a virtual standstill."[53] At least initially, peace in the Persian Gulf came at a steep price for Dubai's merchants. Fortunately for them, such peace was short lived, and new sanctions would present a host of fresh commercial opportunities.

Emirati Sanctions Busting on Iran's Behalf, 1989–1994

In the period from 1989 through 1992, the UAE's trade with Iran was heavily influenced by the Iranians' foreign-financed import spending spree. This spike in Iran's demand for foreign imports occurred shortly after the U.S. government increased the stringency of its sanctions. In the aftermath of those sanctions, direct American exports to Iran did not begin to respond to the Iranian demand for foreign products until 1991 (Figure 5.1). As Figure 5.4 shows, American exports to the UAE and Emirati exports to Iran rose in almost perfect lockstep with one another from 1989 through 1992. Officially, Dubai reexported roughly $2.1 billion worth of goods in 1990, sending $520 million worth of them to Iran.[54] Almost certainly, a substantial amount of above- and below-the-board sanctions-busting commerce taking place in Dubai during this period was done to meet the pent-up demand for American products in Iran. It is also important to note the degree to which Dubai had grown as a global transshipment hub. In 1990, it was reported that nearly 7 percent of the world's total international trade passed through Dubai by land, air, or sea.[55] This placed the world at Iran's doorstep.

On August 3, 1990, Iraq invaded Kuwait. Soon thereafter, the UN Security Council imposed comprehensive sanctions against Iraq, which included a naval blockade of the country. For the UAE, this event sparked a similar contradiction in responses that has been noted in the Iranian case. Although the Emirati government sought to foster a closer security relationship with the United States and repel the Iraqi invasion, something altogether different was going on in Dubai. The comprehensive sanctions imposed by the United Nations against Iraq presented Emirati merchants once again with lucrative sanctions-busting opportunities. Not only could they tap into the same global trade networks they had used to acquire contraband materials to sell to Iran and employ the same regional distribution and smuggling methods they had previously perfected, they could also cooperate with their trade partners in Iran to do it. Traders from Dubai would cross the Gulf to Iranian waters and follow its coastline west until they reached the Shatt-al-Arab waterway, which narrowly separates Iran from Iraq. Once there, a few bribes to Iranian customs and border agents easily allowed traders to cross the Iran–Iraq border.[56] Carrying official papers giving them the right of free transit in Iranian waters, dhows from Dubai could travel across the Gulf unhindered by the naval blockade against Iraq before making their sanctions-busting runs from safely controlled Iranian waters.[57] As a spokesperson for the U.S. Navy concluded, there simply was "no practical way to stop the dhows."[58]

It is notable that this sanctions busting started in the lead-up to an impending conflict with Iraq, in which global opinion was united against Iraq's actions. After the war's conclusion, when international interest in enforcing the sanctions against Iraq waned, Emirati traders' role in sanctions busting on Iraq's behalf only continued to grow.[59] Following the war, cash-starved Iraqis reversed the flow of the sanctions-busting networks that had built up during the conflict to smuggle oil out of their country via Iran to Dubai and the emirate of Fujairah. By 1994, it was estimated that upwards of 10,000 barrels of oil a day were being smuggled out of Iran using these routes, prompting a formal protest by the U.S. government to the United Nations.[60] This case provides additional evidence of the presence of the sophisticated sanctions-busting network that had developed within Dubai. It also demonstrates the willingness of commercial actors to place their economic interests ahead of their government's political interests. Although Emirati soldiers participated in efforts to liberate Kuwait from Iraqi forces, traders from Dubai similarly risked their lives in blockade running to resupply the Iraqi regime.[61]

Emirati exports to Iran began to decline sharply in 1992. As Iran's foreign credit dried up, it lost its means of paying for the high levels of imports it had enjoyed during the preceding four years. The decline in the UAE's exports to Iran corresponds with the same declines experienced by its other leading export partners during this period. Another contributing factor could have been Iran's annexation of two small islands claimed by the UAE in the Persian Gulf, but this appeared to barely affect Dubai's commercial relationship with the country. Emphasizing the continued strength of the commercial ties between Dubai and Iran in 1994, a trade official from Dubai noted, "Iran is an important commercial partner of our country as it takes nearly one-third of our re-exports. Its exports to us are also increasing and most of them are being re-exported to other countries. Iran relies mainly on Dubai to reach other markets."[62] In 1994, the same year that the UAE's federal government signed a defense pact with the United States, Dubai was estimated to have reexported anywhere from $200 to $300 million worth of American-made goods to Iran—constituting roughly 17 to 26 percent of its total imports from the United States.[63] Even if American firms did not know *for sure* that their products were being diverted to Iran, many of them were still profiting from the established sanctions-busting networks that had built up in Dubai. Plausible deniability was the only shield most American firms needed, given the U.S. government's lax enforcement policies.

Explaining the UAE–Iranian Trade-Based Sanctions-Busting Relationship, 1979–1994

The sanctions busting conducted by the UAE on Iran's behalf during this period clearly involved significant levels of market-based trade—some legitimate and some illicit—and appeared to be driven largely by profit-seeking behavior. In this case, three factors highlighted by the hypotheses appeared to play a decisive role in motivating the trade-based sanctions-busting relationship that emerged between the UAE and Iran. Rather than serving as the direct buyer or supplier of sanctions-busting goods, the UAE emerged as a critical middleman for sanctions-busting transactions. Correspondingly, the UAE's geographical proximity to Iran, the strong preexisting commercial linkages it had with Iran, and the commercial openness of Dubai all facilitated in its emergence as a hub for sanctions-busting transactions.

The UAE's geography made it an ideal venue for sanctions busting on Iran's behalf. According to the sanctions-busting theory, a target state's legitimate (that is, observed) trade flows should increase the most with neighboring states with which it does not share a border. Located across the Persian Gulf from Iran, the UAE is only ninety-five kilometers away from Iran at the narrowest point separating the two states. Only 400 kilometers separate Dubai from Bandar Abbas, which grew to become Iran's largest and most important international seaport during this period. Prior to the outbreak of the Iran–Iraq War, roughly two-thirds of Iran's imports came through the ports of Khorramshahr and Bandar Khomeini, which are located near the Iraqi border at the northern edge of the Persian Gulf. Within the first two months of fighting, Iraq had taken possession of Khorramshahr and essentially put the port of Bandar Khomeini out of commission.[64] This dramatically increased the traffic through the far more defensible port city of Bandar Abbas. Trade between the UAE and Bandar Abbas was also assisted by number of strategically located islands sprinkled across the Gulf between the two states.[65] These islands were used to help defend the cross-Gulf trade routes and were also frequently employed by smugglers to evade detection.

The UAE's geographic relationship with Iran presented firms and individual traders with numerous competitive advantages in conducting sanctions-busting trade with Iran relative to other third-party states. First, the sea-routes along the Persian Gulf waters provide for the rapid transport of goods both in small quantities and in bulk between the two countries. Indeed, maritime trade is often cheaper and faster than overland trade routes. Second, Dubai's proximity to Bandar Abbas made it the most efficient trade hub for Iranian traders to use in connecting to global trade networks. Reportedly, it took dhows only an average of one to two-and-a-half days to travel between Dubai and Bandar Abbas during this period.[66] From 1979 through 1994, Dubai grew to become the region's principal transshipment hub—offering Iranian traders global access to goods that sanctions blocked them from directly importing. Third, the short span of largely territorially held waters separating the two countries was ideal for smuggling. Even with its large naval presence in the Gulf during the late 1980s and early 1990s, these trade routes made it prohibitively difficult for the U.S. Navy to interfere with, let alone interdict, sanctions-busting transactions between the two states. Although the UAE did not share a border with Iran, the coastal geography separating the two countries significantly facilitated allowing black market trade to flourish between them in response to the sanctions.

The UAE's proximity to Iran and the ease of maritime commerce between the two countries thus made it one of the most profitable venues for conducting sanctions-busting trade with Iran. The geography separating the two countries was particularly conducive to sanctions-busting trade using the fleets of small shipping vessels common to the Persian Gulf. The regional conflicts that took place during this period (for example, the Iran–Iraq War and the first Persian Gulf War) created additional incentives for traders to employ those fleets for smuggling purposes as opposed to legitimate ones. For both forms of trade, the UAE was thus one of the geographically best-suited candidates to become a major trade-based sanctions buster on Iran's behalf.

Third-party states that have a high degree of trade openness are often best suited to become sanctions-busting venues. This is because they are more likely to possess well-developed trade infrastructures, have access to more expansive trade networks, and offer commercially friendly environments to potential sanctions-busting traders and firms. With respect to each factor, Dubai's emergence as a leading regional transshipment hub made it an ideal place from which to conduct sanctions-busting transactions. Dubai's significant investments in its logistical infrastructure, including the construction of the world's largest human-made port at Jebel Ali, helped make it one of the busiest and well-equipped commercial hubs in the world. The port at Jebel Ali was completed in 1979, and an extensive drydock facility opened soon after at nearby Port Rashid in 1983. Although Dubai had traditionally played a central role in Persian Gulf trade, the new facilities and the Iran–Iraq War helped make Dubai a locus of Persian Gulf trade during the 1980s.[67] During the Tanker War phase of conflict, commercial trading vessels—and especially oil tankers—became military targets for both sides and drew the United States into the conflict.[68] Dubai's drydock facilities, once viewed as a white elephant, received significant business servicing ships damaged by the combatants during this period.[69] Contributing to its free port reputation, Dubai was active in repairing vessels from all sides of the conflict and kept its ports open to all traders that sought to do business in it.[70] Indeed, Davidson contends that "the advanced development of Dubai's Port Rashid and its Port Jebel Ali megaproject had led many Iranian merchants to assume that Dubai would soon become the one convenient stopping point for long-distance shipping and therefore the most sensible location for any long-term commercial base in the Gulf."[71] Dubai offered Iranian traders the easiest, safest access to markets in the rest of the world of any port in the region.

Dubai's institutional innovations also played a major role in Dubai's emergence as the Persian Gulf's preeminent transshipment hub. In 1985, Dubai opened its first free trade zone as an attendant part of the port of Jebel Ali. The free zone model allowed Dubai's Sheikh Rashid to skirt recently imposed federal restrictions on foreign investment and customs laws by creating an administrative territory that would "technically fall outside of UAE jurisdiction."[72] By using the Jebel Ali Free Zone (JAFZA), traders could unload and store their goods in Dubai without paying customs duties for an extended period of time before reexporting or transshipping them elsewhere. JAFZA also allowed firms to repackage, reprocess, or modify the goods being stored in the zone. Although the free zone at Jebel Ali did not become an overnight success, it substantially contributed to making Dubai an attractive transshipment venue. By 1990, JAFZA played host to 298 firms.[73] It also helped create the perfect administrative shelter for firms and individual traders engaged in sanctions busting. It was not until the mid-1990s, however, that the use of the free zone really exploded.

The fact that Dubai managed to maintain good relations with both Iraq and Iran during their war also helped the emirate attract significantly more commercial shipping than it had prior to the war's start. Companies would ship their goods to Dubai in bulk and then use small, safer means of conveyance to forward them on to their final destination.[74] Evidencing this shift, the *Washington Post* reported that even though the number of ships visiting Dubai's ports declined from 3,229 in 1983 to 2,888 in 1986, "the number of dhows and small coastal boats jumped from 6,366 in 1984 to 10,088 in 1986."[75] Dubai's significant capital investments in trade infrastructure and adoption of innovative, business-friendly institutions equipped it to handle far greater amounts of international commerce than it otherwise could have. Combined with the UAE's de facto political neutrality during the Iran–Iraq War, Dubai was in a unique position to act as a transshipment hub for products coming into and going out of the Gulf. Once this role was established, Dubai maintained it even after the hostilities' conclusion. Via Dubai, the UAE was well suited to host sanctions-busting firms or serve as a transshipment point in sanctions-busting transactions on Iran's behalf throughout this politically volatile period.

The last factor to play a key role in the UAE's emergence as a leading sanctions buster was its extensive preexisting commercial relationship with Iran. It was hypothesized that states already engaged in extensive trade with target countries should have significant competitive advantages in exploiting sanctions-busting opportunities. Because of both historical reasons and the Iran–Iraq War, the emirate of Dubai had developed significant commercial ties to Iran on which it was highly dependent. Indeed, a significant portion of Dubai's substantial growth as the leading transshipment hub in the Persian Gulf can be linked to its role as the leading entrepôt for trade with Iran.

The historical linkages between the UAE and Iran stem back to the beginning of the twentieth century when the sheikh of Dubai lured a large number of Persian pearl merchants to relocate to his emirate with promises of duty-free trade.[76] These expatriate merchants prospered in their new home, growing to also monopolize trade involving retail and foodstuff products and becoming part of an influential merchant class in the emirate.[77] This cross-Gulf commercial relocation helped establish Dubai as one of the region's leading free ports and created a sizeable ethnic minority of Persians in Dubai that endures to this day. Indeed, one 2005 report estimated that citizens of Persian descent constitute roughly a quarter of Dubai's population.[78] The historical business ties between merchants in Dubai and Iran appear to have played an influential role in the development of sanctions-busting networks that could operate both above and below the table. During my field visits to Dubai (2005–2009), trips to the district of Diera bore clear evidence of the heavy concentration of Iranian trading firms operating out of the emirate. The bustling dhow-based trade concentrated along Dubai's adjacent Creek also revealed (in plain sight) numerous vessels packed-up with American-made products ostensibly destined for Iranian ports. That community and those practices go all the way back to the period in which sanctions-busting activities first began in 1979.[79]

During the Iran–Iraq War, the UAE was the only Arab state in the Persian Gulf with which Iran did not have a hostile relationship. Given the extent of their cultural and commercial ties to Dubai, the limitations on the alternative options available to them, and the perception of Dubai's seemingly inevitable growth, Iranian merchants chose to focus most of their intra-Gulf trade on the UAE. Thus, commercial ties between Iran and the UAE were strengthened during the first half of the 1980s for reasons exogenous of the U.S. sanctions. When the United States strengthened its sanctions against Iran in the latter parts of the 1980s, the UAE already had an extensive trade relationship developed with the country that could readily handle additional influxes of sanctions-busting trade. Furthermore, many of the same skills, trade routes, and network connections involved in navigating the conflict-prone Gulf during the Iran–Iraq War overlapped with those associated with sanctions-busting trade—especially of the illicit variety. A sizeable commercial constituency thus existed within Dubai that had the interests and ability to exploit the profitable opportunities created by the U.S. sanctions against Iran.

Another puzzling attribute of this case that can be explained by the sanctions-busting theory is that the trade-based sanctions busting conducted by Dubai often came at the cost of the UAE's broader foreign policy interests. The confederal structure of the UAE's government gave its individual emirates much broader discretion in setting their own foreign trade policies and political relationships than is typical in most countries. In response to the oil-rich emirate of Abu Dhabi's primacy over the UAE's federal government, Dubai often chose to pursue maverick policies in pursuit of its own individual interests. Whereas the Abu Dhabi–led government often preferred to support efforts at politically and commercially isolating Iran, Dubai adopted a number of pro-Iranian policies designed to strengthen their commercial ties. For example, the highly visible role played by Dubai in serving as Iran's wartime entrepôt damaged the UAE's reputation among fellow Arab states during the Iran–Iraq War. The $1.5 billion the UAE gave to Iraq at the onset of the war indicates that its government's political interests appeared to coincide with those of Iraq in the conflict. The neutral role the UAE ended up adopting during the war emerged largely by default due to the policy rift between Abu Dhabi and Dubai as opposed to a deliberate political stratagem.

Dubai's sanctions-busting policies on behalf of Iran and Iraq from 1990 through 1994 provide much clearer evidence that the emirate's commercial prerogatives were at odds with the state's foreign policy interests. Following Saddam Hussein's invasion of Kuwait, the UAE's President Sheikh Zayed decided to pursue a closer strategic relationship with the United States.[80] The UAE emerged as a strong supporter of the U.S.-led effort to liberate Kuwait, agreeing to allow U.S. naval vessels to dock in Dubai, contributing troops to the coalition, and footing $3.5 billion worth of the bill.[81] After the war, the UAE sought to maintain the close military ties it had built with the United States. The UAE's security relationship with the United States grew especially salient in light of Iran's declaration of full sovereignty over a set of Persian Gulf islands over which the two countries had an ongoing territorial dispute in 1992.[82] The UAE countered the growing security threat it perceived from Iran by negotiating a defense pact with the United States in April of 1994. Coinciding with this defense pact, the UAE also agreed to allow the United States to preposition troops within Emirati territory, use the port of Jebel Ali as a U.S. Navy port of call, and use Emirati airbases to enforce the "no-fly zone" in Iraq.[83] This arrangement established the UAE as one of the U.S. military's most important staging areas in the Persian Gulf and established the country's importance to U.S. interests in the region. Abu Dhabi's purchases of over $360 million worth of American military hardware from 1992 through 1994 also reflects the closer security cooperation between the two countries.[84] These arrangements suggest a growing view within the UAE's leadership in the early 1990s that the United States could serve as the country's ultimate security guarantor against regional security threats.

Yet even as the UAE's federal government sought substantially closer political and security relations with the United States, Dubai's policies and constituents deliberately undermined the U.S. sanctions against its two greatest regional adversaries: Iran and Iraq. Importantly, this behavior was not politically motivated. Dubai readily welcomed the U.S. Navy to its ports and avidly sought to build up its trade connections with American companies. Instead, Dubai's sanctions busting was driven by its immense profitability—irrespective of the political costs that behavior entailed for the rest of the country.

The other hypotheses highlighted in Chapter 4 did not appear to play a decisive role in influencing the UAE's emergence as a leading sanctions buster on Iran's behalf during this period. The UAE had a relatively small but growing economy at that time, but much of its wealth was based on the extraction and export of fossil fuels. Its small domestic market offered limited opportunities to meet Iran's import demands or absorb excess Iranian exports. Also, the UAE possessed neither a defensive pact with Iran or the United States (until 1994), nor was it governed by democratic institutions. Given that the sanctions-busting theory is probabilistic and that these factors are only partial contributors to the overall attractiveness of a potential sanctions-busting venue, the lack of evidence for them in this case does not limit the potential roles they can play in other cases.

Overall, the sanctions-busting theory provides a compelling explanation for the emergence of the UAE as a leading sanctions buster on Iran's behalf from 1979 through 1994. The UAE's proximity to Iran, the commercial openness of its port city of Dubai, and the close commercial ties that the emirate had to Iran all facilitated in the development of an extensive sanctions-busting relationship between the two countries. Furthermore, the sanctions-busting theory also provides insights to the reasons why some of that trade occurred via legitimate channels although other portions of it occurred via illicit ones. The next section examines how the sanctions-busting relationship between the UAE and Iran changed as a result of Dubai's emergence as a global—and not just regional—transshipment hub and the defense pact alliance the UAE signed with the United States.

The UAE's Sanctions Busting on Iran's Behalf from 1995–2005

The commercial ties between Iran and the UAE only continued to grow stronger from 1995–2005, especially between Dubai and Iran. Iranian firms increased their commercial presence in Dubai substantially, and the emirate became a leading financial center for doing business with Iran and a major destination for Iranian foreign direct investment. Even though the UAE's leadership remained uneasy about the security threat posed by Iran during the latter half of the 1990s, this did not stop the country from increasing its commercial linkages to Iran. Indeed, the UAE's commercial policies, and particularly those of Dubai, toward Iran throughout this period seemed deliberately divorced from their government's security considerations. From 1995 through 2005, the UAE's exports to Iran experienced an almost exponential rate of growth, while its imports from the country grew steadily—excepting a brief spike in 1999 (see Figure 5.3). In some years, Emirati exports to Iran increased by double-digit margins as high as 50 percent. Over this period, Iran's commercial dependence upon the UAE grew increasingly strong. From 1998 to 2002, the UAE's reexport trade with Iran grew from $1 billion to $2.36 billion.[85] In 2003 alone, Iran's bilateral trade with the UAE totaled over $4.4 billion, constituting roughly 13.5 percent of the total trade Iran conducted that year.[86] The sheer volume of reexports from Dubai led some within Iran to call for a ban on Emirati reexports, seeing the cheap imports as undercutting domestic development.[87] Yet, even as the UAE's aggregate trade with Iran substantially increased over this period, these increases were matched by the UAE's broader engagement in international trade and emergence as one of the world's leading transshipment hubs.

Despite the UAE's smaller population and economy, Iran developed an asymmetrical level of commercial dependence on the UAE during this period and, in particular, on the emirate of Dubai. As one Emirati academic concludes, "Dubai is essential to Iran . . . Iran needs Dubai more than the other way round . . . It can deal with the outside world from here and it will need it more and more if there are (trade) sanctions imposed (over Tehran's nuclear program)."[88] Emphasizing this point, an Iranian businessman glibly surmised, "The best place to do business in Iran is in Dubai."[89] The level of commercial interdependence between the UAE and Iran grew to exceptionally high levels during this period—growing, at first, even in spite of the political tensions that existed between the two countries.

Throughout this period Iran also enhanced its previously established sanctions-busting relationships with its European trade partners and developed stronger ties with partners in Asia. U.S. allies such as France, Germany, and Italy all substantially increased their exports to Iran. Notably, the People's Republic of China also emerged as a major Iranian trade partner during this period (see Figure 5.6). The transfer of Hong Kong to Chinese control in 1997, the rapid growth of the Chinese economy, and China's increasing engagement in global commerce all likely contributed to making the country a far more

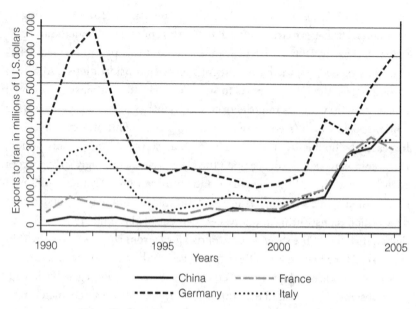

FIGURE 5.6. Other leading exporters to Iran, 1990–2005.
SOURCE: Barbieri et al. 2009.

attractive trading venue for Iran by the late 1990s than it had been previously. China's increasing need for foreign energy supplies also led it to reach out to Iran, signing a number of contracts for the purchase of oil and natural gas and, in defiance of the ILSA, facilitate in the development of Iran's oil fields.[90] The ability to purchase fossil fuels from Iran at below-market costs to meet its soaring energy needs provided the Chinese government with strong incentives to resist American pressure not to invest in or trade with Iran. It is important to note that the deals brokered by the Chinese government with Iran were not meant to provide it with foreign aid; rather, they were engineered to take advantage of the lucrative opportunities the U.S. sanctions created in doing business with Iran. A significant portion of the revenues Iran obtained from exporting fossil fuels to China were, in turn, spent on importing products from the country. From the late 1990s onward, China avidly undermined the American sanctions against Iran—growing into one of Iran's largest trading partners. In terms of the political and commercial incentives driving these states' behaviors, China's emergence as a leading sanctions buster on Iran's behalf is consistent with the sanctions-busting theory.

In adjusting to the enhanced U.S. sanctions during this period, Iran had a number of sanctions-busting options available. This placed greater pressure on third-party venues to provide firms with commercial environments that would allow them to maximize the profitability of their sanctions-busting trade. That the UAE–Iranian commercial relationship only continued to grow stronger during this period indicates the comparatively high profit margins it could offer to sanctions-busting traders. The next section explores the factors that appeared to play an important role in deepening the already established sanctions-busting relationship between Iran and the UAE.

Emirati Sanctions Busting on Iran's Behalf, 1995–2000
In May 1995, the Clinton administration issued Executive Order 12,959, which banned all U.S. trade with Iran. This full embargo did not have nearly the same effect on Iran's commerce as had the one in 1980, as Iran was significantly less dependent on U.S. trade. Yet, before the ban, a wide range of American exports continued to make their way legally to Iran. Furthermore, foreign branches of American oil firms had continued to engage in brisk trade with Iran, which the new ban halted.[91] By the time this new round of harsher sanctions hit, the sanctions-busting network Iran had in place "was a well-greased mechanism."[92] A European diplomat stationed in Tehran at the time gathered that "Iran probably has more ways than most to get around the US ban," adding that "Dubai will be a key" to its efforts.[93] Indeed, a large number of American firms already relied on middlemen in Dubai to sell their products to Iran in 1995—even for goods that had not been sanctioned. Askari and his coauthors assert that Iranians had deliberately sought to become more reliant on Emirati reexports in the lead-up to the sanctions, recognizing that their deteriorating relations with the United States would likely lead to more stringent trade restrictions on direct trade.[94]

The *Washington Post* ran a telling exposé on the effects of the ILSA on the Dubai-based companies that sold American products to Iran.[95] A senior executive at Juma Majid Company, one of Dubai's largest appliance wholesalers, disclosed that before the new sanctions his company had smuggled/reexported roughly 60 to 70 percent of its stock of General Electric (GE) appliances to Iran.[96] The executive observed that abiding by the new U.S. sanctions would cost his company a substantial portion of its business. Given that his company's transactions were taking place outside of the United States, he challenged the notion that the U.S. government could restrict his company's business activities. He further questioned whether his American partner (GE) had a genuine interest in his company's compliance, asking: "Do they [really] agree that we should reduce 70 percent of our sales volume?"[97] The executive's comments reflect that his company had no incentive to comply with the harsher new sanctions unless the U.S. government could credibly threaten retaliation for violating them in ways that would diminish the sanctions busting's profitability. The perception within Dubai was that the U.S. government could not or would not punish sanctions-busting violations; with profit margins as high as 40 percent on the sanctions-busting transactions being conducted, the risk was well worth taking.[98]

This story is also interesting because it touches on the incentives that American firms had to ensure that their regional distributors would comply with the U.S. government's sanctions. In 1995, there were about 200 American companies operating out of Dubai.[99] As Lancaster notes, a great deal of uncertainty seemed to exist among American firms about the extent of their culpability for preventing third parties from reexporting or transshipping their products to Iran. He cites the argument made by Kodak's Dubai branch that, while it could no longer ship directly to Iran, there was nothing to prevent its network of independent distributors from doing so.[100] In their initial response to the sanctions, American companies had strong incentives to turn a blind eye to these types of transactions—perceiving that a "don't ask, don't tell" policy was the most profitable arrangement.[101] Indeed, the prevalence of these sorts of transactions and the legal ambiguity that surrounded them prompted President Clinton to issue the follow-up E.O. 13,059. This order explicitly made American firms responsible for ensuring that their products would not be transshipped or reexported to Iran. Although this measure ended plausible deniability as a legal defense, it still did not stop American companies from trading with Dubai or Dubai's traders from finding increasingly clever ways to mask such transactions.

For example, Hewlett-Packard (HP) formed a regional distribution arrangement with a Dubai-based firm called Redington Gulf in 1997, the primary business strategy of which was to "sell HP supplies to the Iran market."[102] This arrangement turned out to be incredibly profitable for both firms, given their subsequent success in the Iranian market. In 1999, one of HP's general managers reported to a UAE-based newspaper that HP's sales in Iran were growing by 50 percent per year. By 2007, HP is estimated to have captured a 41 percent share of the Iranian printer market.[103] The U.S. government's sanctions policies were clearly not a sufficient deterrent to prevent the company from capitalizing on the profits to be made from continuing to trade with Iran.

As with the first round of U.S. sanctions from 1979 through 1981, the full U.S. trade ban prompted an increase in the amount of smuggling and unrecorded trade taking place between the UAE and Iran. Although American authorities could feasibly monitor large-scale transactions taking place through Dubai's major ports, Dubai's "dhows and the middlemen who stock them [were] almost impossible to regulate."[104] This meant that, once again, smuggling-based trade relationships could readily substitute for legitimate trade channels. As the official trade statistics indicate, the UAE's exports to Iran ended their three-year decline and began to rise steadily once again after 1995. At the same time, American exports to the UAE jumped noticeably after 1995 (see Figure 5.5). This suggests that the end destination of a substantial portion of the American imports being brought into the UAE was being masked. The scope of the sanctions-busting violations taking place could not even be called an open secret, as the phenomenon was readily reported on in the press and commented on by diplomats.[105]

Sanctions-busting firms within the UAE were involved in reexporting more than just American-made kitchen appliances during this period—they also supplied Iran with sensitive dual-use and high-tech products. As an ally of the United States, the UAE had greater access to American dual-use goods than it otherwise would have had. Various news reports concluded that, even after the imposition of the stricter sanctions in 1995, the markets in Tehran were still "flooded with American computers, drilling equipment and parts for everything from trucks to tanks."[106] For example, in 1996 there were reportedly 200 to 300 companies operating in Dubai involved in reexporting $100 million worth of American-made computers and accessories to Iran.[107] Describing the market, a Dubai trader explained, "You can get just about any kind of American computers in Iran now. A PC would be immediately available. For a server you would have to wait a couple of months . . . U.S. sanctions slowed things down and forced importers to use middlemen, so prices jumped some 30 percent, but they really did not stop much."[108] By making it more difficult for Iranians to purchase high-end products directly from U.S. companies, the ILSA made sanctions busting via Dubai even more lucrative for traders located there.

Though the U.S. Department of Commerce's (DOC) prosecution history of export control violations represents only a fraction of the total number of illicit sanctions-busting transactions that took place, they offer some insight into the types of sensitive American goods that were illicitly sold to Iran. An overview of DOC's published enforcement actions during this period reveals that it prosecuted sanctions busters for illicit transactions involving the UAE with respect to the following products: chlorine gas monitors (1998), fire alarm system equipment (1995), impregnated alumina (1995–1996), gas turbine parts (1995–1996), ferrology laboratory equipment (1998), bone densitometers (1998–1999), ethylene vinyl acetate (2002), computer parts (1998–2000), mini photo labs (2001), and a Shimadzu Transformer Oil Gas Analysis System (2000).[109] As the summaries of these cases illustrate, Iranians seeking to acquire high-end American goods frequently used fronts or middlemen in the UAE. As one U.S. official surmised in 1996, "The Iranians have a strong official and commercial presence in Dubai—it is their playground, the most accessible window to the rest of the world, particularly to high technology."[110]

In addition to its direct engagement in sanctions busting on Iran's behalf during this period, the UAE continued to facilitate Iraqi oil-smuggling operations until it finally cracked down on the trade in 1998. Following the trade routes established during the first Gulf War, traders would use barges and dhows to transport Iraqi oil and diesel along the Iranian coastline until they crossed the Gulf to the UAE.[111] Using falsified documentation provided by the Iranian officials, the smugglers would then sell this oil as being of Iranian origin in the UAE.[112] The UAE's decision to partially crack down on the smuggling was based more on environmental and safety concerns than on genuine support for the sanctions' imposition. Many of the dhows and barges used in these smuggling operations were old, in disrepair, and not designed to carry petroleum products. In 1998, several large oil spills along the Emirati coast called international attention to the oil smuggling that was taking place.[113] This led the UAE to outlaw the transport of oil by barges and suppress some of the oil-smuggling activities taking place within its waters—though it continued in diminished levels up until the U.S. invasion of Iraq.

The spike in the UAE's imports from Iran from 1998 and 1999 also presents a conspicuous puzzle (see Figure 5.3). As Askari and his coauthors note, "It is inconceivable" that Dubai could itself absorb $516 million of Iran's nonoil exports (constituting 16.2 percent of Iran's total nonoil exports).[114] There simply were not enough people in Dubai to purchase and/or consume that many carpets, pistachios, and dried figs. Rather, it is much more plausible to assume that a sizable portion of these Iranian imports had begun to be reexported to the United States from Dubai.[115] The trade data support this assertion in that, after the United States lifted its embargo against these products in 2000, the UAE's imports from Iran fell back to what had been their previous levels.

Emirati Sanctions Busting on Iran's Behalf, 2001–2005

Despite the extensive cooperation the UAE offered to the United States following the September 11, 2001, terrorist attacks, the country did very little to curb its sanctions-busting activities. As Figure 5.3 indicates, the UAE's exports to Iran grew at an almost exponential rate during this period. From 2001 through 2005, Iran accounted for between 20 and 25 percent of Dubai's total reexports.[116] An analysis of Dubai's trading sector in 2005 revealed that over 45 percent of the Emirate's traders were involved in exporting products to Iran.[117] Similarly over this time period, the UAE's imports from the United States grew at a staggering rate (see Figure 5.5). Although smuggling continued to play a role in the trade between the UAE and Iran, a larger proportion of the trade began flowing through legitimate channels. Given the increasingly hard-line position the United States took against the Iranian regime following 9/11 and the commitments made by the Emirati government to cooperate with the United States in its "War on Terror," it might seem puzzling that the country's sanctions busters would become more brazen about their trade with Iran during this period.

This dramatic rise in "legitimate" recorded trade between the UAE and Iran can be explained as a product of the burgeoning success of the UAE's various free trade zones (FTZs). For savvy traders, the UAE's FTZs could be exploited to provide cover for their sanctions-busting activities in far more profitable and convenient means than covert smuggling channels. The FTZs, like those at the port of Jebel Ali (JAFZA) and Sharjah International Airport, were established by their emirates to exist outside the customs jurisdiction of the UAE's federal government. They were designed to attract foreign commerce and investment and to minimize the bureaucratic red tape involved in doing business as much as possible. The administrative structures governing the zones were opaque and designed to allow firms that operated out of them to conduct their business free from public oversight. As well, FTZ administrators (who were competing against each other for business) had few incentives to actively police their zones; rather, they had clear incentives to adopt laissez-faire policies to encourage commerce. Because the UAE also had almost no nonproliferation export controls in place to regulate international trade in strategic items and technologies, this made the country's FTZs the perfect venue for conducting gray- and black-market transactions in technologies. This was especially true in Dubai's FTZs, in which sanctions-busting trade with Iran already constituted such a large part of the emirate's legitimate business.

Another sanctions-busting benefit of using Dubai's FTZs is that traders could import, store, and then reexport products via the zones without paying any customs duties on them. They were also allowed to conduct light manufacturing on, repackage, and reprocess the goods they brought into the zones. For traders seeking to mask their products' origins or the ultimate destination of products from their original source country, being able to conduct these activities legally, discretely, and cheaply provided excellent cover for sanctions-busting activities. A company within an FTZ could import an American product, repackage it as a Chinese-manufactured rip-off or equivalent, and then send it on to Iran through legitimate trade channels—thereby avoiding the ire of both the American and Iranian governments. Once the product arrived in Iran, it could then be returned to its original packaging. This form of *reverse counterfeiting* became a popular method of circumventing the sanctions; given the sheer volume of the trade flows passing through Dubai, these transactions were very difficult to detect by American authorities and companies.[118] The tactic was also commonly used by Dubai's smaller dhow traders.[119] Especially at JAFZA, Dubai's largest and most active FTZ, there were so many commercial transactions taking place and so many goods passing through the zone that hiding in plain sight was easy. According to Gary Milhollin and Kelly Motz, this helped to make Dubai "the easiest place in the world to mask the real destination of cargo."[120] It is important to note that most of the sanctions-busting transactions that took place via the UAE's FTZs were legal under Emirati law, irrespective of whether they broke the laws of other governments.

Even with respect to sensitive U.S. exports that required export control licenses, sanctions busters often found it easy to make diversions via Dubai. According to an investigation, the U.S. Department of Commerce "turned down just 2% of applications to export to the U.A.E." from 1999 to early 2004. Moreover, the agency conducted only sixty-three end-user verification checks on sales made to the UAE from 1996 to 1999 and 114 checks from 2000 to 2003.[121] These follow-up checks are conducted to ensure that licensed transactions have not been diverted to third parties and confirm that a licensed product is being used according to its intended end use. Given the UAE's twenty-year history as an active sanction-busting hub, these figures are surprisingly low. In 2005, I observed the reason for these low figures firsthand. Despite all the sanctions-busting trade that was known to be taking place in UAE, the U.S. Department of Commerce had tasked only a single enforcement officer to the country to monitor the end use of sensitive, licensed goods and technologies that U.S. firms were sending to the country. Sanctions busters operating in the UAE thus appear to have needed little subterfuge to obtain sensitive American products because the U.S. government failed to invest the necessary resources to identify, investigate, and punish most violations that took place in the country. Once American goods arrived in Dubai they fell into a black hole as far as most U.S. companies and authorities were concerned. This made Dubai the perfect sanctions-busting haven, as it provided "companies and governments with a vital asset: *automatic deniability.*"[122]

Though the event failed to catalyze immediate policy changes, the 2004 revelation that Dubai served as a key node in the A. Q. Khan proliferation network raised high-profile awareness about the illicit trade flowing through the emirate. Using his global network of connections and the resources of his nuclear fiefdom inside the Pakistani government, Khan peddled his nuclear know-how and coordinating services to help other countries develop nuclear energy and weapons programs.[123] Dubai served as the Khan network's operational headquarters. Though his official post was in Pakistan, A. Q. Khan made forty-four visits to Dubai from 1999 until his network unraveled in early 2004—crossing the Gulf twenty times to visit Iran from Dubai.[124] Two of the companies used by the Khan network were based out of Dubai. SMB Computers, incorporated in JAFZA and having strong commercial ties to Malaysia, was used extensively to transship nuclear technologies and materials to Libya and Iran.[125] The Dubai-based Gulf Technical Industries was used as a front company to provide a cover for the network's illicit purchases coming through the emirate.[126] Given its lax commercial restrictions and almost complete absence of export controls, the UAE was an ideal venue from which to direct the proliferation network's transactions. As Albright and Hinderstein surmised, the Khan proliferation network

> . . . depended on complicated transportation arrangements, mainly to confuse suppliers about the true end use of the item and to evade prying intelligence agencies or deceive them about the final destination for its products. The

international free zone [JAFZA] in Dubai, through which shipments are still subject to few meaningful controls, was particularly critical to the network.[127]

Khan's network played an instrumental role in helping Iran build up its nuclear program's capabilities and almost single-handedly was responsible for the Libyan nuclear program. The network's activities are widely viewed as one of the nuclear nonproliferation community's largest-ever failures, and Dubai played a central role in facilitating its operations.

Though the Emirati government had refused American entreaties to block proliferation-relevant transactions in the past,[128] there is no evidence that UAE's leaders were complicit with or aware of the Khan network's transactions. Clearly, a nuclear-armed Iranian regime is not in the UAE's national security interests. Yet even if these exact transactions were not condoned, the leaders of Dubai had intentionally created a laissez-faire environment that was conducive to them. Indeed, most of the Khan network's transactions did not violate any Emirati laws. Despite the negative publicity that Dubai drew for the part it played in the Khan network, business continued to boom in the emirate and its commercial relationship with Iran, and the sanctions busting it was conducting on its behalf only continued to grow in 2005. The sanctions-busting theory offers insights into why the UAE–Iran sanctions-busting relationship continued to flourish during this period despite all the political disincentives that existed for it.

Explaining the UAE–Iranian Trade-Based
Sanctions-Busting Relationship, 1995–2005

The significant growth in sanctions-busting trade being conducted on Iran's behalf via Dubai during this second case period can be explained by a number of factors according to the sanctions-busting theory. Once again, the UAE's geographic proximity to Iran made it a convenient sanctions-busting venue. The UAE's economy also experienced significant growth during this period, as did its involvement in international commerce. The country's FTZs played a key role attracting far more regional and international investment, multinational corporations (MNCs), and international trade than the country had ever previously experienced. The UAE's economic growth during this period was tied in significant part to its sanctions-busting activities, especially within Dubai. This correspondingly contributed to a growing dependence within the UAE on trade with Iran to sustain its prosperity. Lastly, the UAE's alliance with the United States helped make it a more attractive venue for U.S. firms seeking to circumvent the sanctions against Iran and helped shield it from retaliation for its sanctions-busting activities. The sanctions-busting theory offers a framework for understanding how all of these factors contributed to why the intensity of the sanctions-busting relationship between the UAE and Iran grew stronger during this period.

The UAE's economy grew explosively from 1995 through 2005. Its economy almost doubled in size over this period, in some years experiencing growth upwards of 11 to 12 percent. The period was marked by booms in the UAE's real-estate, construction, and service sectors, fueled by high oil prices and significant inflows of foreign direct investment. Its involvement in international commerce also rose dramatically, with Dubai emerging as one of the most globalized cities in the Middle East. It is almost impossible to separate the early successes of Dubai's economy and its FTZs in this period from the emirate's involvement in sanctions busting. The sanctions-busting opportunities available via Iran provided a highly profitable core around which Dubai's commercial sector was able to grow and expand, funding investments in world-class logistical resources, facilitating innovations in how it catered to foreign investors and businesses, and helping to make Dubai a central node in global distribution networks. The success of Dubai's FTZs encouraged other emirates within the UAE to also create them, many of which subsequently prospered during this period. The expansion of the UAE's FTZs was a critical factor in the overall economic prosperity enjoyed by the country during this period and its continued success as Iran's leading sanctions buster, with the latter being intrinsically linked to the former.

As Table 5.1 illustrates, the number of firms doing business in the UAE's free zones expanded significantly during this period. In JAFZA alone, the number of firms doing business in it grew over 730 percent from 1990 to 2005. By the late 1990s, the administrators of Dubai's ports and JAFZA had gained an international reputation for efficiency and effectiveness in logistics management. In addition to JAFZA, the Sharjah Airport International Free Zone and the Dubai Airport Free Zone both grew rapidly over this period—providing an air-link complement to JAFZA's seaport trafficking. In total, exports (including reexports) from Dubai's free trade zones grew from $2.44 billion in 1995 to $5.1 billion in 2000 and to $14.32 billion in 2004. In just ten years, the emirate's free zones experienced an almost sixfold increase in their export traffic. By the end of 2003, Dubai stood behind only Singapore and Hong Kong as the world's third-largest reexporter.[129]

TABLE 5.1. Growth of the UAE's free trade zones.

Location of free zones	Date established	Firms in 1999	Firms in 2005
Jebel Ali Free Zone	1985	1, 343	2,200
Dubai Airport Free Zone	1996	35	831
Ajman Free Zone	1988	375	1,591
Sharjah Airport International Free Zone	1995	1,000	Over 2,000
Ras al-Khaimah Free Zone	2000	0	1,400

SOURCES: Ghanem 2001, 271; Ajman Free Zone 2005; Dubai Airport Free Zone 2005; "Jebel Ali Free Zone: Free Zone Companies" 2005; Sharjah Airport International Free Zone 2005; Ras al-Khaimah Free Zone 2005.

In addition to the free zones listed in Table 5.1, Dubai initiated an effort to create a plethora of free zones designed to attract foreign investment in the technology, financial, and information sectors. A prototype for the expansion of these sector-specific free zones was the Dubai Internet City (DIC) Zone launched in 2000.[130] The DIC Zone enjoyed significant success in attracting foreign direct investment in the lucrative high-tech market, luring high-profile MNCs like Microsoft, Oracle, Hewlett-Packard, Cisco Systems, IBM, Compaq, Sun Microsystems, and Intel to establish operations in the free zone.[131] The freedom from foreign investment restrictions, taxes on profits, customs duties, and politically motivated trade restrictions (for example, sanctions and export controls) also led a large number of businesses to become incorporated within these FTZs as free zone enterprises. The difference between this second generation of FTZs and their more logistically oriented predecessors is that they sought to attract firms to do business *within* Dubai instead of just *through* it. Although the UAE still lacked a large industrial production base, foreign investment in these free zones provided the country with a rapidly expanding market in the technology and information sectors.

The rapid growth of the UAE's FTZs provided Iran with access not only to the goods produced by companies around the world but access to the companies themselves. The UAE's free zones came to play host to a diverse array of firms from around the world, placing them side-by-side in commercially neutral havens. As an example, Table 5.2 illustrates the heavy presence of Iranian, Indian, and Chinese companies within the JAFZA in 2005. Almost 19 percent of the firms operating out of the JAFZA were of Iranian origin, demonstrating Iranian traders' major presence with the zone.[132] As the text box beside the table suggests, a significant number of leading MNCs also had corporate

TABLE 5.2. Select origins and identities of the firms operating in JAFZA in 2005.

Country	Firms	Percent	Notable MNCs Present in JAFZA
Iran	409	19%	
Japan	84	4%	Acer, Bayer, Black & Decker, Bridgestone,
India	571	26%	Compaq, Daewoo, Daimler-Chrysler, Hewlett-Packard, Honda, Johnson &
Pakistan	112	5%	Johnson, Nissan, Nivea, Nokia, Philips,
China	884	40%	Samsung, Sony, Toshiba, and Xerox
United States	150	7%	

SOURCES: "Jebel Ali Free Zone: Free Zone Companies" 2005 and U.S. & Foreign Commercial Service 2005.

presences within JAFZA. Iranian firms commonly operated right next door to American ones in many FTZs—making coordinating and carrying out diversions remarkably easy.[133] Another common approach used by Iranian sanctions busters was to establish front companies within the FTZs, chartered as "nationless" free zone enterprises. These companies were then used to acquire sanctioned American goods and technologies for reexport to Iran.[134] If Iranian firms simply wanted substitutes for sanctioned U.S. goods, they could also obtain them from one of the many Chinese companies operating in the FTZs as well. Using Dubai as a third-party venue for conducting such transactions was a matter of convenience and cost-effectiveness, not of necessity.

The UAE's dramatic economic growth and emergence as a global commercial hub helped preserve the UAE's status as the leading venue for conducting sanctions-busting trade with Iran despite the emergence of larger-sized commercial competitors. By leveraging its innovative FTZs, Dubai and other emirates within the UAE were able to create commercial environments that proved ideal for sanctions busting. Via their system of innovative institutions that lowered the costs and risks of sanctions busting, the Emiratis were able to leverage the prosperity those activities offered in ways that made their country an even more attractive sanctions-busting venue. The global reputation Dubai gained as a sanctions-busting haven led firms interested in trading with Iran to flock to the UAE in droves by the mid-2000s.

The prosperity that trade with Iran offered came at the cost of the UAE's commercial autonomy. The more the UAE benefited from its trade with Iran, the more costly that disruption of that commercial relationship became. Despite the clear security threats Iran posed and the UAE's closer ties to the United States, sanctions busting was too lucrative for the UAE government to disrupt for political reasons. A 2005 Iranian report concluded that there were over 4,650 Iranian firms operating out of Dubai.[135] News reports from 2005 further estimated that Iranian nationals contributed to roughly 45 percent of the fixed investments in Dubai, citing the involvement of over 400,000 Iranian investors with over $200 billion tied into Dubai's financial and housing sectors.[136] All this helped strengthen the perception that the UAE was one of the safest places to develop sanctions-busting relationships with Iran, as the relationship was too costly for the UAE government to possibly disrupt.

Within the alliance arrangement negotiated between the United States and the UAE, the United States was clearly the more powerful, senior partner. Although the exact terms of the U.S.–UAE defense pact are classified, the agreement included a status of forces agreement, provisions pertaining to troop prepositioning, U.S. naval warship visits, and the use of the al-Dhafra air base.[137] Despite being militarily rather weak, the UAE's strategic location in the Persian Gulf and its advanced port facilities made the country extremely valuable to American interests in the region. In 1995, the U.S. Navy made 300 port call visits in Dubai.[138] The UAE also became one of the American armed services' most popular liberty destinations in the Persian Gulf—with over 110,000 troops visiting the country in 1996.[139] In the years following the first Persian Gulf War (1991 through 2003), the UAE's al-Dhafra air base also played an import role in facilitating the U.S. government's efforts to enforce the no-fly zone in southern Iraq.[140]

Following 9/11, the UAE became an even more important staging and logistical center for the U.S. military's operations in the region. In 1997, there were about 300 American armed service personnel permanently stationed in the UAE.[141] That number grew to 800 personnel prior to the invasion of Afghanistan in 2001 and continued to grow to more than 1,800 servicemen after the invasion of Iraq. Most of these personnel conducted support operations for the U.S. missions in Iraq and Afghanistan.[142] Also from 1995 through 2005, the UAE provided the most frequently visited ports of call for the U.S. Navy out of any country besides the United States. In 2005 alone, Dubai played host to over 500 ship visits from the U.S. Navy.[143] Remarks by U.S. Senator John Warner, Chairman of the U.S. Senate Armed Services Committee, reflect the perceived importance of the strategic U.S. relationship with the UAE: "Whether it's in Afghanistan or Iraq, and the utilization of the facilities in UAE . . . is essential. Absolutely essential. If the UAE felt that they're being mistreated and were to pull back that support, where would [U.S. military support operations] shift? We know not."[144] As Senator Warner's comments suggest, the United States relied heavily on the UAE to support its military presence and operations in the Persian Gulf region and had few alternatives in the region if its relationship with the UAE soured. Senator Warner's remarks also reflect concern about the potential ramifications of alienating the UAE, which attempting to coerce it into complying with U.S. sanctioning efforts would have almost certainly done.[145]

As the perceived importance of the U.S. alliance with the UAE grew, so did the UAE's willingness to brazenly flout the U.S. sanctions against Iran. The fact that the U.S. government did not undertake any significant efforts to convince the UAE to stop sanctions busting reflected that the benefits it received from maintaining a positive alliance relationship with the UAE outweighed the costs of tolerating the UAE's exploitation of its sanctions. The strategic importance of its alliance relationship with the United States thus provided the UAE with greater political cover for its sanctions-busting activities than it had previously enjoyed and far greater political cover than other nonallies had.

As Figure 5.5 illustrates, the United States and UAE traded significantly more with one another during the second case period than the first. Though the changes to the UAE's commercial profile can account for some of that substantial growth, part of it can be positively attributed to the effects the U.S.–UAE alliance had on the countries' trade. As the political relationship between the United States and the UAE got stronger, American firms felt more comfortable trading with and investing in the UAE. By the end of 2005, 500 American firms had established business operations in Dubai—with 150 of them in JAFZA alone. Computer companies like Acer and Supra set up shop in JAFZA, while others like Microsoft, Hewlett Packard, and Oracle opened branches in the media and technology free zone.[146] These corporations' presences in the UAE's free zones was likely the product of the market opportunities available in the UAE, the perceived stability of the U.S.–UAE relationship that made investments in the otherwise unstable region safe, and an opportunistic perspective that Iran's appetite for high-tech goods would *via some indirect means* boost their regional sales. The U.S.–UAE alliance also provided the UAE with far greater access to sensitive U.S. goods than it otherwise would have had. By virtue of several massive arms deals conducted between the United States and UAE under the aegis of their alliance, the UAE was cleared to receive some of the most advanced military technologies the

U.S. government had ever sold abroad.[147] The alliance also provided U.S. firms with a great deal more leeway in exporting controlled dual-use goods and technologies to the UAE than if that strategic relationship did not exist. The UAE offered a prime venue for diverting strategic U.S. goods to Iran because it was so easy to legitimately export those products to Iran's doorstep. The fact that it was *common knowledge* that Dubai was being used as a diversion point to sell sanctioned American strategic goods to Iran, and yet the U.S. government did so little to monitor or restrict the transactions that took place with the country, suggests that U.S. policy makers either made a deliberate policy trade-off or allowed a critical policy failure. The theory presented in this book suggests the former case, but elements of the latter cannot be wholly discounted.

One prominent case, in particular, illustrates how U.S. firms sought to exploit the sanctions-busting opportunities offered by Dubai. When the U.S. energy firm Halliburton decided that it wanted to open a corporate office in Tehran to reestablish its business relationship with Iran in 2000, it chose to work through its Dubai-based subsidiary Halliburton Products & Services.[148] Notably, this move occurred while Dick Cheney was still CEO of the company. Indeed, Cheney was an outspoken critic of the U.S. sanctions imposed against Iran during his tenure at Halliburton—viewing them as bad for American businesses.[149] Speaking to the World Petroleum Congress about the sanctions a month before he joined George W. Bush's presidential ticket, Cheney told the audience: "We're kept out of [Iran] primarily by our own government which has made a decision that U.S. firms should not be allowed to invest significantly in Iran, and I think that's a mistake."[150] His company's move to circumvent the U.S. government's sanctions by working through an independent foreign subsidiary clearly reflects this view. It violated the spirit of the U.S. sanctions by exploiting a legal loophole, if not necessarily the letter of the law.[151] Using a Dubai-based subsidiary made sense, given Dubai's proximity to Iran, the strong commercial ties the UAE had with both the United States and Iran, and the political cover the U.S.–UAE alliance could grant to the firm's activities. In 2005, Halliburton Products & Services Ltd. successfully won contracts from the Iranian government to help develop the oil and gas fields in south Pars.[152] This was the type of transaction that E.O. 13,059 had been imposed to discourage. Although congressional Democrats subsequently conducted hearings and investigations on the deal, the federal government never levied any punishments against Halliburton or its subsidiary for the deal. U.S. policy makers had the mechanisms in place to further go after the firm but did not use them. Following the congressional scrutiny it received, Halliburton actually chose to relocate its corporate headquarters to Dubai in 2006. This is just one prominent example of American firms undercutting the U.S. government's sanctioning efforts and strategically leveraging U.S. allies in doing so.

The UAE had the reputation of being a major sanctions buster on Iran's behalf before the United States formed its alliance with it, and the alliance it brokered with the United States did not change the regime's orientation. Indeed, the alliance only further raised the costs associated with using coercion to obtain the country's sanctions cooperation. As an official from the U.S. Embassy in Abu Dhabi surmised, trying to compel the UAE to adopt the U.S. government's preferred sanctions and export controls vis-à-vis Iran "would be incredibly stupid . . . [The UAE] is the one friend we have in the Gulf, except Kuwait."[153] U.S. policy makers were willing to tolerate a lot in return for the types of military cooperation it was receiving via its alliance with the UAE. Astute firms recognized that both the U.S. strategic dependence on the UAE and the UAE's commercial dependence on Iran were too great for either country to disrupt the sanctions-busting relationship the UAE had formed with Iran. The political cover extended to the UAE only served to further attract firms from other third-party states to conduct their sanctions-busting trade through the country. Both how the U.S. alliance constrained its ability to coerce the UAE into supporting its sanctions and how American and third-party firms exploited those constraints to circumvent the sanctions perfectly illustrate the sanctions-busting theory's counterintuitive predictions in practice.

My theory thus offers a compelling explanation of why the sanctions-busting relationship between the UAE and Iran intensified from 1995 to 2005 despite the apparent political disincentives that existed for the expansion of that relationship. By making its sanctions even harsher, the U.S. government made sanctions busting on Iran's behalf even more profitable for third-party and U.S. firms willing to circumvent them. The UAE's proximity to Iran, its explosively growing economy and heavy engagement in international commerce, its close commercial ties to Iran, and its alliance with the United States all helped make it one of the most profitable venues from which to sanctions-bust on Iran's behalf. The UAE's innovative system of FTZs also helped to increasingly funnel sanctions-busting trade on Iran's behalf through legitimate channels. By the end of 2005, the UAE—and Dubai in particular—had gained a global reputation for being the number-one venue for sanctions busting on Iran's behalf.

How Much Did the UAE's Sanctions Busting Undercut the U.S. Sanctions?

It is difficult to place the success or failure of a given sanctioning effort at the doorstep of any single third-party state's response. The U.S. sanctions have had a variety of different goals over time: the release of U.S. hostages, discouraging Iran's state sponsorship of terrorism, encouraging regime change and democratic reform, and discouraging Iran's pursuit of a potential nuclear weapons capability. Other than the first objective associated with the 1979–1981 sanctioning effort, there is little evidence to suggest that the U.S. sanctions have achieved the objectives for which they were imposed. As Chapter 3 explained, sanctions outcomes are influenced by the aggregate number of states willing to engage in trade-based sanctions busting on the target's behalf and the foreign aid flows the target receives—of which the contributions of any given third-party state may matter or be trivial. Indeed, Iran had multiple sanctions-busting trade partners beyond the UAE that have certainly contributed to its ability to resist the U.S. sanctions.

With that being said, the UAE was uniquely qualified in certain ways to provide Iran with sanctions-busting support that made the sanctions-busting it conducted particularly pernicious to U.S. sanctioning efforts. The case evidence provides strong evidence that the UAE was not just the most profitable venue from which to sanctions-bust on Iran's behalf, but it was also the most affordable market for Iranian traders. Especially during the 1980s, Iran had almost no alternative regional trading partners that could help it circumvent the U.S. sanctions nearly as cost-effectively as the UAE. The UAE's sanctions busting appears to have substantially diminished the overarching economic cost the U.S. sanctions would have imposed had it not been avidly sanctions-busting on Iran's behalf. In subsequent decades, the global sanctions-busting options available to Iran certainly opened up. Yet few countries could match the efficiency, experience, or convenience of the sanctions-busting sector that had developed in Dubai. Especially when the United States imposed complete trade bans, such as in 1995, the UAE offered Iranians the most cost-effective means of obtaining sanctioned U.S. products and/or foreign substitutes. How else could HP have had an over 41 percent market share of Iran's printer market? It is doubtful that this factor alone has prevented the Iranian government from capitulating to the U.S. government's various sanctioning efforts, but it certainly reduced the costs of its obstinacy.

The UAE also appeared to have played an important role in undermining the strategic impact of the U.S. sanctions on Iran. Especially considering the U.S. government's goals of restricting Iran's access to high-tech military and aerospace goods and technologies, fossil fuel exploration and extraction goods and technologies, and nuclear-related goods and technologies, the UAE has served as a siphon for leaking those high-value strategic products to Iran. The UAE government's almost complete lack of export controls, combined with its robust sanctions-busting operations and easy access to U.S. strategic exports, made it an ideal place for the Iranian government or elements thereof to acquire such products. That A. Q. Khan made Dubai the foreign headquarters for his illicit proliferation efforts vis-à-vis Iran was anything but a coincidence. For decades, the Iranian government was able to utilize Dubai as a means for obtaining strategic and dual-use goods without which its economy, energy sector, and national security would have suffered from the sanctions by a far greater magnitude. The inability of the U.S. government to stop the progress of Iran's nuclear program via its sanctions and global diplomatic efforts can be attributed in a nontrivial amount to the role played by the UAE. The sanctions busting conducted by the UAE thus left the Iranian government in a far stronger position vis-à-vis the U.S. sanctions than it otherwise would have had.

This suggests that UAE played an important but not necessarily determinative role in undercutting the U.S. sanctioning efforts against Iran from 1984 through 2005. The UAE's sanctions busting certainly did not convince the U.S. government to give up on its efforts, but it has helped convince the Iranians not to give in to those efforts. Causally speaking, there is strong reason to think that the UAE's sanctions busting on Iran's behalf was a significant reason why the United States largely failed to achieve its sanctions objectives.

Postscript: U.S. Efforts to Curtail Emirati Sanctions Busting from 2006 to the Present

From 2006 onward, a number of events helped catalyze the U.S. and international sanctioning efforts against Iran. The repeated findings by the

International Atomic Energy Agency that Iran has violated its legal commitments under the Nuclear Nonproliferation Treaty, the security concerns Iran's potential pursuit of nuclear weapons raised, the bellicose and antagonizing rhetoric of Iran's President Mahmoud Ahmadinejad, and the Iranian government's violent crackdown after the country's 2009 presidential election have all contributed to the international isolation and ostracization of Iran. These events, along with the U.S. government's renewed political commitment to its sanctioning efforts against Iran, facilitated in a number of UN Security Council resolutions being passed that imposed international economic sanctions on Iran and parties within the country geared toward limiting the development of its nuclear program.[154] These measures created an international legal obligation for all states to impose at least limited sanctions against Iran. The reputation costs of being viewed as supportive of Iran thus grew significantly larger after 2006, encouraging more governments to actively participate in the sanctioning effort and making it more difficult for third-party governments to justify providing cover to firms that sanctions-bust on Iran's behalf. This has offered U.S. policy makers greater leeway in pursuing more proactive policies designed to curb third-party sanctions busting.[155]

In the UAE case, U.S. policy makers undertook a concerted effort to convince the UAE government to crack down on the most egregious sanctions busting that was taking place through that country. They made curbing the UAE's involvement in helping Iran obtain sensitive strategic goods and technologies a key priority, and—to a notable extent—those efforts have been effective. Whereas the UAE continues to actively participate in sanctions-busting trade with Iran, it has limited the scale and scope of the sanctions-busting activities it allows to take place in a number of areas like that one. The approach U.S. policy makers undertook to achieve those concessions, the UAE's response to them, and the impact those efforts had on the sanctions' effectiveness are all potentially instructive. As this postscript reveals, the pressure the United States has brought to bear on the UAE over its sanctions busting has yielded positive but limited results. However, the ultimate return on its investment remains in question.

Revelations about the active role that Dubai played in the A. Q. Khan proliferation network played a major role in shifting the U.S. government's attitude toward the UAE's sanctions busting. From 2007 to 2009, the U.S. Government Accountability Office also found that the UAE was responsible for half (fifteen out of thirty) of the total export control violations that the U.S.

government prosecuted for illegal transshipment of U.S. strategic goods and technologies to Iran—and those were only the cases in which violations were identified and sufficient evidence existed for prosecution.[156] A major priority for the U.S. government thus became encouraging the Emiratis to implement a strategic trade control system that would restrict the legal trafficking of weapons of mass destruction (WMD)-relevant goods technologies via the UAE. The UAE's imposition of strategic trade controls would help prevent Iran from using the country as a legitimate channel for circumventing the U.S. and international sanctions imposed against it on acquiring these products.

Although the U.S. government offered the UAE government technical assistance to aid in its strategic trade control system's development, it also began placing overt pressure on the regime to curtail its sanctions-busting activities. In 2006, Dubai's state-owned ports management corporation, DP World, sought a deal to enter the U.S. market and encountered unexpectedly vociferous opposition. Although the Bush administration and key U.S. policy makers actually supported the deal, fearing the damage that blocking it could cause to alliance relations with the UAE, a vocal bipartisan coalition mounted a concerted effort against it.[157] Citing Dubai's reputation as a sanctions-busting haven among other concerns, opponents to the DP World deal generated so much controversy that it was scuttled.[158] This episode embarrassingly conveyed to the Emirati leadership that there could be salient repercussions for the UAE's sanctions-busting activities.

Also during this period, the U.S. Department of Commerce developed a new category of states posing proliferation risks called "destinations of diversion concerns." This categorization was designed for countries with weak strategic trade controls that engaged in high levels of international trade and were not cooperating with the U.S. government in preventing proliferation activities: in other words, the UAE. This designation would have significantly restricted the UAE from receiving access to high-value U.S. exports and placed all licensed transactions to the country under much greater scrutiny. Threatening the UAE with this designation, which would have had significant commercial and reputational costs for the country, was a powerful but low-profile means of coercing the UAE government. The U.S. government also stepped up its bilateral diplomatic pressure on the UAE, with a continuous flow of high-level U.S. policy makers visiting the country and engaging the Emiratis on this issue.[159]

Lastly, the U.S. government had additional leverage over the UAE in that it was seeking to become the first Persian Gulf state to create a civilian nuclear energy program. The UAE's establishment of an operative strategic trade control system was one of U.S. policy makers' preconditions for signing a civilian nuclear assistance agreement with the UAE in 2009.[160] Concerted engagement across all these issues help place far greater pressure on the UAE to crack down on its lucrative sale of strategic goods and technologies to Iran than ever before.

In addition to the specific pressure that the United States has placed on the UAE, U.S. efforts to obtain multilateral support for its nonproliferation-oriented sanctions against Iran began gaining traction in 2006. The United States successfully lobbied the UN Security Council to pass UNSCR 1737—the first of a series of Security Council resolutions aimed at Iran's nuclear program and individuals, agencies, and companies that facilitate it.[161] UNSCR 1540 (2004), which mandated that all countries impose strategic trade control systems, constituted another important multilateral measure that placed pressure on the UAE to impose restrictions on its trade in proliferation-sensitive items and technologies.[162] The UN sanctions played two important roles. First they added another dimension to the bilateral pressure the U.S. government was placing on the UAE's leadership to crack down on the country's proliferation-sensitive trade with Iran. Secondly, the UN sanctions provided the UAE with political cover in imposing trade restrictions against Iran to minimize the political fallout vis-à-vis the Iranian government. The latter was especially important to Emirati leaders.[163]

The United States' coercive efforts extended beyond just proliferation-sensitive trade. U.S. policy makers also sought to obtain greater Emirati cooperation in preventing the diversion of other U.S. products through the country and in curtailing its financial ties with Iran as part of a broader strategy to financially isolate Iran. Significant domestic opposition existed in the UAE to imposing full-spectrum trade sanctions against Iran. Gaining Emirati support for curtailing its trade with Iran in nonstrategic goods and technologies was therefore an uphill battle. Dubai's position as an emergent global financial center, though, also gave the UAE an important role in financing Iranians' global sanctions-busting activities. In this sector, U.S. policy makers possessed greater leverage in engaging the Emiratis. In a strategy credited to Stuart Levey, then the U.S. Department of Treasury's undersecretary for terrorism and financial intelligence, the U.S. government began efforts to isolate

Iran's banking sector from the international financial system that its traders rely on for international transactions.[164] Given the dominant U.S. role in the global financial system, conducting business via the United States or with U.S. partners is critical for most international banks. This dependence gave the U.S. government significant leverage over foreign banks in compelling them to stop financing sanctions-busting transactions.[165] In 2010, Congress passed the Comprehensive Iran Sanctions, Accountability, and Divestment Act, which significantly enhanced the U.S. Treasury Department's ability to pressure foreign banks to cease their business with sanctioned Iranian entities.

Whereas Treasury's early efforts to obtain the cooperation of foreign banks relied on threats of "naming and shaming" to harm the reputations of banks involved in sanctions-busting transactions, it grew significantly more aggressive in investigating and prosecuting financial institutions for their role in sanctions-busting-related activities. These investigations resulted in substantial financial settlements with a number of banks, such as Lloyds TSB Bank (2009), Credit Suisse (2009), Barclays Bank (2010), ING (2012), and HSBC (2012).[166] Notably, a number of these banks were headquartered in states that shared alliances with the United States. The UAE's strong commercial ties with Iran made the costs of disrupting its financial ties with the country quite significant. At the same time, Dubai's continued growth as a global financial center could have been crippled if its banks were denied access to the U.S. financial sector. Reflecting Dubai's importance and the delicate nature of the issue, Undersecretary Levey made gaining the Emiratis' cooperation in imposing financial restrictions on Iran one of his personal priorities.[167]

In the spring of 2012, the Obama administration grew even bolder in targeting foreign firms involved in busting the U.S. sanctions against Syria and Iran with the issuance of E.O. 13608. The measure empowered the U.S. Treasury Department to identify parties involved in sanctions-busting activities and punish them by revoking their ability to enter the United States, receive any U.S. foreign aid, or do business of any kind with U.S. citizens, firms, or governmental bodies—"effectively excluding them from the U.S. economic system."[168] Although the measure's penalties were harsh, its bite relies on the extent to which foreign firms depend on doing business with U.S. partners. So although the measure placed minimal additional pressure on small, regional traders to stop sanctions busting on Iran's behalf, it placed significantly more pressure on larger corporations that had global business profiles and frequently interact with U.S. firms or the U.S. financial system.

The combined pressures that the United States placed on the UAE resulted in some notable concessions, but they have not persuaded the country to sever its sanctions-busting relationship with Iran. The Department of Commerce's threat of designating the UAE as a diversion risk and the UN sanctions proved to be particularly effective at gaining tangible cooperation from its government.[169] The UAE's most notable response was the adoption of its first comprehensive strategic trade control law in 2007. Since then, it has continued to foster its strategic trade control system's development with the assistance of the U.S. government and has cooperated much more closely with the U.S. government in halting proliferation-sensitive transactions destined for Iran.[170] As an interesting comparison, the U.S. government was also the most successful in getting its North Atlantic Treaty Organization (NATO) allies to deny strategic exports to Cuba even if they refused all other cooperation with the U.S. sanctioning efforts. The UAE's financial sector has also provided fairly substantial cooperation in severing relationships with blacklisted Iranian financial institutions and denying Iranian-based firms with access to letters of credit. The harsh punishments the U.S. government meted out against other foreign banks have helped convince many Emirati financial institutions of the risks associated with doing business with Iran.[171] With the special attention they have received, the U.S. Treasury Department's coercive threats have been quite clearly communicated to Emirati banks.[172] Additionally, the UAE government has expressed its support for complying with the UN-backed sanctions that restrict or ban financial transactions with specific Iranian individuals, firms, and governmental bodies. In early 2012, the UAE's central bank took the major step of asking its financial institutions to cease financing commercial trade with Iran.[173] This significant concession appears to be the result of the unprecedented coercive pressure the U.S. government brought to bear with E.O. 13608, the Emirati banking system's vulnerability to being cut off from the U.S. financial system, and the credibility the United States had gained in imposing substantial fines on the banks of its other allies.

The U.S. government has not been nearly as effective in curbing the rest of the UAE's nonstrategic commercial relationship with Iran. The UAE government's cooperation with U.S. and international sanctions has certainly harmed its sanctions-busting relationship with Iran; however, the UAE and Iran still continue to be one of each other's leading nonoil trading partners. Trade between the UAE and Iran more than tripled from 2005 ($4.2 billion) to 2008 ($14.3 billion) before taking a dip in 2009.[174] The Iranian commercial presence in Dubai remains strong even if the business climate is not as friendly as it once was.[175] The UAE's trade with Iran rebounded from its dip in 2009, with the two countries conducting approximately $15.5 billion dollars' worth of bilateral trade in 2011. It is important to note that that estimate captures only legitimate trade flows. One of the major effects of the UAE government's enhanced cooperation with U.S. sanctioning efforts has been to drive the trade conducted between the two countries back to the illicit and gray-market channels it had previously flowed through. Given the U.S. efforts to block foreign financing for trade deals with Iran and its most recent efforts to deny shippers insurance on transactions with Iran, dhow-based trade has once again emerged as one of the most cost-effective means of sanctions busting on Iran's behalf. Smuggling using high-powered speedboats also grew far more common in the northern emirates of the UAE where the cross-Gulf trip to Iran can be made even more quickly.[176] Unfortunately for the United States, Emirati and Iranian traders have had over three decades' worth of sanctions-busting experience and have readily been able to employ that knowledge in devising innovative ways to circumvent this newest sanctioning effort.

As highlighted in Chapter 1, the UAE government's continued lackluster commitment to sanctioning Iran can be evidenced via its cooperation with Turkish and Iranian traders in facilitating their gas-for-gold deals. This episode illustrates that U.S. pressure rather than a genuine commitment to the sanctions goals has driven the UAE's cooperation with sanctioning efforts against Iran. The cooperation U.S. policy makers obtained from the Emiratis remains largely limited to those issue areas where the United States had the greatest leverage over the country. Notably, what helped stop the flow of gas-for-gold transactions the most have been new rounds of U.S. sanctions backed by executive order and congressional legislation (2012–2013) that impose sanctions on third-party firms providing Iran with precious metals or facilitating in such transactions.[177]

The UAE government has thus far managed to balance between the competing pressures that both Iran and the United States have placed on it.[178] Iran remains both one of the UAE's most important trading partners and its greatest security threat. The United States also possesses significant economic leverage over the UAE and serves as its primary (but not only) guarantor of security. The allure of sanctions busting has historically trumped the UAE's foreign policy interests in supporting at least some of the sanctioning efforts against Iran. In recent years, though, the U.S. government has been more successful in winning the sender-target tug-of-war over the UAE's sanctions-related policies. The higher levels of cooperation the UAE has been providing to the sanctioning efforts against Iran are not guaranteed to last, however; in taking the long view, the Emirati leadership recognizes that maintaining good relations with one's neighbors is both profitable and prudent. The UAE is unlikely to sacrifice its long-term interests on the United States' behalf; it will cooperate with U.S. sanctions to the extent that the United States maintains its high level of coercive pressure and the opportunity costs of cooperating do not grow too large. U.S. policy makers should be pragmatic in terms of what costs the UAE is able and willing to bear in supporting sanctioning efforts against Iran.

Is Achieving Limited Emirati Cooperation Enough?

The U.S. government's efforts to disrupt the UAE and other third-party states' sanctions-busting relationships with Iran appear to have significantly increased their adverse effects on Iran's economy. In just a single ten-day period in the fall of 2012, the Iranian rial's value declined by 30 percent against the U.S. dollar. A 2013 U.S. GAO report concluded that, since 2010, the U.S. and international sanctions against Iran have substantially hurt Iran's oil export revenues, contributed to inflation within the country, and significantly harmed its overall economic performance.[179] The success of U.S. and, more recently, EU efforts to isolate Iran from the global financial system can be mostly credited for the enhanced impact that the sanctions have had. To the extent that the UAE has gone along with those efforts, its cooperation has contributed to Iran's financial isolation. By denying Iranians easy access to strategically valuable products and technologies, the UAE's cooperation has helped raise the costs the sanctions impose on Iran, especially with respect to its nuclear program's progress. At the same time, the UAE continues to be an important trading partner for Iran.

In response to increasingly harsh sanctions and the disruptions to its sanctions-busting relationship with the UAE, Iran responded by diversifying its sanctions-busting portfolio with a number of other countries from 2006 through 2013. These third parties have included Turkey, China, India, Iraq, and Germany. Iran's trade with China, in particular, grew more than fifteen-fold from 2001 through 2011 to approximately $45 billion. Along with South Africa, India, and Japan, China is also one of Iran's leading oil importers. Even in these cases, though, the countries have begun disengaging with Iran in light of the increasingly stringent sanctions measures the U.S. government has begun employing over the past several years. As U.S. and international sanctions increasingly raised the transaction costs of legitimate trade conducted with Iran, it has also once more turned to smuggling and illicit trade as a leading means of sanctions busting. By increasingly cutting off Iran from many other legitimate third-party partners and raising the associated transaction costs of its international trade, U.S. government's aggressive sanctioning efforts have diminished the cost-effectiveness of trade-based sanctions busting as a sanctions resistance strategy for Iran. Given Iran's increasingly limited options, those parties that continue to trade with Iran can charge the country even more exorbitant premiums for their trade. In drawing an increasingly tight noose around Iran's economy, U.S. sanctioning efforts have sought to harness the greed of third-party sanctions busters to make even the trade conducted via major sanctions-busting partners less cost effective.[180] Thus, while third-party firms continue to do business with Iran, their profits increasingly come at the expense of rather than to the benefit of Iran. This strategy, of course, entirely depends on keeping sanctioning coalitions against Iran united and limiting Iran's external trade options, which will be difficult and costly to continue doing in the long run.

Overall, the UAE's limited cooperation appears to have positively contributed to making the sanctions against Iran more effective. Alone, its limited cooperation would likely have little impact on the sanctions' effectiveness because Iran could readily replace its trade. Within the context of the U.S. government's larger successes of gaining international support for its sanctioning efforts, though, the UAE's cooperation has contributed to making Iran's continued resistance of the sanctions more costly. And to the extent that the UAE continues its profitable sanctions-busting trade relationship with Iran, the continued U.S. efforts to commercially isolate Iran will ensure that the substantial profits UAE sanctions busters rake in increasingly come at a punitive cost to their Iranian trading partners.

Summary

This chapter has sought to evaluate the descriptive accuracy of the sanctions-busting theory's account of why and how trade-based sanctions busting occurs. In looking at several different periods of U.S. sanctioning efforts, the evidence revealed that commercially oriented motivations played a predominate role in driving the sanctions-busting relationship that formed between the UAE and Iran. A number of the key factors highlighted by the theory appeared to be strongly associated with what made the UAE such an attractive sanctions-busting venue. This evidence lends credence to its causal account of trade-based sanctions busting. The UAE's sanctions busting was opportunistic and exploitive of its relationships both with the United States and with Iran. Even so, the UAE's self-interested pursuit of commercial gains has—until very recently—served to Iran's benefit. Its behavior in the second period is particularly striking, in that the UAE's sanctions busting deliberately undercut its most important ally's sanctions against a regional rival that both countries perceived as a threat. The case thus provides strong evidence of the counterintuitive effects that alliance relationships can have on sanctions-busting behavior. Overall, the UAE significantly prospered from busting the U.S. sanctions for several decades and faced little backlash for the damage it did to the U.S. sanctioning efforts.

This case offers particularly salient insights into the role of illicit trade in sanctions busting. It was hypothesized that illicit sanctions-busting should occur most readily between target states and their immediate neighbors. In the UAE's case, its proximity to Iran by water and Dubai's central role in Persian Gulf–based trade networks made it a preferential locale for smuggling on Iran's behalf. Building on its existing commercial ties to Iran, its investments in logistical infrastructure, and its business-friendly commercial environments, Dubai helped incubate a regional sanctions-busting and war-smuggling industry from 1979 onwards. After the United States reimposed sanctions against Iran in 1984, this sanctions-busting industry was able to grow in lockstep to service Iran's growing needs. By the time the U.S.- and UN-mandated sanctions were imposed against Iraq in 1990, this sector was well developed and more than capable of also taking advantage of the illicit sanctions-busting opportunities afforded by them. Although smuggling co-existed with legitimate trade between the UAE and Iran throughout the periods analyzed, the success of the UAE's FTZs increasingly allowed sanctions busters to hide their transactions in plain sight as an alternative to smuggling. It is important to note that the role played by illicit trade in states' trade-based sanctions-busting relationships cannot be directly evaluated in the next chapter's statistical analysis. Evidence from this case and other accounts indicate, though, that it can be a major component of the sanctions-busting transactions that take place.[181] As such, the model employed seeks to identify indirect evidence of its presence. What is striking about this case and the findings from the next chapter's analysis, though, is just how much sanctions busting occurs overtly in readily observable ways.

As the postscript analysis discussed, U.S. efforts to curb the sanctions busting taking place on Iran's behalf have grown increasingly successful in recent years. By employing aggressive new sanctions policies and capitalizing on the international community's dissatisfaction with Iran's behavior, U.S. policy makers have brought to bear a broader and more united international sanctioning coalition against Iran than at any point in the sanctions episode's history. These efforts have not been able to completely stop third parties like the UAE from extensively sanctions busting on Iran's behalf, but they have substantially diminished the cost-effectiveness of that strategy for resisting the sanctions. The extent to which the U.S. policy makers have been able to mobilize domestic support for the sanctioning effort against Iran, recruit international support for their sanctioning efforts, and convince third-party governments to tolerate its use of extraterritorial sanctions all align to make the current sanctioning effort against Iran an anomalous case rather than an archetypical one. Even so, policy makers can still extract some lessons about what appears to have finally made the sanctions effective after twenty-plus years of largely ineffectual sanctions policies. It still remains to be seen, though, whether these enhanced sanctioning efforts will be sufficient to achieve the U.S. government's objectives vis-à-vis Iran.

6 Assessing Which Third-Party States Become Trade-Based Sanctions Busters

THIS CHAPTER EVALUATES THE GENERALIZABILITY OF THE sanctions-busting theory's explanation of trade-based sanctions busting using a statistical method of analysis. It analyzes the sanctions-busting trade relationships that third-party states had with target states over the course of the same set of ninety-six U.S. sanctions episodes examined in Chapter 3. The analysis tests the key factors that contribute to whether a third-party state will engage in trade-based sanctions busting on behalf of a target state in a given year. It complements the findings from the previous statistical analysis by identifying the reasons why specific third-party states sanctions-busted on the target states' behalves in each of those sanctions episodes. The results of this analysis offer generalizable insights into the factors that influence trade-based sanctions-busting behavior and can be used to develop a profile of the states most likely to become trade-based sanctions busters in any given sanctions episode.

The results are highly supportive of the trade-based sanctions-busting hypotheses proposed in Chapter 4. The factors that affect the profitability of trade between third-party and target states appear to have the greatest influence over which third-party states become extensive sanctions busters. Along those lines, the results strongly support the hypothesis that U.S. allies should be more likely to bust its sanctions than nonallied states. The results also provide further evidence to suggest that the neighbors of target states conduct a significant proportion of their sanctions-busting trade via illicit or unrecorded channels. The sanctions-busting profile that can be gleaned from this analysis paints a disturbing picture for American policy makers: U.S. sanctions are most likely to be undercut by fellow democracies with which it is allied that also possess large, globalized economies (for example, France, Great Britain, Canada, Japan, and so on). In other words, the closest friends of the United States turn out to be its sanctions' greatest enemies.

Analyzing Trade-Based Sanctions Busters

This chapter employs a data set of the yearly trade relationships that 165 different third-party states had with countries sanctioned by the United States from 1950 through 2002. The dependent variable of this analysis is whether third-party states engage in trade-based sanctions busting on a target's behalf in a given year. Drawing on the factors identified by the hypotheses, a binary time-series cross-sectional analysis is used to identify the variables that are most strongly associated with trade-based sanctions-busting behavior.

The data set is constructed to facilitate analyzing how both sender and target states can influence whether third-party states sanctions-bust on the target's behalf. The structure of the data set is organized around the specific triadic relationships formed among the primary sender (in this case, the United States), the target of its sanctions, and the various third-party states. To create the data set, the observation years in which the United States had imposed sanctions against a target are identified for each of the sanctions episodes. For each U.S.–target pairing in these sanctions episodes, the remaining states in the world are matched with them as third-party states to form individual triadic units. Yearly observations of the triadic units formed between the United States as the primary sanctioner, the target of its sanctions, and every possible third-party state are employed as the unit of analysis.[1] Via this approach, the factors that increase or decrease third-party states' likelihoods of engaging in extensive trade-based sanctions busting in any given sanctions episode can be assessed.

The dependent variable for each triadic observation is the *Trade-Based Sanctions Busting* variable coded in Chapter 3. This variable flags the individual instances in which third-party states engaged in extensive trade-based sanctions busting on a target's behalf in a given year. This approach flags roughly 2.68 percent of the observations as involving trade-based sanctions busting if the sample is limited to only those observations in which bilateral

TABLE 6.1. Most active trade-based sanctions busters.

Third-party states	Sanctions-busting observations	Rank
Japan	328	1
West Germany	242	2
Italy	193	3
France	164	4
United Kingdom	139	5
Germany	129	6
China	121	7
Brazil	64	8
South Korea	59	9
Soviet Union/Russia	58	10
Saudi Arabia	57	11
Singapore	56	12
Netherlands	48	13
Thailand	45	14
India	45	15

trade data for third-party and target states are available.[2] This indicates that only a limited number of third-party states tend to engage in extensive trade-based sanctions busting in most sanctions episodes.

A fairly significant number of states engaged in extensive trade-based sanctions busting at least once, but most of the sanctions busting was conducted by a relatively small number of countries. Out of the total number of third parties for which at least some trade data were available, 45.26 percent (eighty-six) had at least one observation in which they sanctions-busted on a target's behalf. Table 6.1 depicts the top fifteen countries that, in their roles as third-party states, engaged in extensive sanctions busting in the sample. As it shows, Japan, (West) Germany, Italy, France, and the United Kingdom were by far the most active trade-based sanctions busters. If the scores of West Germany and postunification Germany are counted together, Germany was the most active sanctions buster followed closely by Japan. Indeed, the five most active sanctions busters accounted for 47.16 percent of the total amount of sanctions busting that took place in the sample. What's notable is that all of the leading sanctions busters are democratic U.S. allies that possessed large economies and were heavily engaged in international trade. Beyond just these first impressions, however, more rigorous analysis of the factors that motivated these states to sanctions-bust is needed.

To test the sanctions-busting theory's hypotheses, this chapter develops an integrated model of the factors most likely to be associated with trade-based sanctions-busting behavior. For the *Third-Party Economic Size Hypothesis*, the model employs a variable using data on the gross domestic product (GDP) in current-year U.S. dollars for each third-party state in a given year. This GDP variable is logarithmically transformed to reduce its skew and lagged one year to ensure that it is not endogenously related to the dependent variable.[3] One-year lags are used for all the economic variables to ensure that the causal relationships being evaluated run in only one direction. The hypothesis predicts that this variable should be positively associated with third-party states' likelihoods of becoming extensive sanctions busters in the analysis. Third-party states with large economies, like Japan and Germany, should thus be much more likely to extensively sanctions-bust than countries like Guatemala.

To test the *Third-Party Commercial Openness Hypothesis*, the model relies on a measure of the total amount of international trade a third-party state conducts as a proportion of its GDP in a given year.[4] The variable captures the economic importance of international trade to the third-party state's economy. Contrary to the previous measure, this variable does not measure the absolute scale of economic activity in a third-party state; rather, it captures the intensity of its involvement in international trade in relation to its broader economy. Whereas neither the Netherlands nor Singapore possesses large economies, both countries are international trade hubs and operate two of the largest seaports in the world. The extensive involvement of these countries in international trade should have made them highly commercially competitive sanctions busters—explaining their place on the top-fifteen list with countries possessing much larger economies. This hypothesis thus predicts that *Third-Party Commercial Openness* should positively affect the likelihood that third-party states will sanctions-bust.

The *Third-Party Commercial Dependence Hypothesis* is tested via a measure of the salience of the bilateral trade that a third-party state conducts with a target in a given year in relation to the total amount of international trade the third-party state conducts. The *Third-Party Commercial Dependence* variable captures the extent to which a third-party state is dependent on its trade relationship with a target. The greater this level of dependence, the more costly and difficult it should be for third-party governments to disrupt that trade relationship by cooperating with sanctioning efforts. The stronger these ties are, the easier it should also be for target firms to find replacement trade partners in those third-party states. This variable should have a strong, positive effect on third-party states' likelihoods of sanctions busting on a target state's behalf.

According to the sanctions-busting theory's next two hypotheses, a third-party state's possession of defense pact alliances with either the sender or target states should positively affect its likelihood of sanctions busting. In any given triadic observation, four different potential defense pact arrangements can exist for a third-party state: It could have a defense pact with the sender only, a defense pact with the target only, defense pacts with both states, or defense pacts with neither.[5] Whereas possessing a defense pact with a target state provides a target government with political incentives to support sanctions busting on a target's behalf, possessing a defense pact with a sender insulates third-party governments and their firms from reprisals for exploiting sanctions-busting opportunities. Both mechanisms provide firms in third parties and target states with additional commercial incentives to sanctions-bust. The hypotheses thus predict that, compared to not having a defense pact with either state, the possession of defense pacts with the target, sender, or both states should make a third-party state more likely to sanctions-bust. For the model, this variable is coded as a series of dummy variables that capture each of the four categories of alliance arrangements. The analysis compares the effects of possessing only a defense pact with the target, only a defense pact with the sender, or defense pacts with both states to the null condition of possessing defense pacts with neither.

To evaluate the *Target-Third Party Democratic Regimes Hypothesis*, the analysis tests whether the presence of democratic regimes in the target and third-party states influences the likelihood of a sanctions-busting relationship emerging between them. The third-party and target states are coded as possessing democratic regimes using data from the *Polity IV Project*.[6] Because the United States is the sender in all the sanctions cases and it is always a democracy, the analysis can only explain the role played by variation in the target and sender states' regimes. This means that there are four different configurations of target and third-party regime types that can exist within a given triad: The target is the only democracy, the third-party state is the only democracy, both are democracies, and neither is a democracy. The sanctions-busting theory predicts that when the target and third-party states both possess democratic regimes they should be more likely to develop a sanctions-busting relationship than if neither possesses them. To code these different regime-type configurations within the analysis, a series of dummy variables is used to capture each of the categories. The "neither state being democratic" category is employed as the null category for comparison.

The *Target–Third Party Distance Hypothesis* seeks to evaluate the role that distance plays in affecting which third-party states are most likely to sanctions-bust on behalf of a particular target state. The farther away a third-party state is from the target, the more costly and challenging it will be for firms in both countries to establish extensive sanctions-busting relationships. The distance separating target and third-party states is coded using the distance between the states' capital cities, except for states that share land borders for which the practical distance between them is 0.[7] Because countries' capital cities also tend to be their economic hubs and located more centrally within their states, this approach is preferable to using minimum distance measures.[8] According to the hypothesis, this variable is expected to negatively affect the likelihood of third-party states becoming extensive trade-based sanctions busters on behalf of target states.

Whereas the previous hypothesis asserts that third-party states that are more geographically proximate to target states are more apt to sanctions-bust, the *Target–Third Party Shared Border Hypothesis* takes into account the commercial and political incentives that exist to use illicit or untraceable sanctions-busting channels. It predicts that the comparative ease by which traders can engage in cross-border smuggling often makes that approach preferable to conducting legitimate, recorded trade. These incentives exist for both the firms and governments of third-party states that may want to avoid reprisals from sender states or negative publicity that may arise from their sanctions-busting activities. Third-party states are coded as being neighbors to a target state if they share a land border with it or are separated from it by less than twelve miles of water using data from the *Direct Contiguity Data Set*.[9] This hypothesis predicts that being a direct neighbor of a target state makes a third party less likely to sanctions-bust on its behalf using legitimate, observable trade flows. This variable should thus have a negative effect in the analysis.

In addition to the hypothesized variables, several additional control variables are included within the analysis. The first is the size of the target state's economy, which is coded using the logged and lagged value of its GDP (*Target Economic Size*). This is important because the larger a target state's economy is, the better its domestic economy may be able to adjust to the sender's sanctions without the external support of sanctions busters. Secondly, the model controls for the severity of the sanctions imposed against a target state. The literature on this topic is conflicted. Previous work by Caruso suggests that the disruptive effects of harsh sanctions tend to be significant impediments to trade with target states, which may actually prevent states from sanctions-busting on their behalf.[10] In contrast, authors such as Drezner and Kaempfer and Lowenberg argue that the harsher the sanctions imposed against a target are, the greater the commercial benefits of sanctions busting for third parties are apt to be.[11] Using data from Hufbauer and his coauthors' sanctions data set, harsh sanctions are coded as being in place if a target is subject to import, export, and financial sanctions by the U.S. government in a given year (*Harsh U.S. Sanctions*).[12]

Lastly, the effects of time on third-party states' likelihoods of sanctions busting are controlled for in two ways. First, a duration variable (*Duration of the U.S. Sanctions*) is included that accounts for how long a target has been subject to continuous sanctions by the U.S. government in the data set. The longer the sanctions persist, the more time that target states should have to cultivate the most cost-effective sanctions-busting relationships possible with third-party states. Temporal dependence is also accounted for in the analysis by including a count variable for the number of years since a third party has sanctions-busted on the target's behalf (*Time Since Busting*) and the squared and cubed values of that variable.[13] It could be predicted that the longer a third-party state goes without establishing a sanctions-busting relationship with the target, the less likely it will be to do so in the long run.[14]

Analyzing the Results

The analysis of which third-party states engage in extensive trade-based sanctions busting requires the use of estimators that can assess binary outcomes and that are appropriate for analyzing relatively rare events.[15] As such, a basic logit estimator and a more specialized rare-events logit are used to analyze the models. In both cases, standard errors clustered by target states are employed. The effects of temporal dependence are controlled for by the cubic polynomial variables that account for the time since a third-party state last sanctions-busted on a target's behalf.[16] In terms of the sample of cases employed, the analysis focuses on those observations in which trade data between the tar-

TABLE 6.2. Analysis of the causes of extensive trade-based sanctions busting.

	Model 1	Model 2
Third-Party Economic Size	0.722*** (0.042)	0.721*** (0.042)
Third-Party Commercial Openness	0.062*** (0.013)	0.064*** (0.013)
Third-Party Commercial Dependence	4.213*** (1.242)	4.184*** (1.242)
Only a U.S.–Third Party Defense Pact	0.881*** (0.117)	0.880*** (0.117)
Third-Party Defense Pacts with Both	0.764*** (0.218)	0.765*** (0.218)
Only a Target–Third Party Defense Pact	0.839*** (0.268)	0.840*** (0.268)
Only Target Democratic	−0.074 (0.242)	−0.065 (0.242)
Both Democracies	0.500* (0.272)	0.501* (0.272)
Only the Third-Party Democratic	0.039 (0.113)	0.039 (0.113)
Target–Third Party Distance	−0.641*** (0.120)	−0.641*** (0.120)
Target–Third Party Shared Border	−3.286*** (0.948)	−3.281*** (0.948)
Target Economic Size	−0.156*** (0.053)	−0.156*** (0.053)
Harsh U.S. Sanctions	0.008 (0.214)	0.009 (0.214)
Duration of U.S. Sanctions	0.067*** (0.015)	0.067*** (0.015)
Time Since Busting	−0.884*** (0.093)	−0.882*** (0.093)
Time Since Busting^2	0.043*** (0.009)	0.043*** (0.009)
Time Since Busting^3	−0.001*** (0.000)	−0.001*** (0.000)
Constant	−8.423*** (1.614)	−8.414*** (1.614)
Probability > χ^2	0.000	
Observations	83,143	83,143

Clustered standard errors are included below the variable coefficients in parentheses. Asterisks (*, **, and ***) denote statistical significance at the 90, 95, and 99 percent confidence levels using one-tailed tests.

get and third-party state are fully available and exclude cases for which they are missing. Table 6.2 displays the results of using the basic logit estimator in Model 1 and the rare-events logit estimator in Model 2. Both models provide strong support for the sanctions-busting theory's hypotheses. The discussion focuses on the results from Model 1 because both models produce nearly identical results.

An important component of the analysis in this section concentrates on understanding the substantive effects or "real-world" impact that the various variables have on sanctions-busting behavior. This is done by examining how particular factors change the likelihood that third-party states will sanctions-bust under different scenarios. By assuming that all the variables in the analysis take on their mean or modal values in a scenario and then isolating the effects of changing a single variable, its predicted real-world effects in an average scenario can be ascertained.[17] This is done by comparing the predicted probabilities of third-party sanctions busting taking place in two different scenarios to identify differences in the relative risks of its occurrence. It is notable that, given the overall rarity of sanctions-busting behavior, its absolute chances of occurring in average scenarios is quite low (approximately 0.25 percent in a given year). This is consistent with the expectation that third-party states will extensively sanctions-bust only when it is highly profitable for them to do so—which it is not in most typical circumstances. Yet when the factors identified by the theory jointly take on favorable values, the likelihood of a third-party sanctions busting can rapidly increase. The initial analysis focuses on exploring how changes to individual factors alter the relative likelihood of trade-based sanctions-busting occurring in isolation. Subsequently, the analysis explores how changing the factors identified by the sanctions-busting theory in concert can affect the absolute likelihoods of sanctions busting taking place.

The results from the quantitative analysis provide strong support for the first three hypotheses related to third-party states' economic profiles and their commercial relationships with target states. In terms of the *Third-Party Economic Size Hypothesis*, the variable exercises a positive and statistically significant effect on the likelihood of third-party states engaging in sanctions busting. In an average scenario in which all other factors are held constant, increasing *Third-Party Economic Size* by one standard deviation (1.88) from its mean value (17.15) causes the predicted probability that a third-party state will sanctions-bust to rise by roughly 297 percent. If this value is increased instead by two standard deviations, the predicted probability of the third-party state sanctions-busting increases by 1,337 percent. This suggests that possessing a large economy significantly contributes to third-party states' general likelihood of extensively sanctions-busting in any given sanctions episode.

The effects of *Third-Party Commercial Openness* are also positive and statistically significant as hypothesized. Substantively, the effects of changes to *Third-Party Commercial Openness* lead to a smaller but still notable increase in third-party states' likelihoods of sanctions-busting. Holding all other factors constant, increasing the variable by one standard deviation (1.91) above its mean (.19) leads to a 12.5 percent increase in an average third-party state's likelihood of sanctions-busting. This supports the hypothesis that actively trading third-party states are more likely to become extensive sanctions busters than countries that are not very engaged in international trade.

With respect to *Third-Party Commercial Dependence*, the variable positively and statistically significantly affects third-party states' likelihoods of sanctions-busting on target states' behalves. Holding all other factors constant in an average scenario, increasing *Third-Party Commercial Dependence* by one standard deviation (0.04) above its mean (.005) causes its predicted probability of sanctions-busting to increase by 12.5 percent. This means that the stronger the commercial linkage that a third party possesses with a target state, the more likely it is to sanctions-bust on the target's behalf. These findings support the hypothesis that third-party states' commercial dependence on target states increases their likelihoods of sanctions busting on target states' behalfs.

In terms of the defense pact–related hypotheses, the results of the three relational alliance variables should be interpreted together as they constitute a single categorical variable. The reported coefficients for each of these variables represent a comparison between the circumstance they represent and the null condition of the third-party state possessing no defense pacts with either the target or sender states. According to the *Target–Third Party Defense Pact (DP) Hypothesis*, the variables *Only a Target–Third Party Defense Pact* and *Third-Party Defense Pacts with Both* should positively affect the third-party states' likelihoods of sanctions-busting; indeed, both variables have positive and statistically significant effects in the model. Similarly, the *Sender–Third Party Defense Pact Hypothesis* predicts that *Only a Sender–Third Party Defense Pact* and *Third Party Defense Pacts with Both* should be positive. Supporting that hypothesis, the *Only a Sender–Third Party Defense Pact* variable is also positive and statistically significant. This indicates that third-party states that possess any combination of defense pact relationships with the target or sender states will be more likely to sanctions-bust than third parties that possess no such relationships with either state. These findings support both of the hypotheses.

The distribution of substantive effects across the different defense pact arrangements is particularly interesting. Comparing the difference between when a third party only possesses a defense pact with the sender versus possessing defense pacts with neither in an otherwise typical scenario, the predicted probability of a third-party state sanctions-busting is 137 percent greater with the sender defense pact. Making that same sort of comparison using sole possession of a defense pact with the target instead, the third-party state's predicted probability of sanctions-busting is 125 percent greater. On the basis of these findings, it could be expected that when third-party states possess defense pacts with both the target and sender states their likelihoods of sanctions-busting should be significantly greater than possessing only a single defense pact with either state. Instead, a third-party state that possesses defense pacts with both the sender and target states compared to having them with neither has a 112 percent greater chance of sanctions-busting. Although this is still a substantial positive effect, it appears as if possessing alliance relationships with both the sender and target states makes a third party less likely to sanctions-bust than when it has a clear loyalty to one side or the other. One explanation for this is that third-party states with clearly divided loyalties between the sender and target could have their behavior placed under greater scrutiny, because their sanctions-busting looks as if they are favoring their alliance partnership with the target over the sender. This effect does not overwhelm the incentives to sanctions-bust, but it does appear to suppress them to some extent.

With respect to the *Target–Third-Party Democratic Regimes Hypothesis*, the regime type variables also need to be evaluated in conjunction with one another. Each of the three regime type variables test whether there is a statistically significant difference between the arrangement they represent and the null category of neither state possessing democratic regimes. The results indicate that the effects of only the target (*Only Target Democratic*) or only the third-party (*Only Third-Party Democratic*) states possessing democratic regimes are not statistically significant. As the hypothesis predicted, though, *Both Democracies* has a positive and statistically significant effect on third-party states' likelihood of sanctions busting. The strength of this statistical relationship is relatively weak, though, and it sometimes washed out in additional robustness checks. In an otherwise typical scenario, the likelihood of sanctions busting taking place is 112 percent greater if the target and third-party states are both democracies compared to a situation in which neither is democratic. These findings support the hypothesis, but they are not exceptionally strong.

In contrast, the effects of both the geographical hypotheses receive strong support from the analysis. In the case of *Target–Third Party Distance*, the variable has the negative and statistically significant effect on sanctions busting that the sanctions-busting theory predicts. In an average scenario, increasing *Target–Third Party Distance* by one standard deviation (1.61) above its mean value (8.01) causes the predicted probability that a third-party state will sanctions-bust to decline by 65 percent. This is quite a substantial reduction, suggesting that there are significant benefits for potential sanctions busters in being regionally proximate to the target. Yet the results also reveal that directly neighboring a target state makes a third-party state less likely to sanctions-bust on its behalf using legitimate, recorded trade flows. As hypothesized, the effects of *Target–Third Party Shared Border* are negative and statistically significant. Comparing the differences between otherwise identical circumstances in which a third-party state shares a border with a target versus where it is separated from it by 150 miles, the bordering third party state is 7 percent less likely to sanctions-bust on the target's behalf than the neighbor 150 miles away. Given the negative effects distance has been shown to have and the fact that bordering states normally trade significantly more with one another, this finding is quite puzzling unless the roles of illicit trade and smuggling are accounted for. This particular finding provides strong circumstantial evidence that the neighbors of target states conduct a notable amount of their sanctions-busting trade via smuggling and unrecorded trade.

All together, the results of the analysis provide considerable support for the theory's explanation of trade-based sanctions busting. Although the effects of *Third-Party Economic Size* are fairly potent, the results suggest that no single factor drives whether a third-party state will sanctions-bust on a target state's behalf. Instead, a package of factors based on the profile of the third-party state and its commercial, political, and geographic relationship with the target and sender states appear to all influence trade-based sanctions-busting behavior. This suggests that sanctions-busting trade concentrates in those third-party states that—along a range of factors—can provide the most profitable venues for taking advantage of the commercial opportunities that sanctions create in target states. This is evident if we compare an average scenario in which the hypothesized variables are set at their mean or modal values to one in which they are set at moderately favorable values according to the sanctions-busting theory.[18] Comparing these two scenarios, a third-party state is 4,869 percent more likely to sanctions-bust extensively on a target's behalf in the second scenario. Whereas the third party has a negligible chance of sanctions busting in the typical scenario (0.0025), its likelihood of sanctions busting grows to 0.13 in the slightly favorable scenario. This suggests that an alignment of multiple factors must be in place for a third-party state to sanctions-bust extensively.

In terms of the control variables included within the model, they also produced some interesting insights into sanctions-busting behavior. For example, the size of the target state's economy (*Target Economic Size*) does have a negative and statistically significant effect on the likelihood that third-party states will sanctions-bust on its behalf. Taken in concert with the findings regarding *Third-Party Economic Size*, this indicates that sanctions-busting relationships are most likely to emerge between third-party states with large economies and target states with smaller ones. This makes sense, as the third-party states' economies in these circumstances will be best able to accommodate the needs of the target states' economies. Given the competing accounts of how the severity of sanctions affects third-party trade with their targets, it is not necessarily surprising that *Harsh U.S. Sanctions* did not exercise any statistically significant effects in the analysis. Whereas greater sanction-busting opportunities may exist during harsh sanctioning efforts, the disruptive effects they cause may make it more difficult for third-party states to capitalize on them. As such, there is not an appreciable difference between the sanctions busting that takes place during limited versus more extensive sanctioning efforts. As an additional robustness check, the potential impact of the amount of trade the United States continued to conduct with the states it sanctioned was also evaluated. The factor did not appear to have any impact on third-party states' propensity to sanctions-bust in a given sanctions episode.

The variables included to control for temporal effects revealed the presence of two slightly different trends. The *Duration of U.S. Sanctions* variable measures the length of time that the United States had continuous sanctions in place against a target, whereas the *Time Since Busting* variables capture the length of time since a third party had sanctions-busted on a target state's behalf. The effects of *Duration of U.S. Sanctions* are positive and statistically significant in the analyses, meaning that the longer U.S. sanctions persist the more likely third-party states are to bust them. The *Time Since Busting* variables must be interpreted jointly as they are interaction terms. The negative and statistically significant sign on the *Time Since Busting*^{3} variable is the most important indicator of the cumulative effects of a third party not sanctions-busting in a particular sanctions-busting episode. It indicates that third-party states will become increasingly less likely to sanctions-bust on a target's behalf as more time passes without them having done it. Together, these findings indicate that the amount of sanctions busting taking place on a target's behalf is likely to grow the longer the sanctions against it last, but that it is unlikely to involve new sanctions busters that have not done it in the past.

Profiling Trade-Based Sanctions Busters

So is there a consistent profile that can be developed on the types of states most likely to become extensive trade-based sanctions busters? Three key third-party characteristics appear to be associated with sanctions-busting behavior: These third parties possess large economies, they are extensively involved in international trade, and they possess democratic governments. Although the sanctions-busting theory links only the latter factor to trade-based sanctions busting on behalf of democratic target states, democratic institutions are more broadly associated with transparency and protection of property rights that can benefit the commercial competitiveness of third-party states.[19] The role played by these factors all received general support within the quantitative analysis, and anecdotal evidence also supports them. The fact that Japan, (West) Germany, the United Kingdom, France, and Italy are all among the leading sanctions busters in the analysis illustrates this point. These states were not political rivals of the United States actively seeking to undercut its foreign policy agenda. Quite the contrary—they were some of its closest military allies during the Cold War and remained so afterwards. Yet these states were also the greatest commercial competitors of the United States, possessing industries and businesses that overlapped with those in the United States. When the U.S. government severed or disrupted its commercial relationships with target states, foreign firms within those countries were well situated to exploit the vacuum left by U.S. businesses.

Beyond just the three specific indicators identified by the theory, the degree to which third-party states can cost-effectively replace the trade disrupted by a sender's sanctions appears to heavily influence their general aptitude at sanctions busting. The third-party states whose economies could competitively mirror the U.S. economy were ones best able to profit from exploiting the U.S. sanctions. China's placement as the seventh most active sanctions buster also appears to support this point, especially in the later periods analyzed. Although not democratic, China's rapidly growing, export-oriented economy turned the state into a major commercial competitor of the United States in the 1980s, 1990s, and 2000s. Indeed, over 90 percent of the trade-based sanctions busting China conducted in this study occurred after Deng Xiaoping initiated the liberalizing reforms to China's economy in 1978. Generally speaking, then, countries with large, commercially competitive economies should be viewed as much greater sanctions-busting threats than other states.

In any given sanctions episode, there are also a number of relational factors that signal a much higher likelihood of sanctions busting. Third-party states that possess strong, preexisting commercial ties to a target or defense pact alliances with them are significantly more likely to become extensive sanctions busters than other countries. The number of states possessing these close relationships with a target is normally fairly limited, making them useful indicators. Additionally, a target's regional neighbors also appear much more likely to sanctions-bust on a target's behalf than would be more distant states—via legitimate or illicit means. Because the evidence suggests that third-party states sanctions-bust only when a number of factors align to make it highly profitable, possessing one or more of these characteristics signals a much higher than average likelihood of sanctions busting.

The role that sender alliances play in sanctions busting constitutes a more challenging factor to use in identifying potential sanctions busters. Within this analysis, the results indicate that third-party states that possess defense pacts with sender states are much more likely to become extensive trade-based sanctions busters. As the analysis indicates, though, the substantive impact of this effect is not very great if a number of additional factors do not align to make it highly profitable for the third party to undermine its allies' sanctions. Indeed, additional analysis of the data and the results from my related work both point to a powerful interaction between third-party states' commercial interests in sanctions busting and their possession of an alliance with a sender state. Sender states' allies with only limited commercial ties to a target state are actually more likely to curb their trade with it than nonallies, whereas sender allies with strong commercial ties to a target are substantially more likely to increase their trade with it.[20] This means that U.S. policy makers should be the most concerned about allied third parties that possess commercial profiles that make them adept at sanctions busting or that possess strong commercial ties with the target.

What makes the sanctions busting conducted by a sender's allies so disheartening is that such states tend to be the ones that could potentially make the largest contributions to the success of sanctioning efforts if they cooperated with the efforts. By preventing a target from having access to a third party that would otherwise be an active sanctions buster, the sender could tangibly increase the odds of its sanctions' success. Because allies are generally expected to be more cooperative than other states, the perceived defections by allies can also create intra-alliance tensions that are difficult to resolve. In large part, this is because coercive mechanisms that sender states have at their disposal to stop their allies from sanctions busting are apt to only worsen the intra-alliance relationship instead of improving it. The greater the commercial benefits of sanctions-busting for a third-party ally, the more willing a sender government must be to jeopardize its alliance relationship with the third party to stop it from sanctions busting. U.S. policy makers have often—but not always—appeared unwilling to accept the trade-offs involved in coercing their allies to stop sanctions busting to make their sanctioning efforts more effective.

All this suggests that a profile does exist for the types of third-party states that engage in extensive trade-based sanctions busting. The most prolific sanctions busters tend to be third-party states that possess large economies, are intensively engaged in international trade, and tend to possess democratic governments—though the latter factor appears to be the least important of the three. In any given sanctions episode, states that are geographically proximate to the target, have close commercial ties to it, or share a defensive pact with it are also more likely to emerge as extensive sanctions busters. Lastly, allies of sender states that have salient commercial interests in sanctions-busting on a target's behalf also appear particularly apt to become major trade-based sanctions busters. As the conclusion discusses, this information can be used by U.S. policy makers to identify potential sanctions busters and to best leverage the diplomatic efforts they undertake to support their sanctioning efforts.

Summary

The analysis of ninety-six U.S.-imposed sanctions episodes conducted in this chapter provides strong support for the book's theoretical account of why trade-based sanctions busting occurs. An examination of the states that busted U.S. sanctions reveals that although roughly 45 percent of the countries in the world have done it at some point, a small number of states appear to conduct the lion's share of the sanctions busting that occurs. Many of these leading sanctions busters turn out to be U.S. allies that also are its chief commercial competitors, such as Japan, Germany, and Great Britain. The profile of these leading sanctions busters appeared broadly consistent with the sanctions-busting theory's predictions. The statistical analysis revealed that, in the aggregate, the profitability of third-party states as trade-based sanctions-busting venues appears to be the most powerful determinant of which states engage in the activity. All of the theory's major trade-based sanctions-busting hypotheses received support in the analysis. The findings further showed that third-party states that possess defense pacts with targets, senders, or both states are more likely to sanctions-bust than third-party states that lack them. Notably, the analysis also revealed indirect evidence of the trade-based sanctions busting taking place via illicit trade and smuggling conducted by target states' neighbors. Consistent with the sanctions-busting theory's account of trade-based sanctions busting, no single factor in the analysis proved sufficiently strong to drive third-party states to sanctions-bust; rather, such behavior was shown to arise out of a favorable alignment of multiple factors that affect the profitability of trading with target states.

The next chapter comparatively explores the circumstances in which third-party states sanctions-bust via foreign aid instead of foreign trade. An important component of the sanctions-busting theory's explanation of aid-based sanctions busting is that it constitutes a second-best option for third-party governments that would like to assist a target state. If the theory is correct, third-party states should sanctions-bust via trade on Cuba's behalf to the extent they can and only employ foreign aid if the former is not a viable option. In those cases, political motivations should play a much more determinative role in whether third-party states engage in extensive sanctions busting.

7   Sanctions Busting for Politics

Analyzing Cuba's Aid-Based Sanctions Busters

WHEREAS THE PRECEDING TWO CHAPTERS EXPLORED THE motivations and mechanisms of trade-based sanctions busting, this chapter focuses on those states that provide extensive foreign aid to sanctioned countries. Specifically, it examines the role that sanctions busting has played in the Cuban government's efforts to resist U.S. sanctions over the past fifty-plus years. Given its duration, the Cuban sanctions episode represents somewhat of an outlier. Yet the political salience of the episode and the important role that the Soviet–Cuban sanctions-busting relationship has had on the study of the phenomenon makes it a critical case to study and explain. As the analysis reveals, Cuba has actually had the aid-based sanctions-busting support of multiple states over the course of the sanctions and established numerous trade-based sanctions-busting relationships with U.S. allies. Consistent with the overarching theory, the Castro regime appears to have leveraged both trade-based and aid-based sanctions busting in its efforts to resist the U.S. sanctions. More broadly, studying this sanctions episode offers an additional opportunity to learn more about how the U.S. and Cuban governments sought to influence third-party responses to the sanctions and the impact those responses had on the sanctions' outcomes.

The sanctions-busting theory asserts that third-party states should prefer to engage in trade-based sanctions busting and employ only aid-based sanctions busting in a limited set of circumstances. Aid-based sanctions busting takes place when a third-party government has a salient political motive to defeat the sanctions against a target state, when the use of market-based trade is infeasible, and when it can afford to provide the target with extensive aid. In particular, the political motives driving aid-based sanctions busting will tend to involve either a rivalry between a third party and the sender or a broader ideological issue that the third-party government views at stake in the sanctions dispute. Although none of these factors is sufficient to induce aid-based sanctions busting, they should be jointly necessary for a third party to provide a target with significant, sustained aid. In cases where third-party states provided Cuba with extensive sanctions-busting aid, the sanctions-busting theory predicts that all three of these conditions will have been met.

To test the aid-based sanctions-busting hypothesis, this chapter conducts a comparative analysis of the third-party states that provided Cuba with extensive foreign assistance over the past fifty-plus years of U.S. sanctions. Testing hypotheses that employ necessary conditions requires selecting cases on the basis of the dependent variable's value, which, in this case, narrows the analysis down to only those states that appeared to have engaged in aid-based sanctions-busting behavior using the profile developed in Chapter 2. An overview of the sanctions-busting relationships forged by the Cuban government from 1950 until present times indicates that the Soviet Union (1961–1989), China (1962–1966), China (2001–present), and Venezuela (1999–present) all appear to have engaged in extensive aid-based sanctions-busting support on Cuba's behalf.[1] Once it has been demonstrated that the states truly were aid-based sanctions busters, each case is examined to evaluate: (1) whether the third-party government had a salient ideological or rivalry-based motive to defeat the sanctions against Cuba; (2) whether market-based sanctions busting on Cuba's behalf was infeasible to achieve the government's desired goals; and (3) whether the government had the economic means to provide Cuba with extensive assistance. When possible, the case narratives analyze the effects of disruptions to one or more of these conditions on the sanctions-busting aid these countries provided to Cuba. Analyzing these four cases via a "structured, focused comparison" should yield insights about the causes of aid-based sanctions-busting that are far more generalizable than a single case study could provide.[2] This comparative approach constitutes a compromise between the case study and statistical approaches that were used to evaluate the trade-based sanctions-busting hypotheses.

An additionally important part of this chapter's narrative explores the proactive role that the Castro regime played in cultivating and managing its relationships with aid-based benefactors and trade-based sanctions busters. Fidel Castro viewed both types of sanctions busting as complementary strategies for obtaining the resources Cuba needed to sustain itself. When the foreign aid Cuba received was plentiful, it supplanted a significant part of the regime's need for market-based sanctions busting. At the same time, such aid also provided Cuba with additional resources to fund trade with commercially oriented sanctions busters to buy what its benefactors could not provide. When Cuba experienced foreign aid shortfalls, it was forced to tighten its belt and rely more heavily on market-based sanctions-busting relationships. These insights reinforce the importance of jointly studying both aid- and trade-based sanctions-busting assistance within a common explanatory framework. The holistic approach in this chapter also offers an opportunity to evaluate other aspects of the sanctions-busting theory related to the causes and consequences of sanctions busting.

The results provide strong support for the aid-based sanctions-busting hypothesis and for the sanction-busting theory's overarching account of the phenomenon. In three out of the four cases, all the necessary conditions for aid-based sanctions busting posited by the theory are present. Post–Cold War China was the only slightly deviant case, as the Chinese government appeared to use the extensive aid it offered to Cuba as an augment to the commercially oriented sanctions busting it was also providing. Moreover, the withdrawal of these necessary conditions was associated with the severance of the patronage relationships. The Cuban case also illustrates the methods by which target governments can court the patronage of aid-based sanctions busters and balance the support they provide with commercially oriented sanctions busters. Castro's regime exploited both foreign aid and opportunism as part of its sanctions resistance efforts. A lot of work went into Cuba's efforts to cultivate, sustain, and manage its mixed network of external sanctions busters, especially in light of the U.S. government's efforts to disrupt it. This suggests that sanctions busting can be a potent but nonetheless difficult tool for target states to master in holding out against sanctions over the long run.

The rest of the chapter proceeds as follows. The next two sections explore the sanctioning effort against Cuba and how it sustained itself via sanctions busting first during and then after the Cold War. The analysis of the Cold War period highlights the patronage provided to Cuba by the Soviet Union and China, whereas the analysis of the post–Cold War period highlights the patronage provided to it by China and Venezuela. These empirical sections are followed by a summary comparison of the findings from the cases and a discussion of the common strategies Cuba's leadership adopted in leveraging both its aid- and trade-based sanctions-busting relationships. The chapter concludes by discussing the lessons that can be gleaned from how well the U.S. policies designed to prevent Cuba from receiving sanctions-busting support fared in that endeavor.

Busting the U.S. Sanctioning Effort against Cuba during the Cold War

When Fidel Castro overthrew the U.S-friendly Batista regime in Cuba, few could have anticipated that this action would initiate over a half-century of hostilities with the U.S. government. The decisions made by both Castro and U.S. leaders in the early 1960s helped lock both countries into an adversarial relationship that would come to be defined by the U.S. government's sanctioning effort to isolate and undermine Castro's regime. The United States mobilized almost the entire Western Hemisphere in support of its sanctioning efforts and made deterring third-party trade with Cuba a top diplomatic priority until the mid-1970s. In response, Castro was driven to seek external support from third-party governments willing to offer the regime their patronage. Both the Soviet Union and the People's Republic of China extended support to Cuba, though the former was able to do so much more extensively. Over the course of the next thirty years of the Cold War, the Soviet Union would provide Cuba with tens of billions of dollars' worth of sanctions-busting aid that proved crucial to sustaining the Castro regime. As this section reveals, Castro was able to effectively resist the almost unprecedentedly powerful sanctioning effort of the United States via his use of both trade- and aid-based sanctions busting.

The U.S. Sanctioning Effort against Cuba during the Cold War
Before the Cuban Revolution that brought Fidel Castro into power, the United States had enjoyed a close commercial relationship with Cuba. In 1959, the United States purchased over two-thirds of Cuba's exports (mainly sugar) and supplied the country with over three-fifths of its total imports.[3] Although the revolution that Castro staged against the U.S.-backed Batista regime in Cuba ran contrary to U.S. interests, it was not immediately clear what type of relationship Castro's new regime would have with the United States. U.S. rela-

tions with Castro's regime took a dramatic turn for the worse after Castro expropriated American-owned oil refineries in Cuba in June 1960. President Dwight Eisenhower responded by cutting the U.S. sugar import quota from Cuba by 700,000 tons. Castro retaliated several months later by nationalizing hundreds of millions of dollars of U.S. properties in Cuba—including banks, agricultural properties, and mines.[4] Caught in this "spiral of antagonism," the Eisenhower administration moved to sever most American exports to Cuba under the aegis of the Export Control Act of 1949, preventing the sale of all but medical products and foodstuffs to the country.[5] In justifying this action, President Eisenhower claimed that the purpose of the sanctions "was to deny Cuba items, particularly spare parts for American-made equipment, and thus cause costly shutdowns" that would have "a snowballing effect" on the Cuban economy.[6]

U.S. relations with Cuba continued to worsen after John F. Kennedy became president in 1961. The ill-planned Bay of Pigs invasion that President Kennedy approved in the early days of his administration ended in disaster. Castro responded to the failed invasion on April 16, 1961, by publicly declaring that Cuba's revolution had been socialist in nature—which he had not previously done.[7] In February 1962, the U.S. government banned all trade with Cuba under the aegis of a strict set of import restrictions issued by the U.S. Treasury Department and the Trading with the Enemy Act.[8] This led Cuba to seek a stronger security relationship with the Soviet Union, setting up the showdown with the United States over the placement of Soviet nuclear missiles in Cuba in the fall of 1962. After the Cuban Missile Crisis, the U.S. government issued the "Cuban Assets Control Regulations" (CACR). The CACR froze nearly all Cuban assets in the United States, banned U.S. firms and citizens from engaging in almost all types of commercial transactions with Cuban entities, and severely restricted the travel of U.S. citizens to Cuba.[9] This measure effectively prohibited U.S.-owned subsidiaries and companies with American citizens on their boards from trading with Cuba, introducing an important extraterritorial element to the U.S. sanctions. Yet this measure was only one part of a much broader effort to prevent third-party trade with Cuba.

Recognizing that its direct efforts alone might not be sufficient to isolate Cuba, the U.S. government actively sought third-party support for its sanctions. The United States relied heavily on international organizations as part of those efforts. The Organization of American States (OAS) became one of the primary U.S. tools for isolating Castro's regime in the Western hemisphere. In January 1962, the United States successfully lobbied for Cuba's suspension from the organization. Building on its initial success, the United States convinced the OAS membership to approve a full embargo against Cuba in 1964.[10] Other than Mexico, which refused to participate in the sanctioning effort, the OAS embargo proved effective at maintaining the sanctioning effort against Cuba across most of Latin America throughout the latter part of the 1960s.

The United States also attempted to use NATO as a vehicle for rallying third-party support for its sanctions among its Western European allies and Canada. According to Morris Morely, "Washington policymakers believed that the success of the economic embargo would depend, in large part, on Havana's incapacity to locate alternative capitalist trading and financial partners."[11] As such, the U.S. government heavily lobbied its NATO allies to deny the Cuban government military assistance, reduce their purchases of Cuban sugar, limit the trade credits they offered to Cuba, prevent the diversions of American products through their countries, and discourage their firms from trading with Cuba.[12] In contrast to the OAS, U.S. policy makers used NATO only as a forum for lobbying the organization's members to support the U.S. sanctioning effort.

The U.S. efforts at gaining the support of its NATO allies met with mixed success. In general, U.S. efforts were most effective at convincing U.S. allies to curb their exports of strategic goods to Cuba and to deny trade credits to the Cuban government.[13] Originally, officials like Secretary of State Dean Rusk and Walter Rostow in the State Department expected to obtain strong support from NATO allies. Even when the expected levels of cooperation were not forthcoming, they limited their diplomatic efforts to "moral suasion" as opposed to coercion or threats.[14] The reluctance to employ the latter methods stemmed from the perception that the costs of compelling the countries' cooperation would simply be too high. Senator J. William Fulbright, Chairman of the Senate Foreign Relations Committee, conceded as much in 1964, stating: "It is simply not within our power to compel our allies to cut off their trade with Cuba, unless we are prepared to take drastic action against them."[15] This view was shared by other key U.S. diplomats like Secretary Rusk, who publicly advocated against taking a hard-line stance on the sanctions issue.[16] Given its NATO allies' greater strategic importance than those of its Latin American allies, it makes sense that U.S. policy makers would be much more reticent to employ harsh coercion against their NATO allies in which the costs of disrupting alliance relationships were significantly higher. Morely aptly summarizes the prudent approach adopted by U.S. policy makers:

> Although there was considerable "browbeating [of] the Europeans into seeing it our way," both the Kennedy and Johnson administrations exhibited a strongly pragmatic attitude. Ultimately, Washington was not prepared "to put on the screws and initiate a confrontation with [important allies] over Cuba" to a point where long-term political and military relationships were endangered. As a State Department official put it, "there is a limit to which we will jeopardize relations with friendly countries by getting unity with them over something like this."[17]

Despite the damage that the U.S. allies were doing to its sanctioning efforts, U.S. policy makers did not view the costs of compelling their cooperation as worth the potential benefits. Consistent with the sanctions-busting theory's account, the value that the United States placed on maintaining positive relationships with its strategically important allies led it to tolerate their opportunistic sanctions busting.

The United States also sought to exploit Cuba's dependence on maritime trade in its efforts to isolate the country from global commerce. U.S. efforts on this front involved state-to-state diplomacy, the extraterritorial coercion of foreign firms, and the imposition of domestic policies that punished firms that facilitated in trade with Cuba. To put a damper on sanctions busting, President Kennedy vastly increased the U.S. Department of Commerce's oversight and enforcement powers in 1961. Policies were put in place so that cargo vessels visiting the United States with planned stops in Cuba would be searched for strategic goods. The U.S. government also began blacklisting companies found to be violating its sanctions policies.[18] In the midst of heightened tensions with the Soviet Union over Cuba in 1962, the U.S. government invoked the "Battle Act" against Cuba. This measure denied U.S. foreign assistance to countries that allowed their ships or aircraft to transport strategic goods to Cuba and denied port access to foreign vessels trading with Cuba.[19] The executive branch backed up these policies in 1963 with a national security memorandum that disallowed shipping companies engaged in trade with Cuba from carrying cargo financed by the U.S. government.[20] Overall, these policies were largely effective at cutting down the amount of commercial shipping traffic that Cuba received—causing a 61 percent decline in the number of visits Cuba received from ships hailing from capitalist countries from 1962 through 1963. They were particularly effective in gaining the compliance of Liberia, Turkey, Honduras, Panama, Greece, and West Germany, although the shipping industries of Italy, Great Britain, and Spain remained largely undeterred by them.[21]

The U.S. government sought to actively prevent the sanctions busting conducted by Cuba's communist patrons only in one notable instance: the Cuban Missile Crisis. The crisis occurred after U.S. intelligence revealed in October 1962 that the Soviet Union was clandestinely transferring and installing nuclear-armed ballistic missiles in Cuba. This led to a tense standoff between the United States and the Soviet Union that brought the two countries to the brink of nuclear war. Looking for a way to stand firm against the Soviet Union without starting a war, President Kennedy authorized a naval quarantine of Cuba to prevent the Soviets from completing the installation of its missile facilities. President Kennedy deployed U.S. naval forces to the waters surrounding Cuba and authorized them to intercept Soviet vessels trying to reach the country. Although several potential flashpoint incidents occurred during the quarantine, the policy ultimately offered the U.S. and Soviet leaders flexibility to negotiate a resolution to the crisis. Soviet Premier Nikita Khrushchev agreed to the withdrawal of his country's missiles from Cuba in return for commitments from the United States not to invade the island and to withdraw its Jupiter ballistic missiles from Turkey.[22] The U.S. naval quarantine of Cuba was lifted several weeks later. The crisis helped to cement global perceptions that Cuba had become an important battleground in the Cold War competition between the United States and the Soviet Union. Ironically, then, U.S. success in blocking the transfer of Soviet missiles to Cuba opened the floodgates for the deluge of Soviet assistance that would pour into the country over the next three decades.

Throughout the end of the 1960s, the United States kept up its diplomatic pressure on third-party states to maintain their sanctions against Cuba, but their interest in maintaining the embargo waned by the early 1970s. During the Johnson administration (1963–1969), the U.S. government was surprisingly effective at persuading American MNCs to support the U.S. sanctions against Cuba in their business enterprises abroad via "moral suasion."[23] Ideology and appeals to patriotism seemed to have a dampening effect on American firms' pursuit of profits at all costs in this period. In 1967, the United States convinced the OAS to adopt a measure calling on its member states to deny government-financed cargo and docking privileges to ships that trans-

ported goods to Cuba.[24] This proved to be the last significant achievement of
the United States in obtaining multilateral support for its sanctioning efforts.
By the early 1970s, OAS members began challenging the regional sanctions
against Cuba and the U.S. government's ban on its subsidiaries' trade with
Cuba. It became a contentious issue in U.S. bilateral relations with OAS members, like Canada and Argentina, and also within the OAS itself.[25] In 1975,
the United States finally acceded to this pressure in two ways: It assented to
lifting the OAS embargo against Cuba (even voting yes on the measure), and
it lifted its restrictions on U.S. subsidiaries' trade with Cuba. Despite allowing
the multilateral sanctioning effort to collapse, the U.S. government kept the
rest of its unilateral sanctions against Cuba in place.

Over the course of the next decade and a half, U.S. sanctions policies toward Cuba remained largely locked in the grip of a Cold War stasis. Potential
inroads were made toward lifting the sanctions during the Carter administration. In his first two years in office, President Jimmy Carter lifted the restrictions banning U.S. citizens from traveling to Cuba and spending U.S. dollars
in the country. He also lifted prohibitions on remittances to the country by
Cuban Americans. Cuba's involvement in numerous African conflicts during the late 1970s and early 1980s halted the momentum towards relaxing the
U.S. sanctions.[26] In 1982, President Ronald Reagan reinstated the travel bans
and prohibitions on spending U.S. currency in Cuba—once again adopting
a hard-line stance against the Castro regime in Cuba. No other substantial
changes in U.S. sanctions policies toward Cuba occurred until the Cold War's
conclusion.

Cuba's Response to the U.S. Sanctions

The Cuban response to the American sanctions offers insight into both the
pragmatic and political strategies employed by sanctioned states to mitigate
their costs. Due to its significant initial dependence on the United States and
the strength of the sanctions it imposed, Cuba made its response to the sanctions one of the country's greatest national priorities. Although this might not
be true for all sanctioned states, the Cuban case illustrates how a highly motivated target government can mobilize its political and commercial resources
toward obtaining third-party trade and assistance.

For Castro's government, there were few choices available to it in terms of
replacing its lost trade with the United States beyond the Soviet Union. The
Soviet Union's economy was large enough to substitute for that of the United

States; it possessed crucial commodities, such as oil; and it could produce *much* of what the Cuban government needed in terms of manufactured and industrial products. Also, it was the only country powerful enough to contravene U.S. interests in the Caribbean by extending its security umbrella to the country. Just three days after Eisenhower's decision to decrease the U.S. sugar quota by 700,000 tons in July 1960, the Soviet Union responded by announcing that it would increase its sugar purchases from Cuba by that same amount.[27] This signaled that the Soviet Union was willing to engage in tit-for-tat Cold War politics in the U.S. dispute with Cuba. Despite this announcement, the Soviet Union did not immediately offer Cuba major security guarantees or commit itself to offering Cuba substantial amounts of foreign aid. Indeed, Castro would have to work hard to recruit the Soviets' patronage.

When Castro led the revolt against the U.S.-backed Batista regime in 1959, the revolutionary movement had no clearly defined ideological commitment to Marxist-Leninism. Castro's decision to publicly announce the "socialist" nature of the Cuban Revolution during the Bay of Pigs invasion appears to have been a calculated measure designed to place pressure on the Soviet Union to offer the Cuban regime its support.[28] Despite the significance of the announcement, there were still those within the Soviet Union who questioned "the enormous material expenses involved, as well as the political risks to Soviet-American relations" of becoming Cuba's benefactor.[29] Many remaining doubts about Castro's commitment to socialism were dispelled on December 1, 1961, with his dramatic, televised declaration that "I am a Marxist-Leninist and shall remain a Marxist-Leninist until the day I die." Castro's high-profile commitment to communism was designed to put the Soviet Union's reputation at stake in the U.S.–Cuban sanctions dispute. Castro sought to force the Soviets into demonstrating their commitment to the international communist movement by supporting his regime, despite the significant reservations that its leadership had.[30] Although it would be a *vast* oversimplification to say that the U.S. sanctions caused Cuba to adopt communism, the sanctions certainly increased Castro's incentives for associating Cuba with the international political movement. Adopting communism gave Castro the greatest possible leverage in acquiring the foreign support his regime needed to survive.

The combination of the U.S. and OAS sanctions and the patronage it secured from the Soviet Union led to the complete reorientation of Cuba's international trade flows from what they otherwise would have been. In responding to the sanctions, Cuba embraced—and soon learned how to exploit—the assistance offered to it by the Soviet Union. It also fostered close ties with other socialist countries in Eastern Europe and with China. Kaplowitz estimates that, from 1961 through 1973, Cuba conducted 73 percent of its trade with communist states.[31] Precious few of these countries would have been natural trading partners of Cuba absent the embargo. Out of that, trade with the Soviet Union constituted roughly 48 percent of Cuba's annual trade, and trade with China accounted for an average of 9 percent of its yearly totals. A significant proportion of the trade that Cuba conducted with these countries was also subsidized, either directly or indirectly. In 1972, Cuba joined the Council for Mutual Economic Assistance (CMEA), giving it greater access, under favorable terms, to markets in countries like Hungary, East Germany, Czechoslovakia, and Bulgaria. Even before then, however, Cuban trade with these countries had risen substantially relative to its presanctions levels.

Though Cuba's trading partners were predominantly communist countries during this period, it still sought to maintain a positive commercial reputation with the capitalist world. Surprisingly, Cuba gained a sterling reputation for paying off any financing offered to it by foreign governments for its import purchases in full and on time. This made U.S. efforts to tarnish the country's commercial reputation more difficult. From 1963 through 1964, Cuban trade with capitalist countries increased by 80 percent to around $230 million—recovering from their sharp decline caused by the Cuban Missile Crisis.[32] Cuba's commercial relationships with U.S. allies, such as Great Britain, Japan, and Spain, persevered through the sanctions and, in some cases, grew substantially stronger. In forging these trade-based sanctions-busting relationships with U.S. allies, the Castro regime sought to exploit the U.S. government's unwillingness to harshly punish their sanctions busting. Even with the American resentment such trade engendered, Cuba managed to do business with many U.S. allies—though it cost them far higher than it otherwise would have absent the sanctions. The "Cubans were paying well above normal prices for major equipment imports from Western Europe partly because suppliers were jittery over dealing with Havana, fearing U.S. retaliation," and they were often sorely limited in their choice of suppliers.[33] Firms in Great Britain, Japan, and Spain all benefited significantly from the premiums they were able to charge the Cubans. By refusing to buckle to the U.S. government's pressure, those countries profited immensely from their trade with Cuba throughout the 1960s and 1970s.

By the latter part of the 1960s, Cuba's trade with the nonsocialist world had begun to recover but was impeded by the economic hardship the country was experiencing. Cuba's economic troubles in the latter part of the 1960s and early 1970s made the country even more dependent on the foreign aid it was receiving from the Soviet Union. Even so, Cuba still managed to conduct roughly a quarter of its trade with capitalist states in the late 1960s.[34] This figure climbed to 32 percent in 1972 and 41 percent in 1974.[35] These increases occurred in spite of Cuba's dearth of hard currency reserves, as much of its export trade with communist bloc countries involved barter exchanges of sugar for oil, foodstuffs, and/or manufactured goods. The aid that Cuba received from the Soviet Union was often directly used by Castro's regime for his country's commerce with capitalist trade partners. In this way, the Soviet Union was the party actually paying for the rents that trade-based sanctions busters were extracting from Cuba. Cuba's membership in CMEA and growing dependence on Soviet aid, though, would increasingly crowd out its trade with capitalist countries moving into the 1980s.

During the latter part of the 1970s and 1980s, two important trends shaped Cuba's responses to the U.S. sanctions: an increasing dependence on Soviet aid to keep the country's economy afloat and an active involvement in foreign conflicts in support of the international communist movement. Despite the massive foreign aid inflows that Castro's regime was receiving from the Soviet Union, the country's economic development lagged, and it remained highly dependent on the export of commodities such as sugar, nickel, and Soviet oil. Cuba was also heavily involved in overseas conflicts in Africa, supporting communist movements all over the continent.[36] These actions suggest that U.S. sanctions were failing to cow Castro's regime into submission. If anything, the Castro regime's commitment to undercutting U.S. interests abroad only grew stronger as the sanctions persisted. This is important, given that there was no indication that Castro's regime would move in this direction prior to the U.S. government's embargo of the country.

Despite thirty years of U.S. sanctions, Castro's regime remained in power at the Cold War's conclusion and remained unwilling to concede to them. The sanctions had stunted Cuba's economic development, however, and left it highly dependent on foreign assistance to fund its domestic needs and international activism. Still, the Castro regime's ability to withstand multilateral sanctions from almost its entire hemisphere until the mid-1970s is quite notable. The patronage that Cuba received from the People's Republic of China in the early years of the sanctions and long-term support of the Soviet Union throughout the rest of the Cold War were critical to the Castro regime's survival. The following section describes the sanctions-busting aid that Cuba's two leading patrons provided it during the Cold War and the motivations behind it. The proactive efforts undertaken by the Castro regime to obtain and maintain this aid are an important part of the story.

Cuba's Cold War Patrons

Following the U.S. imposition of sanctions against Cuba, both the Soviet Union and the People's Republic of China stepped in to provide it with assistance. Both countries had adversarial relations with the United States and possessed communist governments. After Castro declared that Cuba would join the socialist camp, both countries subsequently shared a common ideological orientation with Castro's regime. Yet important differences existed in the ideological orientations of China's leaders and those of the Soviet Union, which led to the Sino–Soviet split in the early 1960s. This schism created a rivalry between China and the Soviet Union over which country Cuba's loyalties would belong to. Although Castro was able to play the rivals off one another for several years, ultimately China could not afford to provide Cuba with the lavish amounts of aid that the Soviet Union could. This proved to be a costly victory for the Soviets, though, as they would end up spending tens of billions of dollars supporting the Cubans over the next several decades.

The Soviet Union   The Soviet Union clearly does not fit the profile for a profit-seeking, trade-based sanctions buster. Although the Soviet Union had a large economy during the Cold War, it was dominated by the state and bereft of profit-seeking free enterprises. And though the Soviet Union had domestic demands for products (like sugar) that it could not fulfill domestically, its national economic welfare was not generally dependent on international trade. The Soviet Union's relationship with Cuba prior to 1959 would also not suggest that it could profit from sanctions busting on its behalf. The Soviet Union was half a world away from Cuba, and the degree to which it was economically dependent on the state was minimal. Notably, the U.S. sanctions against Cuba took place in the backdrop of one of the high points in the Soviet Union's Cold War rivalry with the United States. Prior to Castro's revolution and the initiation of the U.S. sanctioning effort, the Soviet Union had no close ties with Cuba or security arrangements with the country. Only in the latter part of 1960 did the Soviet Union consent to Castro's requests for security guarantees, and even then it declined to formalize them in a treaty.[37] Thus, the Soviet Union's emergence as the sanctions-busting patron on Cuba's behalf was not a predetermined outcome of the U.S. sanctions.

The Soviet Union's initial intervention on Cuba's behalf provided little indication of the country's eventual largesse. In the first postsanctions trade agreement the Soviet Union signed with Cuba in 1960, it agreed only to purchase Cuban sugar at world prices. For Cuba, this was less than the subsidized price the United States had been paying for its sugar before the sanctions were imposed. The Soviets also agreed to provide Cuba with $100 million in concessional loans to finance the purchase of Soviet industrial equipment and products.[38] Although these agreements were certainly beneficial to Castro's regime, they both offered reasonable economic returns to the Soviet Union. Not until Castro made his two public commitments to socialism in 1961 did the Soviet Union begin providing Cuba with substantial amounts of costly assistance.[39] Castro's announcements, according to Mervyn Bain, reflected a realization that "Moscow could not afford to let the United States overthrow a communist regime for ideological reasons, in general, or more specifically one in such a significant geographic location."[40]

Following Castro's procommunist declarations, the Soviet Union made a number of costly commitments to help ensure Cuba's security and economic stability. To aid Cuba's economy, the Soviet Union began providing Cuba with hundreds of millions of dollars' worth of assistance, subsidized trade, and loans in 1961.[41] Another major part of that commitment was the deal struck to install Soviet nuclear-armed missiles in Cuba following the failed Bay of Pigs Invasion. Soviet Premier Khrushchev underestimated the fierce political backlash the agreement would cause in the United States and the international crisis the move would create. In negotiating a deal with the Kennedy administration, the Soviet leadership marginalized the Cubans from discussions and even failed to inform Castro of the secret terms of the deal.[42] This generated significant resentment within Castro's regime and led to residual political tensions between the two countries that lasted until the latter part of the 1960s. Castro responded by politically drifting closer to the Chinese camp. Yet, in parallel over this period, the Soviet Union also began to provide Cuba with increasingly significant amounts of foreign aid. Duncan estimates that in the period from 1961 through 1967, the Soviet Union provided Cuba with approximately $2 billion in foreign assistance.[43] In the aftermath of the missile crisis, Castro made two in-person visits to the Soviet Union. The first trip, in 1963, culminated in Cuba's formal adoption into the international socialist camp, which gave it greater access to Soviet aid. Castro's second visit to the Soviet Union, in 1964, resulted in a five-year trade agreement between the two countries that offered Cuba highly favorable terms of trade.[44] It is important to note that this agreement would become the model for future trade agreements that would establish the terms of the subsidized trade that the Soviet Union would conduct with Cuba.[45] The Soviet policies adopted during this period helped solidify the view that preventing Cuba from capitulating to U.S. sanctions constituted a vital commitment to which the Soviet Union's Cold War reputation was tied.

By the latter part of the 1960s, the economic turmoil caused by the U.S. sanctions and the Castro regime's failing economic policies made Castro's regime increasingly more dependent on foreign assistance. Pragmatically, Castro sought to reconcile his regime's political relationship with the Soviet Union. In 1966, Soviet aid to Cuba (through subsidies and long-term trade credits) amounted to roughly $365 million, and by 1973 that figure had risen to as much as $600 million a year.[46] Over roughly that same period, bilateral trade between Cuba and the Soviet Union quadrupled.[47] An important milestone in Cuban–Soviet relations came in 1972 when Cuba was admitted into the Council for Mutual Economic Assistance. Cuba's admittance followed another formal visit to the Soviet Union by Castro in which he was also able to secure several hundred million dollars' worth of debt relief and higher subsidized prices for Cuban sugar and nickel.[48] Formed in 1949, the Soviet-led CMEA was used to structure and coordinate trade among its communist member states and integrate their economic activities.[49] By granting Cuba membership in the organization, the Soviet Union offered it access to greater quantities of foreign assistance and provided itself with a mechanism for sharing the burden of supporting Cuba.[50] Given the Soviet Union's domination of CMEA, its members had little choice in the matter. The burden of supporting Cuba would only go on to rise in the 1970s, as the price of oil skyrocketed and the price of sugar bottomed out.[51] During the 1970s, Cuba also received substantial amounts of free military assistance from the Soviet Union that played a key role in supporting the nation's involvement in numerous military engagements in Africa.[52] By the end of the 1970s, the subsidized trade and foreign assistance provided by the Soviet Union and CMEA to Cuba were playing a dominant role in sustaining the country's economy.

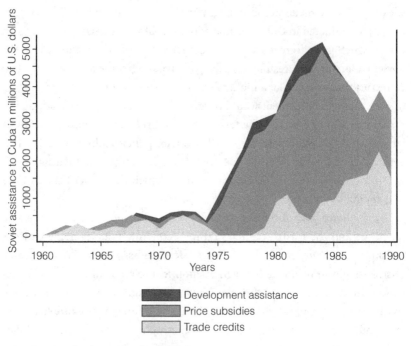

FIGURE 7.1. Soviet assistance to Cuba, 1960–1990.
SOURCE: Leogrande and Thomas 2002, 340–341.

Figure 7.1 provides a fascinating look at how the channels through which Soviet assistance provided to Cuba shifted from 1960 to 1990. These raw data were triangulated by Leogrande and Thomas using a variety of sources, and they constitute one of the most comprehensive accounts of the aid provided to Cuba by the Soviet Union.[53] As the figure shows, most of the Soviet aid to Cuba in the period from 1960 to 1974 came in the form of trade credits. From 1975 through 1990, however, the channels through which the Soviet Union offered sanctions-busting aid to Cuba shifted largely to price subsidies. A large portion of the subsidized assistance came from the Soviet Union's purchase of Cuban sugar at inflated values established as part of the five-year trading agreements. Instead of hard currency, the lion's share of these transactions involved oil-for-sugar barter exchanges at highly favorable terms. Although the Soviet Union had subsidized Cuban sugar at roughly one and a half to two times global prices in the 1960s and 1970s, by the mid-1980s it was trading for Cuban sugar at roughly ten times its global market price.[54] Indeed, Cuba opportunistically exploited these generous subsidies by purchasing foreign sugar at market prices and reselling it to the Soviet Union. The steeply discounted oil that Cuba received from the Soviet Union also became a source of revenue for Cuba. To obtain hard currency for its trade with capitalist sanctions busters, Castro's regime reexported significant quantities of Soviet oil to third parties and pocketed the profits. In 1986, reexports of Soviet oil actually overtook sugar as Cuba's largest export earner.[55] At its peak in this period, trade with the Soviet Union constituted roughly 70 percent of Cuba's overall trade, and it was also receiving approximately $1.5 billion in annual military assistance.[56] The substantial amount of sanctions-busting assistance that the Soviet Union provided to Cuba during this period makes it an extraordinary outlier. Few other countries could have provided Cuba with that level of support even if they had been inclined to.

In looking once again at Figure 7.1, it is also worthwhile to take note of the quantity of development assistance that the Soviet Union provided to Cuba. Notably, this was the category of foreign aid analyzed in Chapter 3, and it appears to have constituted only a minor portion of the sanctions-busting aid the Soviet Union gave to Cuba. It is precisely because aid-based sanctions busters can use so many different channels to provide their assistance that this chapter does not limit its focus to that single category of aid. The variation in methods by which patrons can provide their assistance increase the challenges of identifying such states, especially if their assistance is not as overt as it is in this case. Overall, Leogrande and Thomas estimate that the Soviet Union provided Cuba with a total of $65 billion worth of assistance from 1960 through 1990.[57] It is important to note that these figures do not include military aid that would inflate this total sum by tens of billions of dollars.

For the Soviet Union, supporting Cuba with such lavish support began to place a real strain on its own faltering economy in the latter part of the 1980s. Despite this, the countries' economic relationship remained surprisingly insulated from the variety of reforms the Soviet leadership undertook to reinvigorate its own economic performance. By 1990, however, the sanctions-busting aid being given to Cuba began to be viewed as unsustainable. Reflecting this, the Soviet Union broke its past tradition of signing five-year trade agreements with Cuba and negotiated for only a one-year agreement in 1990. Another striking feature of this agreement was that it set the terms of trade for Cuban sugar exports at market prices—a far cry from the substantially inflated prices from just five years prior.[58] Cuban–Soviet trade declined by approximately 65 percent between 1990 and 1991, and Soviet oil shipments, on which Cuba was utterly dependent, ground to a halt by the end of 1991. Even before the Soviet Union's formal dissolution, it had effectively ceased its extensive aid-based sanctions busting on Cuba's behalf, and it was not a role that any of its successor states would subsequently adopt. It is also notable that, as the Soviets' compulsion to trade with Cuba waned, the CMEA members' subsidized trade with Cuba rapidly dissipated.

Three necessary conditions should have been central to motivating the substantial quantities of sanctions-busting aid the Soviet Union provided to Cuba according to the aid-based sanctions-busting hypothesis. The first relates to a salient set of political motives. The Cold War rivalry between the Soviet Union and United States provides a partial explanation for the Soviet Union's interest in intervening on Cuba's behalf. Notably, though, the Soviet Union did not begin making significant outflows of foreign aid to Cuba until Castro declared Cuba as part of the Marxist-Leninist camp. By making Cuba part of the international communist movement, Castro placed its sanctions dispute within the broader context of the ideologically based rivalry between the world's two leading superpowers. If Cuba succumbed to the U.S. sanctions, it would subsequently be viewed as a victory of the democratic-capitalist forces over those of the communists. Although the Soviet leadership appeared aware of the potential burden they would be taking on in coming to Cuba's aid, declining to support Cuba after Castro's declaration would have hurt the Soviet Union's reputation.[59] Once committed to supporting Cuba, the Soviet Union found itself stuck with an increasingly costly burden that it could not easily shed.

Another dimension to the Soviet Union's ideological motivations pertains to the Sino–Soviet split that occurred during the 1960s in which each country vied for leadership of the international communist movement. Supporting Cuba helped the Soviet Union remain at the vanguard of the international communist movement, whereas abandoning it would have given China a further opening to claim leadership. These considerations were especially salient for the Soviet Union after it backed down during the Cuban Missile Crisis.

As the Soviet Union's commitment to communism faded at the end of the Cold War, so did its commitment to Cuba. "Marxist-Leninism had been a cornerstone of Soviet-Cuban relations," and the Soviet Union's disillusionment with it "meant that one of the key reasons for the relationship's continuation had simply evaporated overnight, as had the importance for the Kremlin of a socialist state in the western hemisphere."[60] Beyond its ideological motivations, the Soviet Union had few other incentives to continue aiding Castro's regime. According to Pavlov, the relationship that the Soviet Union had forged with Cuba had always been more of a marriage of convenience than one borne of true social and political friendship.[61] As the Soviet Union sought to reconcile with the United States, it no longer had a salient strategic or ideological reason to continue providing Cuba with such costly support. In September 1991, Gorbachev publically announced that the Soviet Union would be normalizing its relationship with Cuba. This announcement publically signaled that "ideology was no longer to play a part in the relationship between Moscow and Havana, in a similar way as it did not play a part in Moscow's relationships with other countries."[62] Possessing an ideological stake in Cuba's plight vis-à-vis the U.S. sanctions played a key role initiating the Soviet Union's sanctions-busting aid, and the loss of that motivation appears to have played a similarly important role in its leaders' decision to cease their aid to Cuba.

The second necessary condition posited by the sanctions-busting theory relates to the feasibility of relying on market-based sanctions busting to provide Cuba with the support it needed. If the Soviet Union could accomplish its political ends via commercially beneficial means, it should have done so. The trading relationship between the Soviet Union and Cuba clearly provided lopsided benefits to the Cubans, not the Soviets. The trade deals signed between the two countries, and especially those involving oil-for-sugar bartering arrangements, provide few direct economic benefits to the country. Indeed, Pavlov finds that the supposed "Soviet dependence on imports from Cuba was created by politically motivated and economically unsound decisions" and "was maintained artificially, without any serious attempt to reduce it."[63] Even in his correspondence to Castro, Khrushchev said that his country's assistance to Cuba was done out of "internationalist duty" rather than "mercantilist considerations."[64]

Furthermore, substantial quantities of Soviet trade with Cuba could occur only if they supported it with significant price subsidies. The economic turmoil caused by the U.S. sanctions and the Cuban government's policies meant that the country lacked the independent capacity to pay for the level of sanctions-busting trade it needed to sustain itself, especially with respect to its energy needs. That the Cuban government had to use Soviet aid to fund its sanctions-busting trade with capitalist countries is further proof that such an avenue was not open to the Soviet government.

The last critical requirement for aid-based sanctions busting is whether a third-party government can afford to offer target states substantial foreign assistance. In the Soviet Union's case, it possessed one of the few economies large enough to sustain Cuba with the considerable levels of foreign aid that it needed. Yet, even for the Soviet Union, the burden of sustaining Cuba was not insignificant. By admitting Cuba into CMEA in 1972, the Soviet Union was able to share the costs of supporting the country with its other members. However, the lion's share of the costs associated with supporting Cuba still continued to fall on the Soviet Union. As the costs entailed in supporting Cuba in the 1980s soared, the Soviet Union's economy faced significant turmoil of its own. The Soviet Union's involvement in Afghanistan also grew to become a major drain on the country's resources. By 1990, the Soviet Union could no longer afford to provide Cuba with the lavish support that it once had. This was reflected in the one-year trade agreement the Soviets brokered with Cuba that set the terms of their trade at market prices. The Soviet Union thus lost both the motives and the means to continue sanctions busting on Cuba's behalf even before its dissolution.

The People's Republic of China   The second major instance of aid-based sanctions busting on Cuba's behalf during the Cold War does not even come close to matching the Soviet assistance in scope or duration. The sanctions-busting assistance that the People's Republic of China offered to Cuba in the immediate aftermath of the U.S. sanctions was still significant, though, and it came in the crucial period before the country had solidified its sanctions-busting relationship with the Soviet Union. After the fallout of the Cuban Missile Crisis, there was uncertainty as to whether Castro would shift allegiances to the Chinese ideological camp. The Sino–Soviet rift of the early 1960s and the issue of how the Cuban Revolution fit into their competing visions of the international communist movement provided a tense backdrop to Cuba's relations with both countries. Although Castro flirted with the Chinese, he ultimately realized that the level of support they could afford to provide was nowhere near what the Soviets could. China's patronage of Cuba came to an abrupt end in 1966 via a bitter public dispute between the two countries. Although China continued to be one of Cuba's largest trading partners, China stopped providing Castro's regime with significant foreign aid.

Prior to the Cuban Revolution, the U.S.-backed Batista regime in Cuba had no official diplomatic ties with China, and trade between the two countries had been minimal.[65] Like the Soviet Union, China had an adversarial relationship with the United States. Although the hostilities associated with the Korean War had ended in 1953, relations between China and the United States were still tense. China was also the subject of a sustained sanctioning effort by the U.S. government. After Castro came to power, China made overtures to the new Cuban regime and sought to establish ties with it. The anti-U.S. nature of the Cuban Revolution attracted the Chinese to Cuba's cause, as did its emerging commitments to communism in 1961. Commercially and security-wise, though, China had little at stake in terms of the outcome of the sanctions dispute between Cuba and the United States.

The Chinese government's interest in supporting the Cuban regime was evidenced early in 1960. In response to the U.S. sanctions, China offered to negotiate a long-term trade agreement with Cuba that coincided with the establishment of closer bilateral relations. In an agreement brokered in July of 1960, China agreed to purchase 500,000 tons of Cuban sugar annually for five years at market prices. In return, the Cuban government was to receive 80 percent of its payment in Chinese manufactured and industrial goods—including the shipment of whole factories to Cuba.[66] Although China did need to import sugar, Cuba's distance from China and the prices it paid for Cuban sugar indicate that China could have gotten better deals elsewhere.[67]

One month after Castro's announcement that he was a Marxist-Leninist in December 1961, China publically recognized Cuba's efforts to join the communist camp.[68] Subsequently, China and Cuba expanded their trade relationship even further in 1962—negotiating the exchange of Chinese foodstuffs, chemicals, medicine, and other merchandise in return for Cuban nickel, copper, sugar, and fruit.[69] Following the Cuban Missile Crisis, the Chinese harshly criticized the Soviet Union's decision to back down in the dispute. Castro's disillusionment with the Soviet Union after the incident provided him with further incentives to pursue close relations with China. Castro's shared views on the necessity of armed struggle to achieve revolutionary communist ends also attracted him to China's ideological camp. Lévesque argues that while Chinese leaders recognized that "they lacked the military and economic means to take the Soviet Union's place," they thought their aid could obtain "at least partial support from the Cuban leaders" in their dispute with the Soviets.[70] In February 1963, the Chinese government signed an additional trade agreement with Cuba that extended the country a substantial no-interest, long-term loan. A joint communiqué issued by the countries states that their future economic relationship would seek "to advance the common cause of the two peoples of opposing imperialism and building socialism."[71] This strongly suggests that the sanctions busting that China was conducting on Cuba's behalf was being done not to exploit its commercial circumstance but in furtherance of political goals.

Using the Sino–Soviet rift to his advantage, Castro played off the political rivalry between the two countries in pursuit of more lucrative assistance packages from both states. Castro leveraged the rift to negotiate a higher purchase price for Cuban sugar from China than the already subsidized price the Soviet had agreed to pay in 1965. On the basis of the five-year trade agreement the countries signed in 1965, China agreed to purchase Cuban sugar at over double the international market prices. This agreement was designed to establish a long-term framework for Sino–Cuban economic relations.[72] During the period from 1963 to 1965, the Chinese were also providing the Cubans with substantial quantities of rice—a key food staple for the Cuban people. These shipments peaked in 1965 when Cuba received 250,000 tons of rice from the country. Despite the increasing salience of Cuba's sanctions-busting relationship with China, the Soviet Union continued to be Cuba's largest trading partner by far. Of the total trade conducted by Cuba with communist countries in 1964, 66 percent was with the Soviet Union whereas only 18 percent was with China.[73]

The fine line that Castro strode in balancing Cuba's relations between China and the Soviet Union finally gave way in 1966, when the Chinese government reneged on its trade deal with Cuba—cutting its sugar purchases by 200,000 tons and rice exports by half.[74] In Cuba, this move was viewed as retaliation for Castro's closer movement into the Soviet Union's ideological camp. For their part, the Chinese argued that their decision was based on internal requirements and their need to reallocate aid to Vietnam.[75] The ill will generated by China's broken sanctions-busting commitment quickly burgeoned into a much larger dispute. In public statements, Castro characterized China as betraying his compatriots and the communist cause by refusing to deliver the promised foodstuffs on which Cuba's population depended.[76] He further accused China of seeking to extort and blackmail his country and even of sponsoring a massive propaganda campaign within Cuba designed to challenge his regime's ideological positions.[77] As the rhetorical conflict between the two countries escalated, Castro referred to China as a fascist regime that was engaged in a Goebels-like campaign in his country.[78] The Chinese responded with their own set of public accusations and attempts to discredit the Castro regime in a spiraling war of words.[79] This dispute effectively terminated the Chinese government's aid-based sanctions-busting efforts on Cuba's behalf and would have a long-term chilling effect on the countries' relations.

The evidence in this case appears broadly supportive of the sanctions-busting theory's explanation of aid-based sanctions busting. Given China's almost negligible commercial and political relationship with Cuba prior to 1960, China had few immediate interests at stake in the sanctions issue. For the Chinese, supporting Castro's regime offered the means to advance its anti-imperialist/U.S. political agenda and gain additional support for its ideological dispute with the Soviet Union. Whereas the former was sufficient for the Chinese to extend limited assistance to Cuba from 1960 to 1961, the latter motive appeared to encourage the Chinese to provide much more robust assistance to Cuba from 1962 to 1965. Unfortunately for Cuba, the ideological and political demands of its two largest patrons were irreconcilable, and Castro could not continue appeasing both to their satisfaction. Indeed, the once common metaphor that "Castro's stomach is in Moscow, but his heart is in Beijing" aptly captures Castro's dilemma.[80] Ultimately, Chinese leaders sought unrealistically high levels of political support from Castro in their rivalry with the Soviet Union given his regime's dependence on Soviet aid. Although the Chinese cited ulterior reasons for breaking their sanctions-busting pledge to Cuba, their dissatisfaction with Castro's lackluster political support caused them to deprioritize aiding Cuba. That the rhetorical dispute between Cuba and China took on such a highly ideologically charged tone reflects the fact that those motives had been central to China's sanctions-busting relationship on Cuba's behalf in the first place. By moving toward the Soviet ideological camp, Castro undercut the motives that the Chinese had to continue providing his regime with extensive sanctions-busting aid. The Chinese government's decision to cut back on its assistance to Cuba in 1966 is thus consistent with the sanctions-busting theory's expectations.

In terms of the economic feasibility of market-based trade, several initial agreements that the governments brokered were based on those rates but involved a substantial bartering component. Yet as the Chinese government sought to forge a closer relationship with Cuba and play a greater role supporting the regime, it shifted to offering Cuba price subsidies and subsidized loans. These shifts coincided with the economic turmoil Cuba experienced from 1962 through 1965, which made it all the more dependent on foreign assistance to sustain itself. When the Chinese told Castro that they were cutting their planned rice exports in half in 1966, his government was forced to respond by cutting the Cuban population's daily rice ration similarly in half.[81] In the absence of an alternative patron, China's decision to withdrawal its aid could have undermined Castro's ability to sustain his regime.

Yet Cuba did have a rival patron, and it was a rival that Chinese leaders knew they could not afford to compete against. China did not have the disposable income or the cheap energy supplies that the Soviet Union possessed. As such, China could not afford to fully provide Castro's regime with the support it needed. Because the ideological and political agendas that China sought to promote via its sanctions-busting competed with rather than complemented those of the Soviet Union, Castro was forced to choose the patron who could best afford to provide for his country's needs.[82] Thus, it wasn't that China couldn't afford to provide Cuba with significant sanctions-busting aid—it was that it couldn't provide Cuba with enough to really matter in light of what the Soviets could offer instead. Although the Chinese would continue to trade with Cuba throughout the Cold War, China ceased its efforts to compete with the Soviet Union as a sanctions-busting patron of Cuba after 1966. Although the details are more complex in this case, the findings are still consistent with the theoretical account provided.

Busting the U.S. Sanctioning Effort against Cuba after the Cold War

Rather than serving as an opening for reconciliation, the end of the Cold War actually reinvigorated the hostilities between the United States and Cuba. To hasten the Castro regime's collapse, U.S. policy makers sought to strengthen the multilateral component of their sanctioning effort in the early and mid-1990s. This effort largely failed, leading to far more anger and resentment among the U.S. sanctions-busting allies than it did cooperation. Although Cuba struggled through economic hardship throughout the 1990s, Castro spent the decade laying the groundwork for a new set of patronage relationships. These efforts had succeeded at the turn of the millennium, with Castro securing the patronage of both Venezuela and China. The billions of dollars' worth of assistance that Castro would receive from these two countries over the ensuing decade helped spark an economic recovery in Cuba, which once again placed it on solid footing in resisting the sanctions. The Castro regime was thus far better positioned to weather the transition of power from Fidel to his brother Raúl in 2006 than it would have been during the 1990s. Leveraging both the support of trade-based and aid-based sanctions busters, the Castro regime still remains in power fifty-plus years after the U.S. government first imposed its sanctions against Cuba.

The U.S. Sanctioning Effort against Cuba after the Cold War

Following the U.S. Cold War victory over the Soviet Union, there was an expectation in American policy circles that Castro's regime would soon follow suit in collapsing.[83] From 1989 through 1993, Cuba's GDP sank by somewhere between 35 and 50 percent.[84] Yet when Cuba did not immediately collapse, interest groups capitalized on the perception that Cuba was on the brink of folding to encourage U.S. lawmakers to reinvigorate their sanctioning efforts.[85]

The rhetoric and goals of the U.S. sanctioning effort also changed during this period. Rather than focusing on removing the threat posed by Cuba to U.S. national security, the political justifications for maintaining the sanctions shifted to the need to democratize Cuba and punish the regime's human rights violations.[86] Summarizing the U.S. sanctions' post–Cold War policy objectives, Preeg observes that they were "designed to squeeze the Cuban economy to the point of suffering or collapse whereby the Castro Government is forced to hold democratic elections or is violently overthrown."[87] Implicit within the American stance was that, irrespective of whatever Cuba did to moderate its objectionable foreign policies, the U.S. sanctions would not be lifted until the Castro regime left power.[88] Domestic politics, highlighted by presidential politics in Florida and the lobbying efforts of anti-Castro groups, thus emerged as the chief motivator for U.S. sanctions policies toward Cuba.[89] So, while the Cold War political environment that had defined the U.S. sanctioning effort against Cuba unraveled, the U.S. government's commitment to its sanctions against Cuba remained firm.

Given that a full trade embargo was already in place against Cuba at the end of the Cold War, there were few direct measures the U.S. government could take to tighten its sanctions. Instead, U.S. policy makers focused on reinvigorating the multilateral sanctioning effort against Castro's regime and cutting down on third-party trade with the country. From 1989 through 1991, U.S. foreign subsidiaries' trade with Cuba had grown from $331 million to $715 million.[90] This reflected the fact that Cuba was forced to reorient its trade away from the Soviet Union and members of the CMEA. Driven heavily by presidential politics, the Cuban Democracy Act (CDA) was passed by Congress and signed into law by President George H. W. Bush in 1992. The CDA once again banned U.S. foreign subsidiaries from trading with Cuba and prohibited ships that had visited Cuban ports from docking in the United States for 180 days.

Just as many within the administration had predicted, the legislation inflamed the governments of many of Cuba's third-party trading partners. The CDA evoked strident criticism from Canada, the EU, Mexico, Latin America, and Japan. Canada and Great Britain went so far as to adopt blocking legislation within their own countries that *criminalized* obeying the CDA, with Canada's punishments including up to five years of imprisonment.[91] This created both a diplomatic furor for the U.S. government and an intractable quandary for U.S. businesses abroad: They were forced to choose between angering their host governments and potentially breaking their laws versus violating the laws of their home country. The UN General Assembly actually passed a resolution condemning the U.S. sanctions against Cuba and the new extraterritorial provisions they contained.[92] The CDA engendered a lot of resentment, but that would pale in comparison to Congress's next effort to expand the extraterritorial provisions of U.S. sanctions.

Although the CDA reduced the trade conducted by U.S. subsidiaries with Cuba, it failed to bring about the collapse of Castro's regime. In 1996, Congress passed the so-called Helms-Burton Act.[93] In addition to providing legislative foundations for the U.S. sanctions,[94] the Helms-Burton Act targeted third-party companies that traded or invested in Cuba, prohibited U.S. nationals from engaging in any commercial or financial transactions that *in any way* involved expropriated properties in Cuba, and sought to cut aid to the Russian government equivalent to the amount of assistance it gave Cuba.[95] The legislation's controversial Title III gave U.S. citizens with claims to commercial properties that had been expropriated by Cuba the *right* to sue third parties known to be profiting from those properties in U.S. courts. Title IV also denied U.S. visas to the management-level employees and principal shareholders of such firms. The legislation allowed for presidential waivers of the Title III and Russian aid-related provisions. Due to the legal and logistical uncertainties created by the legislation, many American firms were driven toward choosing foreign business partners that did no business with Cuba at all.

The international response to the Helms-Burton Act was profoundly negative, especially among the closest U.S. allies. After the bill passed, Canada immediately imposed blocking legislation to forbid compliance with the measure and threatened retaliatory legislation that would allow Canadians to countersue American firms in their courts for any losses suffered due to Helms-Burton. In July 1996, the U.S. government barred nine executives and shareholders of Sherritt International, a Canadian mining company that did a substantial amount of business with Cuba, from visiting the United States under the aegis of Title IV.[96] The incensed Canadians followed through with their threat and passed retaliatory legislation in January 1997.[97] Beyond unleashing a torrent of criticism against the measure, all fifteen members of the European Union (EU) passed retaliatory legislation in response to the Helms-Burton Act.[98] The EU formally brought suit against the Helms-Burton Act in the World Trade Organization (WTO) to obtain a ruling against the measure as a secondary boycott that violated international trade law.[99] As a State Department official disbelievingly observed, "Every single European Union member state, even the ones who completely agreed with us on human rights, rejected Helms-Burton."[100] Both on a bilateral basis and via the EU, the dispute with the United States over its extraterritorial sanctions emerged as the leading source of transatlantic conflict during that period.

The measure also invoked the ire of the U.S. allies in Latin America. Working with Canada, Mexico helped lead the hemispheric opposition to the Helms-Burton Act.[101] A resolution with thirty-two cosponsors was brought before the OAS that roundly condemned the extraterritorial measures contained within the Helms-Burton Act and passed with the United States casting the sole dissenting vote.[102] The OAS further asked the Inter-American Juridical Committee (IAJC) to issue a ruling on the legality of the American measure.[103] The IAJC subsequently found that the Helms-Burton Act violated international law on numerous counts. Whereas the OAS had been the vehicle the United States had used to build a multilateral coalition of support for its sanctions in the 1960s, Latin American countries used it to organize their opposition to the U.S. sanctions in the 1990s.

The Clinton administration did its best to manage the political fallout created by the legislation. President Clinton suspended the implementation of the Title III provision in the summer of 1996 to facilitate diplomatic negotiations with the countries it affected. Negotiations with the EU carried into the spring of 1998, when tentative agreement was reached. The EU countries agreed to let their WTO suit against the United States lapse and to adopt a few face-saving concessions in their policies toward Cuba. In return, the

Clinton administration agreed to waive the Title III provision indefinitely and seek to have Congress rescind Title IV.[104] This agreement achieved a tolerable stalemate: The Helms-Burton Act would remain in place, but President Clinton and subsequent administrations would not enforce its extraterritorial provisions.

The international responses to both the CDA and the Helms-Burton Act illustrate how U.S. efforts to coerce third-party support for its sanctions can be fraught with difficulty. Although the U.S. legislation was directed at all countries' trade with Cuba, the United States took the political concerns of its close allies (Canada and members of the EU) more seriously than those of other countries. Those were also the countries to push back the hardest against U.S. efforts to coerce their cooperation. Even though hard-liners within Congress viewed the acquisition of third-party support as crucial to their sanctions effort, the Bush and Clinton administrations balked at the damage that fully pursuing such measures would have on the U.S. alliance relationships. As the sanctions-busting theory suggests, intra-alliance politics heavily constrained the U.S. ability to prevent trade-based sanctions busting by its close allies.

In 1998, President Clinton relaxed many of the restrictions regarding remittances and travel to Cuba and allowed direct flights to Cuba from the United States to resume, as those measures were still under presidential jurisdiction. Similar to the Iranian case, the Sanctions Reform and Export Enhancement Act of 2000 lifted the sanctions on sales of food and medicine to Cuba. This legislation opened up a large gap in the U.S. sanctions regime. A GAO report notes that in response to the lifting of sanctions on these products alone, U.S. exports to Cuba rose from $6 million in 2000 to over $350 million in 2006.[105] Despite the erosion of the sanctions, the second Bush administration enacted new policies in 2004 (an election year) that reimposed stringent restrictions on travel to Cuba, reduced the amount of money U.S. travelers could spend in Cuba from $167 a day to $50 a day, and further clamped down on remittances.[106] Following President Barack Obama's election, he lifted a number of the restrictions on travel to Cuba by citizens with family in the country and relaxed the stringent limitations on remittances. In 2011, he further relaxed the travel restrictions to the country and the ceiling on remittances.[107] Overall, the U.S. sanctioning effort against Cuba remained markedly strong until 2000, at which point the vigor with which the sanctions were pursued began to fade.

Cuba's Response to the U.S. Sanctioning Efforts

Facing the withdrawal of Soviet support, the Cuban economy underwent a period of substantial contraction. Cuba faced severe shortages of oil, food, and consumer goods. The loss of the Soviet Union's oil subsidies hit Cuba especially hard. Cuba was almost wholly dependent on foreign energy supplies, and it could not afford to continue its prior levels of energy consumption without subsidies.[108] In his 1991 address to the Cuban Communist Congress, Castro expressed the uncertainty that Cuba faced in terms of the export markets for its sugar and ability to purchase oil.[109] The sudden withdrawal of Soviet aid forced Castro to declare a period of economic emergency that placed the country at a wartime level of austerity. From 1992 through 1993, Cuba teetered on the brink of collapse. To survive, Castro pursued a three-pronged strategy that included initiating capitalist reforms within Cuba, opening up the country to foreign investment, and courting the assistance of new third-party benefactors.

As part of a package of domestic response measures, Castro initiated a series of liberalizing reforms to the Cuban economy. These reforms occurred in the wake of the Cuban sugar industry's collapse in the early 1990s, which had previously been the country's primary domestic revenue source.[110] The reforms included allowing farmers' markets to open up around the country, legalizing private holdings and purchases using U.S. currency, allowing citizens to become self-employed, and amending the country's laws to become more attractive to foreign investment.[111] Castro also sought foreign assistance in cultivating the country's underdeveloped tourism sector. As the 1990s progressed, tourism overtook sugar as Cuba's primary source of hard currency.[112] Castro further found creative ways of paying off foreign creditors through debt-for-equity swaps in joint-venture projects or state-owned enterprises, which were especially popular among Mexican investors.[113] By legalizing the use of dollars, Castro opened up the floodgates for Cubans to receive overseas remittances. Conservative estimates place Cuba's yearly inflows at around $800 million during the mid-1990s; these emerged as a valuable source of hard currency for the country.[114] After enduring severe hardship during the early part of the decade, the Cuban economy began a steady recovery by the latter half of the 1990s.[115] Despite the positive trajectory of Cuba's economic turnaround, the country still suffered from a chronic lack of energy supplies and access to sufficient capital to fund its economic development.

Lacking the commercial wherewithal to solve these problems, the Cuban government once again relied on the political acumen of Castro to secure foreign assistance.[116] Castro's efforts focused on rekindling Cuba's past relationship with China and cultivating a new alliance with Venezuela's Hugo Chávez. A major part of those efforts included a proactive campaign to reconcile with China after the divisive schism that had soured the countries' relations since 1966. Castro's efforts to restore China as a major Cuban patron in the 1990s met with mixed success. Whereas Castro would have liked China to have immediately stepped in to fill the void left by the Soviet Union, reconciling the lingering rift between the countries took time. Castro had more success in forging a close relationship with Venezuela's ambitious and ideologically sympathetic president. The close relationship that Castro forged with Chávez would result in billions of dollars' worth of assistance throughout the 2000s.

Especially prior to the aid-based sanctions-busting relationship that Castro established with Venezuela, Cuba's trade-based sanctions-busting relationships played a critical role in the regime's survival. It is important to note that the commercial ties between Cuba and Russia remained intact after the Soviet Union's dissolution. Russia inherited Cuba's $20 billion debt to the Soviet Union and many of the direct commercial linkages that had tied the two countries together. Trade between the two countries continued in large part out of inertia through the mid-1990s. As Russian firms found more profitable trading opportunities elsewhere, though, bilateral trade between the two countries atrophied. Whereas bilateral trade between the Soviet Union and Cuba had amounted to approximately 4.4 billion pesos in 1991, equivalent trade between Cuba and Russia comprised only 500 million pesos in 1998—a decline of nearly 89 percent.[117] The adjustment of the Russo–Cuban trade relationship to market-based terms reveals just how important the Soviet subsidies had been in sustaining that trade relationship during the Cold War. The Russian government continued to broker oil-for-sugar deals with Cuba until 1999, at which point all future negotiations were turned over to the private sector.

As Cuba's trade relationship with Russia waned during the 1990s, its trade relationships with Western countries steadily rose—especially with Canada and the EU. From 1991 through 2006, trade with Canada constituted roughly 10 percent of the total foreign trade that Cuba conducted. Canadian firms also invested heavily in Cuba's mining sector.[118] According to Kirk and McKenna, "The commercial bottom line . . . [was] the driving force" behind Canada's relationship with Cuba, and the country's trade with Cuba was so lucrative because of "the lack of U.S. competition."[119] This helps explain why Canada responded so strongly to U.S. efforts to curb its sanctions-busting relationship with Cuba. A large number of EU members, including Spain, Italy, and the Netherlands, also sought to exploit the commercial opportunities available in Cuba. Even after the passage of the CDA, Cuba conducted 45 percent of its total trade with the EU in 1994.[120] The large commercial stake that so many European countries had in Cuba created significant incentives for their governments to defend their sanctions-busting relationships against U.S. efforts to disrupt them. The EU's total share of Cuba's international trade remained high throughout the 1990s, until it began to decline somewhat in the early 2000s.[121] Rather than being the result of U.S. coercion, this reflected Cuba's burgeoning sanctions-busting relationships with China and Venezuela, which offered it far more favorable terms of trade.

Fidel Castro continued to display the same sort of flexible, pragmatic approach toward resisting the U.S. sanctions that he had during the Cold War. With the loss of Cuba's primary sanctions-busting patron, Castro set out to find new ones that could fill the void left by the Soviet Union. In the interim, he relied heavily on commercially oriented sanctions busters, which allowed his regime to weather a period of hardship that could have been even worse and potentially led to his regime's downfall. The liberalizing reforms that Castro introduced were geared toward making the country more attractive to foreign businesses and investors. In seeking to restore Cuba's relationship with China and forge a new aid-based sanctions-busting relationship with Venezuela, Castro sought to exploit the few potential patronage opportunities that existed for his regime. Although forging these aid-based sanctions-busting relationships required significant political investments by Castro, he succeeded in winning both governments' support.

In 2006, Cuba experienced its first major transition of power since the Revolution in 1959. Due to illness, Fidel transferred his presidential authorities to his younger brother Raúl Castro, who was serving as Cuba's vice president. Raúl officially ascended to the presidency after Fidel declined to stand for reelection in 2008. Although Raúl Castro has initiated more aggressive economic reforms than his brother, Cuba has largely remained committed to its socialist model of governance and economics. The transition of power had little effect on U.S.–Cuban relations or the U.S. sanctioning effort, as it was perceived as a continuation of the existing Castro regime.[122] Under its new leadership, Cuba appears to be just as committed to resisting U.S. sanctions as it was under Fidel.

Cuba's Post–Cold War Patrons

This section examines Cuba's aid-based sanctions-busting relationships with the People's Republic of China and Venezuela and how they formed. The Chinese case represents a difficult test for the sanctions-busting theory, as it exemplifies the sometimes fuzzy distinctions between trade- and aid-based sanctions busters that occur when governments can only partially accomplish their political sanctions-busting objectives via commercial means. Although China began providing Cuba with substantial amounts of foreign aid in 2001, it had already established a strong trade-based sanctions-busting relationship with the country. Most aspects of this case are consistent with the sanction-busting theory, but the case suggests that foreign aid can sometimes be used to augment sanctions-busting trade relationships, not just as a substitute for them. Venezuela's emergence as Cuba's replacement patron for the Soviet Union is far more consistent with the theory. A combination of oil wealth, ideology, and political ambition led Hugo Chávez to become Cuba's chief patron after he was elected president of Venezuela in 1998. Both countries have played important roles in reviving Cuba's economy and helping to sustain the regime through what could have been a tumultuous transition of power between the Castro brothers.

The People's Republic of China   The China of the 1990s was far different from the China of the 1960s that had offered Castro's regime its patronage. Notably, China had undergone substantial reforms that had shifted its ideology and economy to a more market-based orientation that emphasized economic growth and development. Except for the Tiananmen Square protests in 1989, China's communist government successfully weathered the Cold War's conclusion. By the late 1990s, China's economy was booming, and it was politically stable. Its success stood in marked contrast to Russia, which was caught in the midst of a devastating economic crisis. For the world's remaining communist states, China's success offered validation to those that argued that the communist model was still viable and need not be abandoned. Although it was not an outright political adversary of the United States, China's meteoric economic growth made it into a rival for natural resources, economic markets, and political influence in Latin America.[123] Flush with resources and sharing an ideological affinity that appeared increasingly endangered, China appears to have been well-situated to step into the Soviet Union's role as Cuba's leading patron had it chosen to do so.

Relations between China and Cuba had remained strained right up until the Cold War's conclusion. The diplomatic acrimony between the two countries had been renewed following China's invasion of Vietnam in 1979. Castro ardently criticized the Chinese incursion and infamously referred to China's Deng Xiaoping as "a caricature of Hitler."[124] As the chief architect of China's economic reforms that emphasized market reforms and an export-driven model of economic growth, Xiaoping has been credited with establishing the framework for China's economic success. Castro viewed such reforms with deep skepticism, as he perceived them as inconsistent with his and Mao Zedong's original vision of Marxist-Leninism. Thus, important ideological and political differences separated Cuba and China in the latter part of the 1980s. A critical turning point for Sino–Cuban relations occurred in 1989 when Castro unexpectedly offered his public support to China's government after it cracked down on the Tiananmen Square protests.[125] This signaled Castro's interest in a rapprochement with the Chinese and would lay the groundwork for his subsequent efforts at reconciliation. Whereas the Soviet Union had not abandoned its assistance to Cuba in 1989, growing pressures within the CMEA were placing the future of Cuba's economic relationships in jeopardy. Castro's decision to try to mend relations with China after twenty-plus years of enmity can readily be understood in this context.

After the Soviet Union's collapse, Fidel Castro sought additional opportunities to reconcile with China. According to Chen, Castro resumed making regular dinner visits to the Chinese Embassy in Havana in 1991 after a twenty-four-year hiatus. He also reportedly went out of his way to accommodate China's President Jiang Zemin when he briefly visited Cuba in 1993. During the visit, Castro heavily engaged Jiang on socialism- and economic-related issues.[126] When Chinese Premier Li'Peng visited Cuba in October 1995, Castro purportedly greeted the Chinese leader with a "bear hug."[127] Castro's efforts to reconcile with the Chinese culminated with his first-ever trip to the country in November 1995. Economic issues were the primary focus of Castro's meetings, part of which included a request for higher levels of Chinese technical assistance.[128] Evidencing his commitment to healing his ideological rift with the Chinese, Castro even publicly praised China's economic reforms during the visit.[129] Castro hosted a high-level visit by then-Secretary of the Chinese Communist Party Hu Jintao in 1997 and another visit by President

Jiang in 2001.[130] When Castro made a return visit to China in 2003, he was warmly welcomed by both leaders, and Hu remarked that "As socialist countries led by the Communist parties, China and Cuba share the same ideals and faith." These remarks and the agreement on bilateral economic cooperation that Castro received during the trip illustrate the success of his efforts to reconcile with the Chinese.[131] In comparative perspective, Castro's proactive diplomacy and high-level exchanges with Chinese officials throughout this period mirrored his efforts to secure Soviet foreign assistance during the mid-1960s. These activities are illustrative of the proactive approach that Castro's regime adopted toward building relationships with potential patrons. Following in his brother's footsteps, Raúl Castro traveled to China in July 2012 to secure new assistance for Cuba.[132]

China's post–Cold War policy of keeping its total foreign aid disbursements a secret makes assessing the amount of aid the country has given to Cuba a considerable challenge.[133] As such, China's assistance to Cuba can be assessed only in a piecemeal fashion. Much of the foreign aid China has provided to Cuba reportedly involves concessional loans or credit lines, a significant portion of which appear geared toward financing the purchase of Chinese products. During the period of Sino–Cuban reconciliation in the 1990s, the aid that China offered Cuba was rather limited. As part of Castro's visit to China in 1995, for example, he was able to secure a $3 million economic grant and $8 million in scientific and technical assistance.[134] Although such aid was certainly useful to Castro's cash-strapped regime, it was nowhere near the previous aid levels his government had grown accustomed to from the Soviet Union. As relations between the two countries improved, China's generosity grew in kind—with 2001 appearing as a watershed year. During President Jiang's April visit to Cuba, the Chinese government agreed to extend $380.5 million in preferential loans to Castro's regime and signed a broader cooperative agreement.[135] The Chinese also agreed in 2001 to help Cuba modernize its armed forces and provided it with extensive disaster relief after the country was struck by a hurricane.[136] In the following years, the Chinese government continued to provide Cuba with concessional loans at favorable rates (3 percent per annum over twenty years).[137] In 2009, the Chinese extended Cuba a $600 million credit line to finance the purchase of ten grain ships and modernize Cuba's ports and communications infrastructure. It also gave Cuba $9 million as an outright donation.[138] In 2012, China pledged to provide Cuba with additional interest-free loans, financial aid, and further technical assistance.[139]

Beyond just the aid that China provided to Cuba, it also grew to become one of Cuba's leading trade partners over this period. During Cuba's period of severe economic contraction in the early 1990s, China's share of Cuba's trade declined. This trend reversed trajectories by the end of the decade; by 2006, Cuba was conducting roughly 17 percent of its total trade with China—with the majority of that trade coming in the form of Chinese imports.[140] With its booming, export-oriented economy, China's leaders aggressively sought out new markets for their country's products and new sources of natural resources in the late 1990s and early 2000s. Cuba was only one of many Latin American countries in which China sought to develop larger export profiles during the period.[141] The extensive commercial relationship that China developed with Cuba was in large part market based, and its sanctions-busting trade with the country certainly helped substitute for U.S. trade. It is also notable that a significant portion of the loans and financial assistance extended to Cuba were tied to the purchase of Chinese exports. For example, $150 million of the extensive loan package offered to Cuba in 2001 went to financing the purchase of a million Chinese-manufactured color televisions.[142] This suggests that a notable portion of the Chinese aid given to Cuba was the result of mixed political and commercial motives.

It is difficult to categorize China's sanctions-busting relationship with Cuba as being only trade based or aid based from 2001 onward. Although the Chinese government had the requisite motivations and budgetary surpluses to become a sanctions-busting patron on Cuba's behalf by the early 2000s, it had already established a fairly extensive commercially oriented sanctions-busting relationship with Cuba. China's predilection for sanctions-busting trade was highlighted in Table 6.1, and it only grew larger throughout the 2000s. Yet rather than forgoing the foreign aid option, the Chinese government chose to become additionally generous with the foreign aid it offered Cuba. Within the theory's explanation of trade-based sanctions busting, it is argued that politically motivated third-party governments can adopt policies, like subsidies or concessional loans, to encourage sanctions-busting trade. What can separate aid-based from trade-based sanctions-busting relationships is how much these policies are responsible for driving bilateral commerce between third parties and targets and their ultimate cost to target governments. In the

Soviet Union's case, its economic exchanges with Cuba were unequivocally aid based. The difficulty with categorizing this case is that China appears to have adopted a hybrid strategy that balances fairly extensive outlays of costly foreign aid with profitable sanctions-busting trade. Interestingly, China also appears to have developed a similar approach in the sanctions-busting approach on North Korea's behalf in recent years as the latter country grew increasingly dependent on Chinese trade in addition to Chinese aid. A careful examination of the factors associated with China's decisions to offer both aid-based and trade-based sanctions-busting support may thus suggest a useful revision to the originally proposed sanctions-busting theory.

In terms of China's political motivations to aid Cuba, simply sharing a common communist orientation was insufficient motivation for the Chinese to offer Cuba extensive foreign aid after the Cold War's conclusion. And although U.S.–Chinese relations during this period involved competition and occasional tensions, the two countries' relations lacked the hostility that had defined the U.S.–Soviet relationship. It was not until Castro—through a significant diplomatic effort—healed over the political and ideological divisions that had grown between his country and China that the latter began providing Cuba with significant foreign aid. By the early 2000s, Chinese leaders were much more inclined to find common cause with Cuba in terms of its ideological orientation and economic plight. Indeed, a significant rhetorical component of the Sino–Cuban reconciliation involved China's efforts to convert Cuba to their economic model and the message that Cuba could learn from China's example.[143] Whereas Castro's economic reforms were far more limited than China's, he publicly recognized the success of the Chinese model and deeply engaged Chinese leaders on these issues. The groundwork Castro laid during the 1990s bore fruit in the subsequent decade when China demonstrated a much stronger ideological and political association with Cuba as part of the remaining communist camp. By forging these stronger ties with Castro's regime, China also placed itself in a position in which it had a greater perceived responsibility for the country's welfare. The ideological component to the Sino–Cuban relationship partially helps explain why China did not step into the role as a major aid-based sanctions buster until the 2000s.

China could have continued to serve solely as a trade-based sanctions buster on Cuba's behalf akin to Italy or Spain, but Cuba's economic weakness constrained the extent to which it could even afford to rely on trade-based sanctions busting and the extent to which trade-based sanctions busting could benefit its sanctions resistance efforts. By the early 2000s, China's economic prosperity offered its government the resources to employ foreign aid more actively as a tool of economic statecraft. With its renewed political imperative to support Castro's regime, China's leadership perceived that trade alone was insufficient to achieve its objectives in sustaining Cuba. Rather than forsaking the opportunity to continue profiting from its trade-based sanctions busting on Cuba's behalf and the attendant benefits it provided to Cuba, Chinese leaders chose to supplement its trade with additional offerings of foreign aid. For the Chinese government, this decision was far less costly than pursuing an aid-based sanctions-busting option in isolation; in fact, the aid it provided to Cuba appeared to have bolstered the strength of its trade-based relationship with the country. Through extending generous concessional loans to Cuba to finance the purchase of Chinese goods (as highlighted by the television deal already cited), Chinese leaders could both aid Cuba and obtain a domestic commercial return for its export-oriented industries. By adopting a hybrid approach, the Chinese government was able to play a much larger role as a trade-based sanctions buster on Cuba's behalf than it otherwise would have. The political and commercial benefits that China received from augmenting its sanctions-busting trade with sanctions-busting aid illustrates that sanctions busters will not forsake trade-based sanctions-busting opportunities even when the use of foreign aid becomes necessary to achieve their political objectives. Rather than being a pure drain on China's economy, as the Soviet Union's assistance to Cuba was, China's sanctions-busting strategy on Cuba's behalf appears to have provided it with significantly more positive economic returns.

The Chinese case illustrates that the conceptual division between trade- and aid-based sanctions busters can sometimes be ambiguous, but it also reinforces the importance of jointly studying both phenomena. Just as ideological differences led to the divisive dispute that severed China's sanctions-busting relationship with Cuba during the 1960s, reconciling those differences proved crucial to China's reemergence in that role in the 2000s. That political reconciliation coincided with a period of unprecedented economic prosperity in China, providing its government with the resources to provide Cuba with more generous sanctions-busting aid. China's additional ability to exploit the commercial opportunities created by the U.S. sanctions against Cuba led it to adopt a hybrid sanctions-busting strategy. Although China provided the Cuban government with significant foreign assistance, a significant portion of it went toward strengthening its trade relationship with the country. That Cuba's trade relationship with China grew significantly during the 2000s in response supports the sanctions-busting theory's assertion that targets will forge the strongest trade-based sanctions-busting relationships with the third parties that offer them the best deals. Most aspects of this case are thus consistent with the sanctions-busting theory, but the findings indicate that third-party governments may offer extensive sanctions-busting aid to target states even when a purely commercial option exists if additional aid is needed to accomplish their political objectives.

Venezuela   Venezuela was an unlikely candidate to become Cuba's chief patron after the Cold War's conclusion. For one, Venezuela did not have the long-standing political or ideological ties to Castro's regime that China and Russia did—just the opposite, in fact. Castro had supported a revolutionary movement to overthrow Venezuela's government in the 1960s, leading Venezuela's government to become an ardent supporter of the hemispheric sanctioning effort against Cuba.[144] Venezuela also possessed a weak commercial profile for sanctions busting, as the country remained plagued by poverty and had few industries that could provide equivalent alternatives to sanctioned U.S. goods. Yet the country also had one vital resource that Cuba was in critical need of: oil. When Hugo Chávez was elected president in 1998 with a socialist domestic platform and an internationalist, anti-American foreign policy agenda, he made strengthening Venezuela's ties to Cuba a national priority.[145] In building stronger political and commercial ties with Cuba, Chávez sought to associate himself with Castro's revolutionary legacy and the regime's socialist ideology.[146] By 2005, Chávez had turned Venezuela into Cuba's leading patron, offering it an estimated $1.7 billion worth of yearly oil concessions. This sum dwarfed the entire U.S. aid budget to Latin America in 2005.[147] The Chávez regime continued to support Cuba even since Fidel Castro stepped down from power. With Chávez's recent passing, however, it remains uncertain whether Venezuela will sustain its patronage of Cuba in the long run.

Castro played an active role in cultivating the sanctions-busting relationship between his country and Venezuela. In the early 1990s, Cuba experienced crippling energy shortages as it dealt with the loss of its Soviet-subsidized fuel supplies. Oil-rich Venezuela had a natural market in nearby Cuba, but Cuba lacked the currency to purchase it. Castro first met Hugo Chávez in 1994, offering him a warm reception in Cuba after his release from imprisonment that stemmed from a failed coup attempt in 1992.[148] Castro formed strong ties with the ambitious Chávez, who thought to take over the aging Castro's mantle as Latin America's leading anti-American revolutionary. Chávez's "Bolivarian" ideology emphasized South American unity in standing up to American imperialism on the international front and socialist principles and strong central governance domestically.[149] Chávez's ideological views were heavily influenced by his study of the Cuban Revolution, by Castro's writings and speeches, and, later on, by his direct interactions with Castro himself. For Chávez, Castro's regime represented a model for putting his political ideas into practice.[150]

The relationship that Castro forged with Chávez paid off when Chávez was elected president of Venezuela in 1998. As president, Chávez took up an adversarial stance toward the United States and adopted an internationalist foreign policy heavily influenced by his "Bolivarian" ideology.[151] As an extension of that ideology, Chávez viewed forging a closer relationship with Cuba a national priority. Whereas Castro had to actively court the attentions of the Chinese, he had a much more enthusiastic partner in Chávez. Evidencing this close relationship, Chávez made thirteen trips to Cuba from 1999 to 2005.[152] In the first year of his presidency, Chávez negotiated his first of several deals with Cuba to help supply the country with oil. As part of the deal struck in October 1999, Venezuela entered into a long-term joint venture with Cuba to refit and operate what had been an unused Soviet-era refinery in Cuba. Venezuela would eventually supply this refinery with 70,000 barrels of oil per day.[153] The deal was particularly significant for Cuba, as 1999 marked the last year of its oil-for-sugar swaps with Russia.[154] In October 2000, Chávez followed up with a more extensive arrangement brokered during Castro's first visit to Venezuela in over forty years. During a speech commemorating the visit, Castro remarked, "I came here not looking for fuel, though Venezuela has a lot of it, but seeking understanding and brotherhood."[155] Ultimately, he succeeded at getting more of all three than he could have hoped for. As part of the Convenio Integral de Cooperación, Chávez agreed to supply Cuba with 53,000 barrels of oil per day at preferential rates in exchange for technical assistance and the services of approximately 20,000 to 30,000 Cuban doctors, educators, and coaches.[156] Given Cuba's dearth of hard currency, allowing Castro to barter services for oil was a major boon to his regime. These oil shipments subsequently accounted for roughly a third of the Cuban regime's energy supplies.[157] Venezuela went from having an insignificant economic relationship with Cuba prior to Chávez's taking power to being Cuba's most important sanctions buster almost overnight.

Chávez's generosity proved to be a domestically unpopular move. In 2002, Chávez was briefly deposed by a coup, and the regime that came into power ordered Venezuela's state oil company to suspend its oil shipments to Cuba.[158] Though Chávez restarted the shipments after he was reinstated, Venezuela's state oil company (PDVSA) was subsequently crippled by a major strike in 2003.[159] The Cuban oil shipments sparked significant controversy in Venezuela, as its citizens questioned why they were not instead receiving higher pay or greater social benefits from the country's oil wealth. The Cuban government also fell far behind on its oil payments to PDVSA,[160] which Chávez's government showed scant interest in collecting.[161] Riding the wave of internationally high oil prices, Chávez remained undeterred in using his country's oil as a diplomatic tool.[162] Even before being elected president, Chávez had expressed his provocative views on the utility of oil in international politics, stating: "Oil is a geopolitical weapon and these imbeciles who govern us don't realize the power they have, as an oil producing country."[163] Having—at least temporarily—resolved his country's domestic issues, Chávez saw to it that Venezuela would rapidly reemerge as Cuba's largest and most important economic partner. Toward that end, Venezuela announced in 2005 that it was upping its promised shipments of oil to Cuba to 90,000 barrels per day as part of a broader trade package with the country.[164] This deal allowed Cuba to use long-term, low-interest-rate credit to pay the cost of approximately 40 percent of the oil shipments, while counting the bartered services of the Cuban professionals continuing to serve in the country for the other 60 percent of the cost.[165]

Although the close personal relationship between Hugo Chávez and Fidel Castro played an undoubted role in Venezuela's generous support to Cuba, the transition of power in Cuba has not lessened its generosity. Raúl was greeted warmly in Venezuela when he made his first official visit to the country on becoming president in 2008; more important for Cuba, the subsidized oil shipments from Venezuela have continued unabated. Estimates from 2008 indicate that Venezuela provided Cuba with over 100,000 barrels of oil per day, which amounted to over $3 billion worth of aid. Cuba has also continued to receive other forms of assistance, such as $150 million in aid to build a petrochemical complex in Cienfuegos.[166] By 2011, Venezuela's oil shipments to Cuba had grown to over 115,000 barrels per day at an estimated value of $3.5 billion. This accounted for nearly all of the foreign oil that Cuba imported, which comprised roughly two-thirds of the island's daily oil consumption.[167] Although Venezuela was not providing Cuba with the level of oil surpluses that the Soviet Union once did, there are remarkable parallels in the extent of Cuba's dependence on both patrons for its energy needs. In 2011, Hugo Chávez was diagnosed with an unspecified cancer and chose to receive his treatment in Cuba.

Hugo Chávez's ideology and adversarial stance toward the United States appear to be the leading motivations for the sanctions-busting aid Venezuela provided to Cuba during his presidency. On the basis of his ideological views, Chávez found common cause with Castro in supporting Cuba's socialist-based defiance of the United States and its decades-long sanctioning effort. In the same vein as Castro during the Cold War, Chávez viewed supporting leftist-leaning political movements across Latin America as part of an ideological obligation to spark socialist revolutions across the region. Chávez envisioned forming "an axis of power" with the Castro regime that would be the vanguard for the broader political movement that would eventually serve to "counterbalance the global dominance of the United States."[168] Chávez's widespread use of oil diplomacy across Latin America was indicative of the broad movement he sought to spark.[169] In particular, busting the U.S. sanctions against Cuba offered Chávez a low-risk, high-profile means of publicly standing up to "American imperialism" as part of the ideological imperatives he espoused. Defeating the U.S. sanctioning effort thus became a means for Chávez to legitimize his international political movement and Venezuela's position at the forefront of it. It is notable that, when the coup attempt against Chávez occurred in 2002, cutting off Venezuela's oil-based assistance to Cuba was one of the first policies enacted.

With respect to the affordability of aiding Cuba, Venezuela's substantial oil reserves and the high price of oil provided a vast pool of resources for the Chávez regime to draw on in funding its sanctions-busting assistance. At the same time, much of Venezuela's population remained mired in poverty, and the poverty problem actually grew worse under Chávez's tenure as president.[170] The domestic opposition to Chávez's use of Venezuela's oil wealth on foreign assistance suggests that such aid could have been productively employed on domestic objectives. Yet the broad authority Chávez exercised over

Venezuela's oil resources allowed him to dictate their use. With the price of oil buoyed so high over much of Chávez's presidency, he could afford to divert substantial resources toward his foreign policy prerogatives without significantly jeopardizing his domestic base of support.

As for the final criterion, a clear case can be made that Chávez could not accomplish his political goals via commercially oriented sanctions busting on Cuba's behalf. Prior to Chávez's election, Cuban purchases of Venezuelan oil were very limited—as was all bilateral trade between the two countries. Cuba simply could not afford to purchase large amounts of Venezuelan oil at market prices. It was only after Chávez began offering Cuba oil under highly subsidized terms, which included oil-for-services bartering provisions, that trade between the two countries really took off. The sanctions-busting assistance that Venezuela provided to Cuba was also important in helping Cuba's economy solidly recover for the first time since the withdrawal of Soviet aid, which sanctions-busting trade alone was unlikely to have done.[171] Given Chávez's ideological commitments and the broader movement he hoped to start, simply keeping Cuba from the brink of collapse was not enough. To achieve Chávez's political objectives, the sanctions busting his regime conducted on Cuba's behalf had to demonstrate that countries that were a part of Chávez's movement could successfully stand up to the United States with Venezuela's support. Relying on trade alone was therefore not a viable option. Overall, the Venezuelan case appears to strongly conform to the theory's predictions regarding the conditions that are required for third-party states to become extensive aid-based sanctions busters.

Following Chávez's death in March 2013, there was a great deal of uncertainty concerning whether Venezuela's patronage of Cuba would continue. In a closely contested election, Chávez's handpicked successor Nicolás Maduro was elected president of Venezuela. It was thought that, if Maduro had lost the election, his rival would have substantially cut back on the assistance the Venezuelan government provides to Cuba. At least at the beginning of his presidency, Maduro has continued his predecessor's policy of supporting Cuba with generous foreign assistance programs. Venezuela's economic problems, however, have made it increasingly difficult to fund all the international aid initiatives that Chávez had launched—forcing Maduro to scale at least some of them back.[172] Aid to Cuba has not faced substantial cuts, though, and Maduro has continued to emphasize maintaining close relations with the country. It is also notable that the Venezuelan opposition movement, which grew increasingly active following Maduro's election, has highlighted Maduro's continued patronage of Cuba as one of its major grievances with his regime.[173]

Comparing Cuba's Patrons

The four cases of extensive aid-based sanctions busting from the Cuban sanctions episode provide strong support for the sanctions-busting theory. Each of the cases offers interesting insights into the necessary conditions identified by the theory and how those factors appeared to influence the third-party governments' behavior. Whereas only the Cold War cases offer the opportunity to evaluate the effects of withdrawing the necessary factors for sanctions-busting aid, those cases suggest that they are also critical for sustaining patronage relationships. Looking at the Castro regime's approach toward courting sanctions-busting aid across all four cases yields further insights about effective strategies for obtaining patrons. Lastly, the narrative analysis of the U.S. government's sanctioning efforts reveals the stark challenges it faced in preventing both trade- and aid-based sanctions busting on Cuba's behalf.

In terms of the political motivations that drive aid-based sanctions busting, ideological motivations and/or adversarial relations with the U.S. government appeared to be present in all four cases. The governments of all Cuba's patrons shared similar ideological orientations with the Castro regime. Whereas Castro's failure to align closely enough with China in its ideological schism with the Soviet Union contributed to the end of the patronage relationship, ideological imperatives were what motivated China to assist Cuba in the first place. As the only noncommunist regime to provide support to Cuba, Venezuela is slightly different than the other three cases. Yet the strong similarities between Chavez's Bolivarian ideology and the version of communism that Castro implemented in Cuba make the ideological motivations for Venezuela's patronage probably the strongest of any of the cases. In their earlier writings on "black knight" sanctions busters, which drew heavily on the Soviet–Cuba case, Hufbauer and his coauthors had suggested that such aid was likely a by-product of the Cold War.[174] The fact that third-party governments provided Cuba with their patronage both during and after the Cold War suggests the phenomenon is not limited solely to international systems with bipolar distributions of power. The findings across all four cases provide strong evidence that third-party states will extend significant sanctions-busting assistance to target states only if they have either a strong ideological stake in the target defeating the sanctions or an adversarial relationship with the sender that they can link to the sanctions' outcome—or both.

The evidence for the sanctions-busting theory's assertion that third-party governments engage in aid-based sanctions busting only if trade-based sanctions busting is not a viable option was not fully supported by the analysis. In the Cold War cases of China and the Soviet Union, the state of Cuba's economy was such that it could not have sustained extensive commercially oriented sanctions-busting relationships with either country. Indeed, the evidence revealed that Castro's regime actually had to rely on the aid it received from the Soviet Union to fund its sanctions-busting trade with other capitalist countries. Just as Cuba relied on the Soviet Union to provide it with oil supplies that it could not afford to purchase at market prices, the regime developed a similar dependency on Venezuela. In the Soviet and Venezuelan cases, neither country had an extensive trade relationship with Cuba before starting to provide it with sanctions-busting aid. The post–Cold War China case offers the most conflicting evidence regarding this criterion. China developed a commercially oriented sanctions-busting relationship with Cuba that preceded the aid-based sanctions-busting relationship it formed with the country. The evidence also showed that a significant portion of the aid China provided to Cuba appeared oriented toward supporting its trade relationship with it. This suggests that aid-based and trade-based sanctions busting are not necessarily mutually exclusive options if the former supports the latter, and trade-based sanctions busting alone is insufficient to achieve a third-party government's goals in supporting a target state. This finding is consistent with the expectation that third-party states should preferentially engage in trade-based sanctions busting if it is feasible but indicates that third-party governments may augment their trade with aid if they perceive additional benefits from doing so. Generally, though, the evidence across the four cases has supported the theoretical expectation that third-party governments view sanctions-busting aid as a second-best alternative to sanctions-busting trade.

The last hypothesized provision relates to whether third-party governments can afford to become aid-based sanctions busters. Not all countries can afford to provide sanctioned states with extensive, sustained foreign assistance. Out of the four cases, three involved great powers, and one involved an oil-rich state in a period of premium-priced oil. Cold War China was the patron government with the greatest limitations on the aid that it could afford to provide Cuba. The Chinese government was cognizant of these limitations, especially in comparison to what the Soviet Union could offer Cuba. Part of how Chinese leaders justified their decision to cut their government's aid to Cuba was that it could not afford to also offer such assistance to Vietnam (which was also subject to U.S. sanctions). The Soviets effectively priced the Chinese out of the competition to become Cuba's chief patron, which contributed to China's decision to renege on the sanctions-busting commitment it made to Cuba. Even in the Soviet case, the costs of supporting Cuba ultimately became an unsustainable drain on the country in the late 1980s. In each of the cases evaluated, the third-party states that offered Cuba their patronage had relatively large pools of resources to draw on, and, when the limits of those resources were reached, the governments ceased their aid.

Another major takeaway from this chapter's analysis is that courting sanctions-busting patrons can be a difficult challenge for target leaders that requires a significant investment of effort. To court the Soviet Union's support, Castro was driven to adopt a Marxist-Leninist ideology for his new regime in Cuba. This ended up paying off in a significant way, as this ideology helped Castro obtain sanctions-busting support from China and Venezuela as well. Yet, at the same time, taking this action earned Castro the long-term enmity of the United States, which has steadfastly remained committed to its sanctions even after the Cold War's conclusion. Castro also made significant diplomatic investments in courting potential patrons. In the Soviet, Venezuelan, and post–Cold War Chinese cases, Castro was proactive in developing personal relationships with the countries' leaders through hosting VIP visits or going abroad. Many of the most generous aid packages Cuba received came as a result of Castro's foreign trips. This aspect of Cuba's success has a theoretically important implication. The three necessary conditions identified for aid-based sanctions busting to occur are by no means sufficient ones. Even if a third party might have the incentives and ability to offer its patronage to a target state, the inertia involved in initiating such a relationship may prevent its emergence. Proactive diplomatic efforts by target leaders can thus play a crucial role in convincing potential patrons to start offering their assistance.

The last major insight from the analysis relates to the obstacles that the U.S. government confronted in seeking to prevent third-party governments from sanctions busting on Cuba's behalf. During the early part of the Cold War, the U.S. government was successful in gaining the support of most Latin

American countries for its sanctions. It failed, however, to obtain the support of its key strategic allies like Japan and Great Britain who preferred to exploit the profitable opportunities the sanctions created. Eventually, even the Latin American allies of the United States revolted against its sanctioning efforts in the mid-1970s. Following the Cold War's conclusion, Canada and a number of EU countries swooped in to exploit the desperate position of Castro's regime following the withdrawal of the Soviet Union's aid. Instead of cooperating with U.S. sanctioning efforts, U.S. allies actively undermined them via their trade-based sanctions busting. Although this infuriated U.S. policy makers, the costs of compelling their cooperation proved far too high. Measures like the Cuban Democracy Act and the Helms-Burton Act ended up only angering the governments of the U.S. sanctions-busting allies rather than curbing their sanctions-busting trade. The U.S. government's policies put policy makers in the ironic position of criticizing its democratic allies for "immorally" trying to profit from their trade with the communist regime their sanctions were designed to bring down and replace with a democratic, free-market–oriented government.[175] Ultimately, the U.S. government had no options that were appreciably better than tolerating its allies' sanctions-busting despite the adverse effects it had on the sanctions' chances of success.

Although the U.S. government tried several different ways of clamping down on third-party trade with Cuba, it never developed a clear policy for preventing sanctions-busting aid to the country. The U.S. government has not been blind to the Castro regime's reliance on such aid. A 2006 commission chaired by Secretary of State Condoleezza Rice observed that Castro's regime "is working with like-minded governments, particularly Venezuela, to build a network of political and financial support designed to forestall any external pressure to change."[176] This acknowledges that the Castro regime's patronage relationships were a key impediment to U.S. economic sanctions' success. Although the Helms-Burton Act contained a provision designed to compel Russia to stop providing any lingering aid to Cuba, that policy was a misplaced afterthought to the decades of sanctions-busting assistance the Soviet Union provided Castro's regime. It is also telling that since the legislation's passage three successive presidents have refused to implement the provision. Overall, the U.S. government did not have any real mechanisms for disrupting the assistance that China, the Soviet Union, and Venezuela provided to Cuba. Just as the U.S. government could do little to stop the sanctions-busting trade conducted by its allies, it has similarly been incapable of preventing its adversaries' sanctions-busting aid. Over the past fifty years, the U.S. economic sanctions against Cuba have been undermined by friends and foes alike, and it has had little recourse to prevent it.

Conclusion

This chapter examined how the Castro regime leveraged sanctions-busting support to survive over five decades of U.S. sanctions and the factors that motivated third-party states to provide the country with their sanctions-busting assistance. The comparative analysis evaluated the sanctions-busting theory's hypothesis that third-party states would become extensive aid-based sanctions busters only if they had a salient ideological or rivalry-based motivation, they could afford to provide extensive foreign aid to another country, and the use of sanctions-busting trade was infeasible. The analyses yielded strong support for this hypothesis in analyzing the patronage relationships that Cold War China, the Soviet Union, and Venezuela formed with Cuba. The only inconsistent finding related to the case of post–Cold War China, which provided extensive foreign aid to Cuba as an augment to its commercially oriented sanctions-busting trade relationship with the country. These findings offer illustrative support for the explanation of aid-based sanctions busting but suggest that third-party governments sometimes use it as a supplement to trade-based sanctions busting when the latter is feasible but incapable of fully achieving its leaders' political objectives.

The case narrative also revealed how Castro's regime balanced the use of both trade- and aid-based sanctions busting to endure the hardships imposed by the U.S. sanctions. Fidel Castro had to actively work to court the latter but relied on the former to supplement the aid his country received. In the absence of patrons during the 1990s, Castro's regime was forced to become solely reliant on trade-based sanctions busting. Such circumstances are indeed those faced by most target states, most of the time. The survival of Castro's regime in the period immediately after the Cold War illustrates how even economically impoverished countries can use trade-based sanctions busters to sustain themselves. Third-party sanctions busting played an unquestionably crucial role in the Castro regime's ability to survive the U.S. sanctions against otherwise daunting odds. Despite its best efforts, the U.S. government was unable to find an effective solution to the myriad of challenges that third-party sanctions busting posed to the effectiveness of its sanctioning efforts. The Cuban sanctions episode illustrates the importance of jointly studying trade- and aid-based sanctions busting, as both phenomena are closely inter-linked in terms of their causes and consequences.

8   Implications and Conclusions

THIS BOOK HAS SOUGHT TO EXPLAIN WHY ECONOMIC sanctions have such a poor track record of success even when they are employed by the world's most powerful country. It demonstrates that the failure of U.S. sanctioning efforts is often closely linked to the sanctions-busting behavior of external actors, via both their trade and foreign aid. Commercial motivations primarily drive third-party states to become extensive trade-based sanctions busters, whereas salient political motivations are required for third-party governments to become aid-based sanctions busters. As such, the profiles of the types of states most likely to sanctions-bust using either approach tend to be quite different from one another. The analysis shows that both types of sanctions busting undermine sanctioning efforts in different ways, allowing them to serve as substitutes for one another but also allowing them to reinforce one another when jointly present. Although the findings suggest that preventing the emergence of trade-based sanctions busters is quite difficult for sender states, there are more reasons to be optimistic about countering the corrosive effects of aid-based sanctions busting. Even if third-party sanctions busting cannot be stopped, the findings suggest that the phenomenon can be readily anticipated and that more effective sanctions policies can be adopted to address the challenges it poses. The rest of the chapter summarizes the book's aggregate findings on the causes and consequences of sanctions busting, discusses their policy implications, and concludes by discussing the findings' implications for future research.

Summarizing the Causes and Effects of Sanctions Busting

Third-party states' responses to economic sanctions are subject to significant variation. Economic sanctions can impose a myriad of disruptions and additional costs on third parties' trade with target states, but they can also create lucrative commercial opportunities for those states positioned to take advantage of them. Sanctions disputes have political spillover effects that influence third-party responses as well. Beyond third-party governments' direct incentives in having sanctioning efforts succeed or fail, they may also be subject to lobbying and/or coercive pressure by sender and target governments seeking their support. Third-party states' responses to economic sanctions are thus jointly driven by the commercial interests of their constituents and the foreign policy interests of their governments. For third-party states that can significantly profit from engaging in sanctions-busting trade, the commercial interests of their constituents in sanctions busting can be bolstered by their governments' interests in defeating sanctioning efforts against a target state. Even when third-party governments can politically benefit from supporting the sanctions against a target state, the commercial interests of their constituents will tend to override those considerations when sanctions busting on a target's behalf is highly profitable. As such, the third-party states most likely to become trade-based sanctions busters are those countries that offer firms the most profitable venues from which to sanctions-bust on a target's behalf. A counterintuitive implication of this is that the political cover offered by alliance relationships can also help make third-party allies of sender states significantly more profitable venues for sanctions-busting firms.

The findings from the three empirical chapters that explored the causes of sanctions-busting support all of the trade-based sanctions-busting hypotheses that were tested. The detailed analysis of sanctions-busting relationship that emerged between the UAE and Iran demonstrated how profit-seeking firms were the leading agents that forged that relationship. Firms from Iran, the United States, and the rest of the world flocked to the UAE to circumvent the sanctions that the U.S. government had imposed on Iran. Via its geographical relationship with Iran, its preexisting commercial ties to Iran, the laissez-faire commercial environment fostered by Dubai, and the alliance relationship it formed with the United States in 1994, the UAE emerged as the ideal middleman for sanctions-busting transactions with Iran. The statistical analysis of ninety-six U.S.-imposed sanctions episodes revealed that the best predictors of whether third-party states would become trade-based sanctions busters were those factors that affected their profitability for sanctions-busting firms. Third-party venues with large, open economies, that have close preexisting commercial ties with the target, and that are geographically proximate to the target proved to be more attractive sanctions-busting venues. Interestingly, the analysis also provided circumstantial evidence to suggest that third parties neighboring target states are more likely to sanctions-bust via illicit trade as opposed to legitimate trade. The most counterintuitive finding to arise from the analysis is that U.S. allies are over 100 percent more likely to become trade-based sanctions busters than are other states. In the final analysis of the sanctioning effort against Cuba, additional evidence showed that close U.S. allies were actively engaged in undercutting its sanctioning efforts. Both during and after the Cold War, Great Britain, Canada, Japan, and Spain actively profited from the lucrative opportunities the U.S. sanctions policies created in Cuba. The U.S. government could do little to stop its allies' opportunistic behavior, as the costs of coercing their cooperation were simply too high for the returns they expected to receive. Altogether, the empirical analyses provide an exceptionally high degree of support for the sanctions-busting theory's explanation of trade-based sanctions busting.

The theory of sanctions busting also explains the reasons why third-party governments offer extensive foreign aid to target states. Initially, it was theorized that aid-based sanctions busting occurs only when the following criteria are met: (1) Third-party governments have a salient political interest in preventing the success of sanctioning efforts; (2) the third-party governments can afford significant foreign aid outlays; and (3) employing a trade-based approach is infeasible. In three out of the four cases of aid-based sanctions busting on Cuba's behalf (Cold War China, the Soviet Union, and Venezuela), all three of the theorized criteria were present. In the post–Cold War China case, however, the analysis revealed that the Chinese government opted to provide Cuba with extensive foreign aid as a supplement to the trade-based sanctions busting it was conducting on Cuba's behalf.

The findings from the hybrid sanctions-busting relationship that China developed with Cuba and North Korea in the 2000s offer useful insights in revising the sanctions-busting theory's initial explanation of aid-based sanctions busting. In some cases, third-party states engage in both trade-based and aid-based sanctions busting if their political objectives in supporting a target state cannot be achieved via sanctions-busting trade alone. In the Cuban case, the political incentives of the Chinese government in supporting Castro's regime changed *after* it had already established a trade-based sanctions-busting relationship with the country. In the North Korean case, developing a sanctions-busting trade relationship with North Korea became necessary as North Korea grew increasingly cut off from the other sources of external trade and aid. The aid China was willing to offer North Korea could not make up for all the shortfalls that North Korea experienced. Only by adding a trade-based sanctions-busting component to its aid packages could China continue to fulfill its goals of preventing North Korea from destabilizing. In both cases, the commercially oriented trade China engaged in with the targets it aided helped offset some of the costs associated with aiding them. This stands in stark contrast to the extensive aid packages that the Soviet Union granted to Cuba during the Cold War, which actually subsidized Cuba's sanctions-busting trade with Western third-party states. For third-party states, engaging in hybrid sanctions-busting strategies can be less costly than relying on extensive aid-based sanctions busting alone, even if it is more costly than relying on a purely trade-based approach. Possessing distinct profiles for the types of states most likely to become either aid-based or trade-based sanctions busters in a given sanctions case is still very useful, but this suggests that sometimes those profiles will overlap.

Having a unified account of why both aid-based and trade-based sanctions busting occur is vital because both types of sanctions busting exercise powerful, independent effects on sanctions outcomes. The analysis of sanctions busting's consequences showed that, when target states have even a single trade-based sanctions buster supporting them, this can dramatically reduce the likelihood that a sanctioning effort will succeed. When a target has multiple trade-based sanctions busters supporting it, it appears that sanctions almost never succeed. Aid-based sanctions busters make substantial contributions to the total amount of foreign aid that target states receive, but changes in the quantity of aid they offer may not totally dictate whether a target's total foreign aid in a given year rises or declines. To properly capture the effects that foreign aid inflows have on sanctions outcomes, it is necessary to assess the changes to the aggregate amount of foreign aid that target states receive. The analysis revealed that sanctioning efforts against target states whose foreign aid inflows grow in a given year are less likely to succeed. Conversely, sanctions against target states experiencing declines in their foreign aid inflows are more likely to succeed. Jointly, the impact of a target state receiving sanctions-busting trade and positive inflows of sanctions-busting aid can almost completely undercut any chance of U.S. economic sanctions being effective in a given sanctions episode.

Taken together, the evidence in this book leads to a surprisingly stark conclusion about the countries most responsible for undercutting U.S. sanctioning efforts. The countries most likely to engage in aid-based sanctions busting are wealthy U.S. adversaries that have an ideologically driven motive to defeat its sanctions. Countries such as the Soviet Union and China typify this category of sanctions buster. In contrast, the countries most likely to engage in trade-based sanctions busting are those with large, open economies that possess preexisting commercial ties to target states and alliance relationships with the United States and/or target states. Being geographically proximate to target states and possessing a democratic regime (if the target is also a democracy) can also positively affect third parties' likelihood of becoming trade-based sanctions busters. Generally speaking, countries such as Japan, Germany, the United Kingdom, Italy, and France match these criteria most closely. Because trade-based sanctions busting is far more common than aid-based sanctions busting and even a single trade-based sanctions buster can undermine sanctioning efforts, this implies that many of the closest U.S. military allies constitute the greatest threats to its economic sanctions' success.

Beyond just the United States, the findings from this project potentially shed light on the sanctions-busting phenomenon for other countries that employ economic sanctions as well. Indeed, the United States has been shown to actively engage in trade-based sanctions busting when other countries employ sanctions.[1] Cases like the Berlin Airlift illustrate that the U.S. government has also engaged in aid-based sanctions busting in the past. Thus, although sanctions busting tends be discussed with scorn by U.S. policy makers, whether the activity is "good" or "bad" depends on one's perspective and interests in a given sanctions dispute. Lacking its unparalleled coercive capabilities and its role as an international financial hub, no other countries have the ability to bring the same level of coercive pressure to bear as does the United States in preventing sanctions busting. As such, the fact that the U.S. government has so frequently been unable to prevent sanctions busting suggests that all other countries' sanctions are similarly vulnerable to it—if not more so. This implies that sanctions busting is an endemic problem for all governments and international institutions that seek to employ economic sanctions in pursuit of their policy prerogatives. The explanatory framework provided in this book should thus be relevant to understanding sanctions busting's causes and consequences in the wider population of sanctions cases.

Understanding and Addressing the Policy Problems Posed by Sanctions-Busting

For U.S. policy makers, the findings offer a number of relevant insights in how to cope with the challenges posed by sanctions busting. From a diagnostic perspective, they provide clear evidence that third-party sanctions busters have played a continuous spoiler role in undercutting U.S. sanctioning efforts over the past sixty years. Armed with knowledge on why sanctions busting occurs and the profiles of the states most likely to engage in it, policy makers can better anticipate what the third-party responses to their economic sanctions will be like. For example, if a potential target state has close commercial ties to several third-party neighbors with large, open economies, the likelihood that one or more of those states will end up becoming a trade-based sanctions buster is relatively high. Policy makers can use this information to predict how many states are likely to sanctions-bust on a target's behalf and which third-party states those are likely to be. If it appears that numerous states are likely to bust sanctions in a particular case, the findings from this book indicate that sanctions are unlikely to be effective, and a different policy option should likely be chosen. Alternatively, policy makers can selectively target likely trade-based sanctions busters with intense diplomatic or coercive pressure to prevent them from sanctions busting. Even when U.S. sanctions are imposed for largely symbolic reasons, understanding how they will affect their targets' commercial relationships with other countries can be important.

Another critical insight is that once extensive sanctions busters have emerged on a target's behalf a sender can often do little else to make sanctions successful. Especially once a number of trade-based sanctions busters have emerged on behalf of a target state, sanctioning efforts become dramatically less likely to succeed. A salient takeaway from this is that, in some cases, sender states are better off conceding that sanctioning efforts have failed as opposed to allowing them to linger on in a costly stalemate. In the case of Cuba, for example, U.S. exporters and consumers have been excluded from a neighboring market that they could otherwise substantially benefit from. Instead, the U.S. government's policies allow American firms' foreign rivals to profit from the lucrative opportunities its sanctions have created, or they drive American firms to take their business operations elsewhere. Once policy makers have identified that their sanctioning efforts have been undercut, giving up on them may often be the best option.

For those busted sanctions cases that policy makers cannot or will not give up on, the findings suggest several strategies for remediating the damages done by trade-based sanctions busting. The Whac-A-Mole nature of trade-based sanctions busting means that, even if the U.S. government can curtail the sanctions busting conducted by a particular state, such trade can readily pop up elsewhere in response. The U.S. government's more recent approach vis-à-vis Iran of augmenting its trade sanctions with strategies designed to financially isolate the country appears promising. This strategy dramatically enhanced the pressure that U.S.-led sanctioning efforts placed on Iran's economy. Yet there is likely a limited number of sanctions cases in which the U.S. government can exert that same degree of pressure. If U.S. policy makers seek to apply their recent lessons learned from the Iran case more widely, history suggests that such behaviors will generate significant political backlash from third-party governments. It could also undermine the U.S. role as the world's preeminent financial hub, as it may make working through less restrictive financial centers far more attractive for foreign banks and firms. At least in the case of Iran, though, this strategy has appeared effective at exacerbating the economic costs that the U.S. trade sanctions impose, along with imposing a myriad of new costs on Iran's economy. Policy makers should be cautious, though, about rushing to employ the most recent strategies from the Iranian sanctioning effort to all U.S. sanctioning efforts.

The UAE cases study also provided a number of potentially important insights into how the improved enforcement of U.S. economic sanctions can enhance their effectiveness. As the UAE case study indicated, U.S. firms played an important role undercutting the U.S. government's sanctioning efforts when doing so was both legal and illegal. By imposing sanctions policies that allow U.S. firms or their subsidiaries to legally circumvent its sanctions, U.S. policy makers encourage firms to move their business operations outside the United States or find foreign trade partners that could help them continue to trade indirectly with sanctioned states. Stricter sanctions policies that fully apply to the commercial activities of U.S. citizens, firms, and their foreign-owned subsidiaries can at least outlaw domestic parties from undercutting their home government's sanctioning efforts. Secondly, the U.S. government should invest significantly more resources in the monitoring and enforcement of its sanctions. Given the sheer number of outstanding economic sanctions and strategic trade controls that the U.S. government has on the books, monitoring compliance with these regulations can be an overwhelming task. As I saw firsthand in the UAE case, the resources required to monitor—let alone enforce—the sanctions busting taking place on Iran's behalf far outstripped the resources the U.S. government invested in the task for many years.

Lastly, the U.S. government needs to enact harsher civil and criminal penalties for violations of its sanctions by domestic firms, and they need to be applied regularly and consistently when violations are identified. If the perception among firms is that the punishments for being caught sanctions-busting are tolerably low, then risking such violations becomes just another cost of doing business for pursuing lucrative trading opportunities. The high-profile fines being leveled against many of the major financial institutions that facilitated in money laundering and/or sanctions-busting trade are a good start, but prosecuting the individuals responsible for the violations would also send a stronger message. The incredible amount of sanctions busting that continued to take place on Iran's behalf by U.S. firms even after President Clinton made it illegal under E.O. 13,059 illustrates that outlawing sanctions busting will not stop it in the absence of real enforcement. Harsh, credible, and consistently employed penalties will likely be needed to deter firms from engaging in the otherwise highly lucrative business of sanctions busting. By emphasizing the comprehensive implementation and strict enforcement of U.S. economic sanctions, policy makers can cut off a leading source of sanctions-busting trade without needing any third-party cooperation.

A certain amount of tension exists between the recommendations that U.S. policy makers should abandon failing U.S. economic sanctions for the good of U.S. business interests and that they should also crack down on U.S. businesses that engage in sanctions-busting activities. Current U.S. sanctions policies create a nebulous environment in which the costs of sanctions busting are far less certain than the potential benefits. This environment fosters higher levels of both unintentional and intentional sanctions-busting violations. In terms of the former, the U.S. government's myriad of ever-changing sanctions and strategic trade control policies make it difficult for firms, and especially small businesses, to remain informed and understand their compliance obligations. With respect to the latter, firms may perceive a low probability of being caught and punished for violating sanctions due to the U.S. government's sometimes lax and uneven enforcement.[2] This fosters an attitude toward compliance with sanctioning efforts in which compliance is an action to be evaluated in terms of costs, benefits, and risks instead of as an absolute requirement for doing business. Although the policy costs of this attitude may be low in some sanctions cases, its systemic effects will also influence compliance with the U.S. sanctioning efforts that policy makers prioritize. This was especially evident in the Iranian and Cuban sanctions episodes, as U.S. policy makers cycled through periods of apparent ambivalence toward their sanctions and those in which they made the sanctions a priority. Imposing or leaving in place weakly implemented, poorly enforced, and frequently violated economic sanctions will adversely affect those sanctioning efforts that U.S. policy makers are truly committed to having succeed. As the statistical analyses reveal, sanctioning efforts that persist past about thirteen years rarely ever succeed. To make U.S. sanctioning efforts less costly and more successful, U.S. policy makers should impose and maintain fewer sanctions but far more rigorously enforce those they deem as priorities.

In counteracting the corrosive effects of aid-based sanctions busting, the U.S. government can potentially be more successful in recruiting multilateral cooperation from foreign governments. Because the states that engage in extensive aid-based sanctions are often motivated by their adversarial relations with the United States, they will be very difficult to dissuade. Although aid-based sanctions busters can provide a large amount of the foreign aid a target needs to survive, they can almost never afford to provide all that a target may need.[3] As such, the U.S. government can counteract the effects of aid-based sanctions busters by convincing the other third-party governments that aid target countries to reduce their foreign assistance. Cutting off their foreign aid to target states is apt to be far less costly (budgetwise, economically, and politically) for third-party governments than participating in sanctioning efforts via restricting their trade and/or investment relationships with a target. As such, the U.S. government should be able to obtain far more multilateral cooperation—with far less effort—from third-party governments when it asks them to cut off their foreign aid to target states instead of imposing trade sanctions.

Much more directly, the U.S. government can also stop offering aid to the states it sanctions. For example, the U.S. government provided North Korea with over $1.2 billion in combined food, energy, and medical assistance since 1995 in aid efforts that ran concurrently to its sanctions.[4] Even as the U.S.

economic sanctioning efforts helped cripple and isolate North Korea's economy, it undercut its own sanctions' effectiveness with the aid it provided to the country. In other words, U.S. sanctions contributed to the economic and humanitarian crises in North Korea that subsequently required U.S. foreign aid to remedy, which in turn undercut its sanctions' chances of success and left a hurting stalemate that continues to contribute to the humanitarian crises North Korea's citizens face.

Cutting off aid to sanctioned states is also apt to be effective in the longer run because it can place additional pressure on targets' patrons (if they have them) to replace aid shortfalls from other donors if they want their sanctions-busting efforts to continue to be effective. As in the Soviet Union's case, this can bleed a sanctions-busting patron dry over time as it becomes responsible for paying a larger share of the burden in supporting a target state. Because third-party patrons are almost always adversaries of the sender state, this strategy will be dually beneficial in making the sanctions more effective and sapping the strength of rival third parties. For example, this suggests that by denying aid to North Korea Western donors can make China pay an increasingly steep price for continuing to sustain the country—potentially to the point where it is no longer willing to bear those costs.

The policy recommendations that flow from this analysis also raise significant ethical and humanitarian concerns. Indeed, they run counter to the broader international movement to impose "smart sanctions" that minimize their adverse consequences on innocent populations in target countries.[5] Reducing or cutting off foreign aid to sanctioned states can exacerbate the damages and misery they inflict, and oftentimes those costs will be concentrated on constituencies in target states that have little control over the policies for which the sanctions were imposed. Before embarking on a strategy to deny target states foreign assistance, especially in areas like basic food and medical assistance, U.S. policy makers should carefully consider whether the potential human costs are worth the goals being sought by the sanctioning efforts. In many cases, those prospective costs may be too high. This also reinforces, however, that economic sanctions should not be considered a comparatively innocuous alternative to the use of military force; rather, they are a less direct but often far more corrosive policy tool that degrades the health, social, political, and economic welfare of their targets' populations. If U.S. policy makers commit to using economic sanctions, it may be better to employ harsh sanctioning efforts in an effort to rapidly achieve their goals than to allow them to persist unproductively in painful but survivable stalemates.

The last key policy-relevant insight relates to the adverse and often inadvertent effects that U.S. sanctions have on U.S. alliance relationships. Given the profiles of the closest U.S. allies and the political cover their alliance relationships with the United States offers them, they are often the best-positioned states to profit from the sanctions the United States imposes. As the analyses repeatedly revealed, U.S. efforts at coercing these states to refrain from taking advantage of sanctions-busting opportunities usually generate intra-alliance conflict and tend to be unsuccessful. Moreover, the profits allied sanctions busters earn provide them with salient interests in ensuring the U.S. sanctions' continued persistence. Rather than being partners in pursuing shared policy objectives, U.S. allies have incentives to impede the sanctions from being successful. The fact that U.S. sanctions encourage the closest U.S. allies to forge stronger commercial relationships with its adversaries can have consequences that extend beyond whether sanctions succeed or fail. In some cases, the U.S. government deems it appropriate to follow up its sanctions with the use of military force against a country it has sanctioned.[6] If U.S. allies have strong commercial ties to a target state, they may be far more likely to oppose the use of military force against those countries than they otherwise would. For example, French companies substantially profited from undercutting the sanctions against Saddam Hussein's regime in Iraq. Reportedly, Saddam Hussein's regime even preferentially selected trade partners in France that "espoused pro-Iraq views."[7] France emerged as a vocal opponent to the U.S. invasion of Iraq in 2003. In part, the country's opposition to the war could have been influenced by the significant commercial benefits it was receiving via its sanctions-busting trade with Hussein's regime. Overall, the potential for intra-alliance rifts adds to the growing list of indirect effects that scholars have identified regarding the use of economic sanctions.[8]

Directions for Future Research

The findings from this project contribute to a number of different areas of scholarship that are ripe for future research. Foremost, they contribute to the ongoing effort to better understand the broad set of consequences sanctions have on their targets and how their externalities also affect third-party states.

Initial work in this area has examined how sanctions affect the trade of states neighboring sanctioned countries with the rest of the world, their effect on neighboring states' corruption and involvement in transnational crime, and third-party states' likelihoods of attacking target states.[9] Aspects of this project suggest that further research into the political consequences of economic sanctions on third-party states' relationships with targets and senders states is important. For example, do trade-based sanctions busters develop closer political ties with target states and grow more hostile toward sender states? This could be a significant issue, given the findings regarding alliance dynamics this book has already uncovered. Also, studying how sanctioned states, such as Iran and Iraq, can work together to defeat sanctioning efforts constitutes a promising avenue of inquiry.

Another popular line of inquiry has explored the role that selection effects play in influencing sanctions outcomes. Various works have shown that merely threatening sanctions can sometimes be sufficient in convincing a target state to concede to a sender's demands and that some senders make empty threats that they fail to follow through on.[10] By implication, this suggests that the attempts at coercion that actually result in sanctions being imposed represent more intractable disputes. Potentially, the prospective sanctions-busting options available to target states could play a role in determining their susceptibility to sanctions threats. Once threatened with sanctions, target leaders can prepare for their imposition by lining up potential sanctions-busting partners. Senders could be deterred from threatening or following through on imposing sanctions if it looks as if target states could receive extensive sanctions-busting support.

An additional contribution of this book has been in adopting a more integrated approach toward understanding how different types of economic statecraft can interact with one another. Although David Baldwin stakes out a broad concept of what constitutes economic statecraft, the research agendas of economic sanctions and foreign aid have tended to remain siloed—especially in the quantitative study of the subjects.[11] This project has shown that changes in the amount of foreign aid flows that countries receive influence the success of sanctioning efforts, but being sanctioned could also affect the foreign aid flows that recipient states receive more generally. Gaining a deeper understanding of how aid-based sanctions busters and the efforts of sender states affect the aid flows that target states receive is another area of inquiry that could yield salient insights. Recent works by Glen Biglaiser and David

Lektzian on how economic sanctions affect the foreign direct investment flows of sanctioned states and by Paolo Spadoni on the impact of overseas remittances constitute other lines of inquiry complementary to those explored in this book.[12] Ultimately, the full spectrum of targets' commercial relationships could affect whether the sanctions imposed against them succeed or fail.

The book's findings regarding the effects of alliances also provide an interesting complement to previous work that has explored the comparative susceptibility of allies to economic coercion. Drezner argues that, because economic sanctions do not threaten the security of allied targets as much as adversarial targets, allies face fewer costs in conceding to sanctions.[13] When it comes to imposing sanctions, then, senders are advantaged in squaring off against their allies. The findings related to trade-based sanctions busting in this book, however, predict exactly the opposite: Senders face significant disadvantages in preventing their allies from undercutting their sanctions. This paints a complex picture of intra-alliance relationships, in which even close allies seek to exploit one another to the extent they can without jeopardizing the overarching viability of their alliance. Alliance relationships appear to incentivize far more exploitive behaviors than they do cooperation when it comes to economic sanctions.

Because U.S. policy makers show few signs of abandoning their reliance on economic sanctions any time soon, further research into the array of consequences that they have and the determinants of their success remains an important task. Reducing the humanitarian consequences that economic sanctions have on their targets is only one dimension of making sanctions smarter. For policy makers, finding an appropriate balance between the adverse costs citizens bear due to sanctions and maximizing their sanctions' prospects for obtaining quick, favorable resolutions constitutes another dimension by which sanctions policies can be made smarter. Addressing the problems posed by sanctions busting is one step in that direction, but far more needs to be done.

REFERENCE MATTER

Notes

Chapter 1

1. Lister 2012.

2. These gold export statistics and those above were obtained from Pamuk 2012.

3. Pamuk 2012.

4. Kandemir 2013.

5. For example, see Dubowitz and Ottolenghi 2013.

6. For more on the A. Q. Khan proliferation network and the role Dubai played, see Albright and Hinderstein 2005, 120 and Corera 2006.

7. Stolberg 2010.

8. Baldwin 2002.

9. Baldwin 1985.

10. See Baldwin (1985, 1999/2000) and also Most and Starr (1989) for more on the substitutability of these foreign policies.

11. Hufbauer et al. 2007 and Morgan et al. 2009.

12. See the sanctions data sets created by Hufbauer et al. (2007) and Bapat and Morgan 2009, 1082. Pape (1997) argues that the success rate of economic sanctions is more likely in the single digits. Nincic (2005) further argues that economic sanctions are poor policy instruments for compelling rogues states into reforming.

13. For example, see Whang 2011.

14. For an excellent discussion of why policy makers employ sanctions, even knowing their poor track record of success, see Baldwin 1999/2000.

15. Richard Haas (1997), for example, has been especially critical of the U.S. over-reliance on economic sanctions.

16. These figures are calculated via the ninety-six episodes of U.S.-imposed sanctions from 1950 through 2002 using Hufbauer et al.'s (2007) data set.

17. Galeano 2012.

18. Askari et al. 2003b, 167–169.

19. Hufbauer et al. 1997.

20. Johnson-Freese 2007.

21. Krauss 2007.

22. For example, see U.S. Department of Commerce, Bureau of Industry and Security Export Enforcement 2010.

23. Mueller and Mueller 1999.

24. Kaempfer et al. 2004.

25. For more on the various negative effects that sanctions have on their targets, see Wood 2008; Peksen 2009, 2011; Peksen and Drury 2010; Peterson and Drury 2011; and Allen and Lektzian 2013.

26. Van Bergeijk 1994, Caruso 2003, and Slovov 2007.

27. Andreas 2005.

28. Early 2012.

29. In her seminal book, Lisa Martin (1992) argues that powerful states must coerce much of the cooperation they seek in imposing multilateral economic sanctions against a target country.

30. Pilger 2000.

31. For more on the impact of the sanctions against Iraq, see Alnasrawi 2001, Katzman 2003, and Iraq Survey Group 2005.

32. See Bueno de Mesquita et al. (2004) for the former and Moravcsik (1997) for the latter.

33. As such, the analysis does not include the use of sanctions imposed for purely commercial purposes, such as trade sanctions imposed by the U.S. Trade Representative under Section 301 of the Trade Act of 1974.

34. This approach mirrors the one taken by Lisa Martin in *Coercive Cooperation* (1992).

35. See Hufbauer et al. 1990, Drury 1998, Drezner 2000, Nooruddin 2002, and Lektzian and Souva 2007.

Chapter 2

1. Previous studies, such as Curovic 1997 and Askari et al. 2003a, have similarly employed this type of triadic model.

2. Some economic sectors within sanctioned states can benefit from sanctions. If sanctions reduce the foreign competition faced by import-competing sectors, they might actually improve their business prospects. In general, though, economic sanctions are viewed as inflicting far more aggregate costs on their targets' economies than they provide compensatory gains.

3. Askari et al. 2003a, Kaempfer and Lowenberg 1999, and Drezner 2000.

4. For an excellent discussion of this dynamic, see Kaempfer and Lowenberg 1999.

5. Once again, see Askari et al. 2003a, Kaempfer and Lowenberg 1999, and Drezner 2000.

6. For example, see Parrish 1998, Kaplowitz 1998, and Sutherland and Canwell 2007.

7. For more on the economic and political impact of foreign aid, see Dalgaard and Olsson 2008, Hansen and Headey 2010, Licht 2010, and Selaya and Thiele 2010.

8. Hufbauer et al. 1990, 2007.

9. See Hufbauer et al. 1990. More detail on what types of aid count as "black knight" assistance was provided in Hufbauer et al. 2007, but the actual coding of the variable remained identical.

10. For examples of studies that could not find a direct link between the black knight variable and sanctions success, see Drury 1998; Drezner 1998, 2000; and Hufbauer et al. 2007. Lektzian and Souva 2007 had one of the studies that found the expected negative effect of the black knight variable on sanctions success.

11. McLean and Whang 2010.

12. For example, see Spadoni 2010 and Lektzian and Biglaiser 2014.

13. For an effort to explain these countries' sanctions policies toward South Africa and the factors affecting trade with South Africa during the sanctions, see Kaempfer and Lowenberg 1989 and Kaempfer and Ross 2004.

14. Hufbauer et al. 2007, for example, code the U.S. sanctioning efforts as a success. For a contrary view, see Levy 1999.

15. For example, Venezuela President Hugo Chávez broadly publicized the assistance his government provided to Cuba.

16. Finding hard numbers on China's foreign assistance to North Korea is exceptionally difficult, as both governments have tended to keep those figures confidential.

17. Choo 2008, 345.

18. Ibid., 352.

19. Ibid., 349.

20. Haggard and Noland 2007, 13, and Manyin and Nikitin 2011, 22.

21. Choo 2008, 348.

22. Ibid., 363–367, and Manyin and Nikitin 2011, 22.

23. Manyin and Nikitin 2011, 22, and Haggard and Noland 2007, 28.

24. Gill 2011, 4, and Lee 2013.

25. Institute for Far Eastern Studies 2012.

26. Nanto and Chanlett-Avery 2010, 55–58.

Chapter 3

1. Portions of this chapter draw on arguments originally developed in Early 2011.

2. For examples, see Martin 1992; Drury 1998, 2005; Drezner 1999, 2000; Kaempfer et al. 2004; Allen 2005; Cox and Drury 2006; Hufbauer et al. 2007; Ang and Peksen

2007; Hafner-Burton and Montgomery 2008; Bapat and Morgan 2009; Lektzian and Souva 2007; and McLean and Whang 2010.

3. For examples, see Martin 1992, Drezner 2000, and Bapat and Morgan 2009.

4. For a clear statement of the core assumptions of the liberal paradigm, see Moravcsik 1997.

5. For more on how leaders balance competing domestic and foreign policy prerogatives, see Bueno de Mesquita et al. 2004.

6. For example, see Morgan and Bapat 2003 and also Kastner 2007.

7. Kirshner 1997.

8. Some information about the parties' resolve can be obtained during the stage in which senders threaten to impose sanctions (for example, Drezner 2003 and Whang, McLean, and Kuberski 2013), but that information remains incomplete if the sender follows through with imposing the sanctions and the target resists them.

9. Van Bergeijk and van Marrewijk 1995.

10. For example, see Bueno de Mesquita et al. 2004 and Escribà-Folch and Wright 2010.

11. Kaempfer and Lowenberg 1999.

12. This argument draws on transaction cost economics. For more on this theory, see Williamson 1985 and Dyer 1997, 536.

13. Van Bergeijk 1994 and Caruso 2003.

14. Kaempfer et al. 2004 and Escribà-Folch and Wright 2010.

15. For example, see Lektzian and Sprecher 2007 and Peterson and Drury 2011.

16. For more in-depth discussions on the U.S. use of extraterritorial sanctions, see Martin 1992, Rodman 2001, and Shambaugh 1999.

17. For example, see Andreas 2005, 2008.

18. Kharas 2008 and Desai and Kharas 2010.

19. For example, see Kosack and Tobin 2006; Chong, Gradstein, and Calderon 2009; Hansen and Headey 2010; and Selaya and Thiele 2010.

20. For example, see Kaempfer et al. 2004; Bueno de Mesquita and Smith 2007; Wood 2008; Licht 2010; and Escribà-Folch and Wright 2010.

21. Kosack and Tobin 2006, 210.

22. Kharas 2008.

23. Ibid., 1.

24. Kosack and Tobin 2006.

25. Many constituents may not even be aware that the benefits or subsidies they are receiving are made possible only by foreign aid, either directly or indirectly. With their expectations established as such, they may view continuing to receive their foreign-aid–enabled benefits as entitlements and not as a privilege made possible by foreign aid.

26. Manyin and Nikitin 2014, 11, 13–15.

27. Noland and Haggard 2005, 104.

28. See NKNET 2011, 20, and Noland and Haggard 2011, 57.

29. Manyin 2005, 9–12.

30. Dalgaard and Olsson 2008.

31. Licht 2010.

32. Hufbauer et al. 2007.

33. Box-Steffensmeier and Jones 2004.

34. Van Bergeijk and van Marrewijk 1995.

35. For a detailed discussion of how the composite indicators of *Success Scores* are coded, see Hufbauer et al. 2007, 185. They code *Policy Result* as a four-point (1 through 4) ordinal variable in which a 1 denotes a complete failure and a 4 a total success. They similarly code *Contribution* as a four-point (1 through 4) ordinal variable in which a 1 denotes that sanctions negatively contributed to the final outcome and a 4 denotes they played a decisive role. For a sanctions episode to be coded as a success, it must have received scores of 3 or above for both variables. Sanctions episodes that were still ongoing as of 2002 are coded as continuing to persist in a stalemate.

36. Barbieri et al. 2009.

37. For a more detailed description of these coding procedures and the results of alternative ways of coding the aggregate sanctions-busting variable, see Early 2011.

38. For more on what forms of aid qualify as ODA, see OECD 2008.

39. For more on the operationalization of the net aid transfer measure of ODA, see Roodman 2011.

40. This approach means that the amount of foreign aid that countries receive can be negative in some years, as they may be paying more interest out on past concessional loans than they received than they receive in new aid (Roodman 2011). This transactionally based conceptualization of foreign aid flows appears to best capture the aspects of foreign that can help or a hinder a target's efforts to resist economic sanctions.

41. Kharas 2008.

42. Target states are coded as democracies (*Democracy*) if they score as a 7 or higher on Marshall and Jaggers's (2009) *polity2* variable.

43. For more on the potential way that alliance relationships can affect sanctions outcomes, see Drezner 1999. To code the alliance variable, the model employs data on defense pacts from the ATOP data set (Leeds, Long, and Mitchell 2002).

44. Hufbauer et al. 2007, 60–61.

45. Ibid.

46. Ibid., 185.

47. Ibid., 66–67.

48. Summary statistics for all the variables are in the Online Appendix.

49. Box-Steffensmeier and Jones 2004.

50. This is done as per the recommendations of Carter and Signorino (2010).

51. A large number of additional robustness analyses were conducted using alternative model and variable specifications, which support the results depicted in Table 3.1.

52. This scenario assumes that the sanctions have been in place for three years and the target has experienced no change in its foreign aid flows. All other factors are held constant at their means.

53. Additional robustness analyses were conducted using alternative ways of operationalizing Δ *Foreign Aid*, including analyzing changes in foreign aid flows as a proportion of target states' GDP values. The findings remained consistent with those presented.

54. This graph and the prediction probabilities are calculated via the same typical scenario used to assess the substantive effects of *Trade-Based Busters*.

55. As Barber 1979 notes, one of the challenges associated with long sanctioning efforts is that their goals frequently shift over time. This can adversely influence senders' ability to achieve their goals and make efforts to measure sanctioning efforts' success more difficult.

Chapter 4

1. Portions of this chapter draw from Early 2012.

2. Blumenfeld 1991, 131.

3. Indeed, the issue of whether multilateral support makes sanctions more or less effective has been a topic of major debate (Drezner 2000, Hufbauer et al. 2007, Morgan et al. 2009, and Bapat and Morgan 2009). One can summarize these findings by saying that, even in a best-case scenario, having an additional third-party state cooperate in imposing sanctions will only marginally contribute to the sanctions' likelihood of success.

4. Martin 1992.

5. Ibid.

6. Drezner 1999, 41.

7. For more on this enforcement dynamic between sender firms and sender governments, see Morgan and Bapat 2003.

8. For more on the transaction costs involved in conducting international trade, see Dyer 1997, 535–536, and Anderson and Wincoop 2004.

9. For more on this, see Van Bergeijk 1994, 1995; and Caruso 2003.

10. According to Anderson and Wincoop's 2004, 691–692, definition, trade costs "include all costs incurred in getting a good to a final user other than the marginal cost of producing the goods itself."

11. For more on extraterritorial sanctions, see Shambaugh 1999 and Rodman 2001.

12. For a more detailed discussion, see Kaempfer and Lowenberg 1999.

13. It is possible for foreign aid to benefit particular donor constituencies. For example, a donor state's agricultural sector may commercially benefit from its government's provision of international food aid. As such, leaders may obtain some domestic

political benefits from providing foreign aid to targets. This is counterbalanced by the fact that providing extensive foreign aid to another country can be domestically unpopular.

14. For example, see Li and Sacko 2002; Keshk, Pollins, and Reuveny 2004; and Kastner 2007.

15. Li and Sacko 2002, 33.

16. Abdelal and Kirshner 1999, and Kastner 2007.

17. Drezner 2000, 84.

18. Morgan and Bapat 2003

19. Rodman 1995, 106.

20. These costs could be the benefits the third-party government would receive if the sanctions against the target were successful or the damage undermining a sender's sanctioning effort could have on the third-party government's relationship with it.

21. Limão and Venables 2001.

22. Compensating third parties for the trade they lose as a result of cooperating with sanctioning efforts is difficult and expensive. It can quickly multiply the costs involved in imposing sanctions on the order of several magnitudes. Sender states thus tend to rely on coercive tactics instead. For more on sender governments' incentives to use coercion in obtaining international sanctions cooperation, see Martin 1992.

23. For example, see Leeds 2003.

24. Leeds et al. 2000.

25. Snyder 1997, 180.

26. Ibid., 356.

27. Leeds 2003.

28. Long 2003.

29. For previous analyses of the gas-pipeline sanctions, see Jentleson 1986, Martin 1992, Shambaugh 1999, and Rodman 1995, 2001.

30. Martin 1992, 211–220.

31. Shambaugh 1999, 99.

32. Martin 1992, 224.

33. See ibid., 228–234, for a more detailed discussion.

34. Long 2003.

35. Dixon and Moon 1993, 11.

36. For more on the democratic peace theory as it applies to economic sanctions, see Cox and Drury 2006 and Hafner-Burton and Montgomery 2008.

37. These are a common product of findings from studies that employ gravity models of international trade; see Hufbauer et al. 2007, Long 2008, and Early 2012.

38. Blumenfeld 1991, 119, and Andreas 2005.

39. Kaempfer and Ross 2004.

40. Andreas 2005.

41. See Dadak 2003 and Drezner 2000.

42. Iraq Survey Group 2005, 24–27.

43. Most of the available data come in the form of comprehensive case studies. For several very good examples, see Dadak 2003, Andreas 2005, and Iraq Survey Group 2005.

44. Hufbauer et al. 2007, 59–60.

45. See OECD (2008) for a complete list of what counts as ODA.

46. For example, see Schraeder, Hook, and Taylor 1998; Alesina and Dollar 2000; Bueno de Mesquita and Smith 2007; and Licht 2010.

47. Dreher and Fuchs 2011.

48. Hufbauer et al. 2007, 59–60, also make this point in offering an explanation for why "black knight" assistance might be given.

49. For more on the Arab League Boycott, see Weiss 2006 and Hufbauer et al. 2007, 8.

50. Leogrande 1996, 331.

51. Blumenfeld 1991, 55.

52. Molotsky 1996.

53. For more specific details on the Berlin Airlift, see Parrish 1998, Miller 2005, and Sutherland and Canwell 2007.

54. Miller 2005, 180.

55. Ibid., 3.

56. Bilirakis 1998.

57. See U.S. Department of State 1949, 5; Clay 1962, 51–52; and Miller 2005, 112–113.

58. Great Britain also contributed to the airlift operations but at much lower levels (Miscamble 1980 and Shlaim 1983–1984).

59. George and Bennett 2005.

Chapter 5

1. George and Bennett 2005, 166–167.

2. See Gerring 2004, 349.

3. Corera 2006 and Montgomery 2005.

4. See Malloy 2001, 93–98, and Eizenstat 2004, 1.

5. Carswell 1981–1982, 253.

6. For more details, see Askari et al. 2003b, 188–189; Malloy 2001, 93–98; and Eizenstat 2004, 1–2 .

7. Estelami 1999.

8. Askari et al. 2003b, 188–189.

9. Malloy 2001, 100, and Askari et al. 2003b, 188.

10. Katzman 2007.

11. Downey 1998.

12. See Downey (1998), Shambaugh (1999), Rodman (2001), and Eizenstat (2004) for more on the foreign policy considerations at stake in imposing extraterritorial sanctions.

13. Eizenstat 2004, 3–5, 8–9.

14. Clawson 1998, 89.

15. See the full text of Executive Order 13,059 (1997) for the full range of restrictions it imposed.

16. This legislation was passed with the support of significant lobbying by American agricultural interests.

17. Campbell 2000.

18. Hufbauer et al. 2007, 152.

19. Estelami 1999.

20. See Malloy 2001, 97, and Eizenstat 2004, 1.

21. Carswell 1981–1982, 254.

22. Ibid.

23. Askari et al. 2003b, 196–197.

24. Ibid., 213.

25. For more detailed analysis, see Amuzegar 1997 and Askari et al. 2003b, 211.

26. Figures cited in Levin 1981.

27. Imports to Iran are only shown because oil constitutes an overwhelming proportion of Iran's exports. Japan, China, and France are all leading destinations for Iranian oil.

28. Askari et al. 2003b, 176.

29. The strong resurgence of American trade with Iran in the years after the complete trade ban was lifted in 1981 demonstrates this point. Also see Hosenball 1987.

30. O'Sullivan 2003, 62.

31. Shehadi 1981, 16, and Ibrahim, 1980.

32. Richey 1982.

33. Vicker 1980.

34. Ibrahim 1980.

35. For several discussions on the motives of Dubai's traders, see "Dubai Smugglers Still Voyaging to Iran" 1980 and Ibrahim 1980.

36. "Dubai Smugglers Still Voyaging to Iran" 1980.

37. See "Despite Fighting, Dubai Smugglers" 1980, Ibrahim 1980, and Auerbach 1980.

38. Vicker 1980.

39. Ibrahim 1980.

40. Gray 1983.

41. Cockburn 1982a.

42. Cockburn 1982b.

43. Davidson 2008, 114–115.

44. "Dhows in Gulf Slip by Iraqis" 1984.

45. Naylor 2001, Chapters 16 and 17.

46. Valentine 1989.

47. Fisk 1987.

48. Walker 1987 and Suro 1987.

49. Suro 1987.

50. Fisher 1988.

51. Ibid.

52. "Dubai's Merchants Find Market" 1989.

53. Cowell 1988.

54. Harper 1991.

55. Ibid.

56. "Smugglers Run Blockade" 1990.

57. Coll 1990.

58. "Smugglers Run Blockade" 1990.

59. For an example case, see Fares 1994.

60. Sieff 1994.

61. This behavior is consistent with cases noted in Barbieri and Levy 1999.

62. "Trade with the UAE" 1994.

63. Lancaster 1995.

64. Ibrahim1980.

65. These islands, for example, include Abu Musa, the Tunbs, and Hormuz.

66. "Dhows in Gulf" 1984.

67. Peterson 2003, 138.

68. The war made not just trade with Iranian and Iraqi ports more dangerous but also trade with ports that were closer to where the conflict occurred.

69. For a more extensive discussion of the Tanker War, and especially the U.S. involvement in it, see Entessar 1988, 1439–1447.

70. For news reports of vessels from both sides of the conflict being repaired in Dubai, see Fisk 1987, Cowell 1988, and Davidson 2008, 227.

71. Davidson 2005, 158.

72. Davidson 2008, 115. For a more expansive discussion of Free Trade Zones, see Emadi-Coffin 2002.

73. Davidson 2005, 139.

74. Slavin 1987 and Hiro 1988.

75. See Weintraub 1987.

76. For a detailed discussion of the relocation of the pearl merchants from Lingah to Dubai, see Heard-Bey 1982, 244–245; Al-Gurg 1998, 4–10; and Al-Sayegh 1998, 88–90.

77. Al-Sayegh 1998, 88.

78. This figure was cited in "Luring Minds and Money" 2005.

79. I confirmed this in the various interviews I conducted.

80. Rugh 2000, 259.

81. Peterson 2003, 140.

82. For more on the UAE–Iran territorial dispute regarding the Tunbs and Abu Musa, see Al-Roken 2001 and Gause 2000, 228.

83. Katzman 2005, 4.

84. Foley 1999.

85. Rahman 2004.

86. Ibid. 2004.

87. "Official against Ban" 2005.

88. Quoted in Irish 2007.

89. Quoted in Wright 2008.

90. Dorraj and Currier 2008, 72–73, and Gundzik 2005.

91. "Iran Hits Back" 1995.

92. Swibel 2004a.

93. Wright 1995.

94. Askari et al. 2003b, 198.

95. Lancaster 1995.

96. The products were smuggled to avoid Iranian authorities preceding the American sanctions, not American or Emirati ones.

97. Lancaster 1995.

98. Swibel 2004a.

99. Wright 1995.

100. Lancaster 1995.

101. Stewart 2008 asserts that this perspective still existed within the American business community in the UAE as of 2008.

102. This quote was taken from the company's website and reported in Stockman 2008.

103. Stockman 2008.

104. Wright 1995.

105. Lancaster 1995, Wright 1995, "Dubai: A Booming Entrepot" 1996, and Swibel 2004a.

106. Taubman 1997.

107. This figure was estimated by a trader involved in the computer transshipment business in Dubai and was reported in a story by the *Reuters News* service (Sedarat 1997).

108. Sedarat 1997.

109. These cases were retrieved from press releases published by the U.S. Department of Commerce's Bureau for Industry and Security about the investigations enforcement actions the agency had undertaken in response to export control violations. See U.S. Department of Commerce, Bureau of Industry and Security Export Enforcement 2010. Also see Swibel 2004b.

110. "Dubai: A Booming Entrepot" 1996.

111. Worsnip 1998.

112. "Iraq's Shipping" 2002.

113. "Emirates Vows to Crack Down" 1998 and "Dhows Use Iran" 1998.

114. Askari et al. 2003b, 197–198.

115. Ibid., 198.

116. Rettab and Morada 2005, 10, and Rettab, Morada, and Abdullah 2005, 18–19.

117. Rettab and Morada 2005, 18.

118. These insights were garnered from fieldwork conducted in the UAE in the fall of 2005.

119. Stewart 2008.

120. Milhollin and Motz 2004.

121. Swibel 2004a.

122. Emphasis added by author; see Milhollin and Motz 2004.

123. Montgomery 2005.

124. Corera 2006, 118.

125. Salama 2004.

126. Corera 2006, 144.

127. Albright and Hinderstein 2005, 120.

128. In 2003, officials in Dubai refused to interdict a shipment of sixty-six spark gap triggers being transshipped to Pakistan from South Africa via Dubai. Spark gap triggers are dual-use goods that can be used in medical equipment to break up kidney stones or as high-speed detonators for nuclear weapons (Milhollin and Motz 2004 and Swibel 2004a).

129. See Dubai Chamber of Commerce and Industry (DCCI) 2005 and Huifen 2004.

130. "Dubai Technology" 2005.

131. For the source of these company listings, see Economist Intelligence Unit 2005, 22; Keivani, Parsa, and Younis 2003, 29; and Rosenthal 2005.

132. These figures were collected by the author from the online JAFZA Corporate Directory in the fall of 2005; see "Jebel Ali Free Zone: Free Zone Companies" 2005.

133. In one case in which a U.S. firm involved in sanctions busting was actually caught by the U.S. government, the U.S. firm was literally a couple of doors down from the Iranian firm that it sold sanctioned medical supplies to in an FTZ (Stewart 2008).

134. "Dubai: A Booming Entrepot" 1996.

135. "Luring Minds and Money" 2005.

136. "Official against Ban" 2005 and "UAE Stock Exchange Tumbles" 2006.

137. Katzman 2008, 4.

138. Jehl 1997.

139. Scarborough 1997.

140. Katzman 2005, 4.

141. Jehl 1997.

142. Katzman 2008.

143. Goodwin 2006.

144. Warner 2006.

145. The context for Senator Warner's remarks was the contentious debate over whether the U.S. government would approve a deal to allow an Emirati firm named DP World to manage twelve U.S. ports in 2006.

146. U.S. & Foreign Commercial Service, 2005.

147. Katzman, 2008, 5.

148. Alden 2003 and O'Clery 2004. Although the subsidiary was based in Dubai, it was officially incorporated in the Cayman Islands.

149. Lake 2005.

150. Cheney 2000.

151. Ivanovich 2005 and Lautenberg 2005.

152. Lake 2005.

153. Swibel 2004a.

154. These resolutions include: UNSCR 1737 (2006), 1747 (2007), 1803 (2008), 1929 (2010), and 2049 (2012).

155. These insights arose out of numerous conversations with members of the U.S. sanctions policy community.

156. U.S. GAO 2010, 16.

157. Warner 2006.

158. Sanger 2006 and Early 2010.

159. Wright 2008. This point was also reinforced in the interviews I conducted with U.S. diplomats in 2009 and 2010.

160. For more on this deal, see Early 2010.

161. The UN sanctions imposed against Iran were passed via the following UN Security Council resolutions: UNSCR 1737 (2006), UNSCR 1747 (2007), UNSCR 1803 (2008), and UNSCR 1929 (2010).

162. For more on this, see Stinnett et al. 2011.

163. This observation was shared with me in discussions with UAE officials in 2010.

164. Wright 2008.

165. For an overview of the application and efficacy of financial sanctions, see Feaver and Lorber 2010.

166. Hayes et al. 2012, Protess and Silver-Greenberg 2012, and U.S. GAO 2013.

167. Wright 2008.

168. Krauland et al. 2012.

169. This observation was gleaned from interviews with U.S. diplomats and Emirati officials in 2009 and 2010.

170. Shaheen 2010, Early 2010, and Stinnett et al. 2011.

171. Kumar 2010 and Hall 2012.

172. Sadjadpour 2011, 24, and U.S. GAO 2013, 18.

173. Sleiman 2012.

174. These trade statistics were obtained from Barbieri et al. 2009. The sharp decline in the UAE's trade with Iran was also a product of 2009 global recession, which struck Dubai particularly hard.

175. Over 8,000 Iranian-owned businesses were estimated to have been operating out of Dubai in the late 2000s. These numbers have declined some due to the UAE's enhanced cooperation with the sanctions, but they remain quite high.

176. I obtained this insight from interviews in Dubai in May 2009. For more on the dhow-based smuggling taking place via Dubai, see Foroohar 2010 and Sadjadpour 2011.

177. Katzman 2013.

178. For a discussion of the UAE's strategic challenges, see McGovern 2009.

179. U.S. GAO 2013, 27–42.

180. This insight arose from discussions with members of the U.S. sanctions policy community.

181. Naylor 2001 and Andreas 2005.

Chapter 6

1. If the United States has multiple, overlapping sanctioning efforts in place against a target in a given year, those efforts are aggregated to count as a single sanctioning effort. This is done because there is no way to distinguish for which specific set of sanctions the sanctions busting may be taking place. For more on using this triadic coding approach, see Early 2009.

2. If cases in which trade data are missing are instead assumed to be nonbusting observations, this figure declines to 1.97 percent of the total observations.

3. The GDP data used in this analysis comes from Gleditsch's *Expanded Trade and GDP Data* (2008).

4. The bilateral trade data used in this analysis come from Barbieri et al. 2009.

5. Data on which states possessed defense pacts with one another were obtained from the ATOP Data set (Leeds et al. 2002).

6. Marshall and Jaggers 2009.

7. These data were obtained from EUGene; see Bennett and Stam 2000.

8. To reduce the skew in the distance variable, the variable is logarithmically transformed. Because the base distance values contain observations of 0, 1 was added to all of the observations beforehand.

9. Version 3.1 of the data set is used; see Stinnett et al. 2002.

10. Caruso 2003.

11. Kaempfer and Lowenberg 1999 and Drezner 2000.

12. Hufbauer et al. 2007.

13. This approach follows the advice of Carter and Signorino 2010.

14. Summary statistics are available in the Online Appendix.

15. For more on the use of rare events logit, see King and Zeng 2001.

16. Carter and Signorino 2010.

17. For the *Duration* and *Time Since Busting* variables, it is assumed that the sanctions were in place for three years and the target had not busted during those first three years.

18. To do this, I increase *Third-Party Economic Size*, *Third-Party Commercial Openness*, and *Third-Party Commercial Dependence* by one standard deviation above

their means, decrease *Target–Third Party Distance* by one standard deviation below its mean, and assume that the third-party state has defense pacts with both the target and sender and that both the target and third-party states are democracies.

19. For more on the relationship between democracy and international trade, see Morrow, Siverson, and Tabares 1998 and Mansfield, Milner, and Rosendorff 2000.

20. See the additional analyses in Early 2012.

Chapter 7

1. Several key historical summaries were consulted as part of this review: Morely 1987, Kaplowitz 1998, and Askari et al. 2003b.

2. George and Bennett 2005, Chapter 3.

3. Kaplowitz 1998, 31–32.

4. Ibid., 112–113.

5. Ibid., 40.

6. Eisenhower 1965, 622; Morely 1987, 121, also quotes this passage.

7. Pavlov 1994, 18.

8. Kaplowitz 1998, 48.

9. Askari et al. 2003b, 129.

10. According to State Department officials, the U.S. diplomats applied significant pressure on Latin American countries to support the OAS embargo. See Morely 1987, 176, 445; and Kaplowitz 1998, 59, 67–68.

11. Morely 1987, 123.

12. Morely 1987, Chapters 4 and 5, provides a detailed discussion of U.S. diplomatic efforts to obtain the support of its NATO allies, drawing extensively on archival and firsthand accounts.

13. Morely 1987, 238.

14. Ibid., 191–192, 196.

15. Ibid., 215.

16. Ibid., 201.

17. Ibid., 238.

18. Ibid., 190.

19. Kaplowitz 1998, 49.

20. Ibid., 63–64.

21. Morely 1987, 197–203, and Kaplowitz 1998, 64.

22. For more on the Cuban Missile Crisis, see Allison and Zelikow 1999 and Dobbs 2008.

23. Morely 1987, 211.

24. Kaplowitz 1998, 73.

25. "U.S. Opposes" 1971 and Morely 1987, 274–275.

26. For a review of Cuba's involvement in Africa in this period, see Falk 1987.

27. Pavlov 1994, 13.

28. Lévesque 1978, 31–32, and Pavlov 1994, 18–20.

29. Pavlov 1994, 21–22.

30. Lévesque 1978, 30–34; Pavlov 1994, 22–25; and Bain 2007, 20–21.

31. Kaplowitz 1998, 77.

32. Morely 1987, 213.

33. Ibid., 238.

34. Kaplowitz 1998, 77.

35. Morely 1987, 267.

36. Falk 1987.

37. Pavlov 1994.

38. Phillips 1960a and Duncan 1985, 31.

39. Pavlov 1994, 17–24.

40. Bain 2007, 21.

41. For a discussion, see Szulc 1962.

42. Bain 2007, 22–23.

43. Duncan 1985, 39.

44. Tanner 1964 and Duncan 1985, 44.

45. Bain 2007, 22.

46. "23% of Cuba's Trade" 1967 and Stern 1974.

47. Bain 2007, 31.

48. Lévesque 1978, 167.

49. Most of the CMEA's members were geographically located in Eastern Europe. Besides Cuba, Vietnam and Mongolia were the only other non-European countries granted membership in the organization.

50. "Cuba Becomes Full Member of Soviet Economic Bloc" 1972.

51. Volsky 1979, 55.

52. Volsky 1979 and Falk 1987.

53. Leogrande and Thomas 2002.

54. Bain 2007, 31–32.

55. Kaplowitz 1998, 119.

56. Purcell 1991/1992, 142, and Bain 2007, 47.

57. Leogrande and Thomas 2002, 342.

58. Bain 2007, 60.

59. Lévesque 1978, 22.

60. Bain 2008, 54–55.

61. Pavlov 1994, 248–249.

62. Bain 2007, 63.

63. Pavlov 1994, 80.

64. Ibid., 26.

65. In 1958, the Batista regime in Cuba sold only 50,000 tons of sugar to China (Phillips 1960b).

66. Ibid.

67. Szulc 1965.

68. Lévesque 1978, 60.
69. "China and Cuba Sign" 1962.
70. Lévesque 1978, 91.
71. "Red China and Cuba Sign Pact on Trade" 1963.
72. Szulc 1965.
73. Hofmann 1965.
74. "Cuba May Profit" 1966.
75. "China Cuts Back Trade" 1966 and Lévesque 1978, 117.
76. "Castro Charges Peking" 1966 and "Cuba May Profit" 1966.
77. Lévesque 1978, 116.
78. Joseph Goebels was a high-ranking official within Nazi Germany who was responsible for the Nazi Party's massive propaganda machine. See "China Uses Methods of Goebels" 1966.
79. "Castro Charges Peking" 1966 and Schwartz 1966.
80. Karol 1970, 386.
81. Lévesque 1978, 117.
82. Schwartz 1964 and "Castro Charges" 1966.
83. Smith, 1996, 99, and Morely and McGillion 2002, 22.
84. Preeg 1999, 23, and Askari et al. 2003b, 114.
85. In particular, the Cuban American National Foundation (CANF)—a group representing a strongly anti-Castro contingent of Cuban exiles—played a significant role in convincing Congress and the executive branch to take a hard-line stance against Cuba. See Haney and Vanderbush, 2005; Kaplowitz, 1998, Chapters 7–9; and Morely and McGillion, 2002, 10–22.
86. Smith 1998, 535–537, and Morely and McGillion 2002, 3–6.
87. Preeg 1999, 33.
88. Smith, 1998, 536.
89. Kaplowitz 1998, 203–206, and Haney and Vanderbush 2005, 168–170.
90. During the 1980s, U.S. subsidiary trade with Cuba had hovered around $250 million a year. See figures in Kaplowitz and Kaplowitz 1992 and Kaplowitz 1998, 152.
91. Kaplowitz 1998, 153–154.
92. Smith 1998, 536.
93. The Helms-Burton Act has received significant attention from both the scholarly and policy-making communities; see Haney and Vanderbush 2005, Kaplowitz 1998, Morely and McGillion 2002, Eizenstat 2004, Shambaugh 1999, Fisk 2000, Smith 1998, and Roy 2000.
94. This meant that they would require an act of Congress to subsequently lift them.
95. Morely and McGillion 2002, 101–103.
96. Sanger 1996.
97. Kaplowitz 1998, 185.
98. Kaplowiz 1998, 167, and Morely and McGillion 2002, 120–130.
99. Sanger 1998.

100. Quoted in Morely and McGillion 2002, 111, who obtained the quotation from a confidential interview.

101. Preston 1996.

102. Rohter 1996.

103. Morely and McGillion 2002, 108.

104. Sanger 1998.

105. U.S. GAO 2007, 3.

106. Ibid., 72.

107. Sheridan 2011.

108. Askari et al. 2003b, 125.

109. Pavlov 1994, 243.

110. For more on the collapse of the Cuban sugar industry, see Pollitt 1997, 2004.

111. Rieff 1996 and Smith 1996.

112. Monreal 2002, 78.

113. Pérez-López 1996/1997, 9.

114. Rieff 1996, 65.

115. From 1991 through 1999, Cuba's foreign debt in hard currency rose from $6.38 billion to $11 billion (Leogrande and Thomas 2002, 338).

116. Fletcher 1996.

117. Leogrande and Thomas 2002, 334–335.

118. Roy 2000, 85.

119. Kirk and McKenna 1997, 162.

120. "Europeans Agree" 1996.

121. Barbieri et al. 2009.

122. Spadoni 2010, 54.

123. Rohter 2004.

124. Ratliff 2004, 10.

125. Chen 2007, 26–27.

126. Ibid., 28–29.

127. Walker 1995.

128. Ibid.

129. Faison 1995.

130. Chen 2007; Rosenthal 2003.

131. Rosenthal 2003.

132. "China Pledges Financial Aid to Cuba's Castro" 2012.

133. For more on the difficulty of assessing Chinese foreign aid flows, see Lum et al. 2009 and Grimm et al. 2011.

134. Faison 1995.

135. "China Grants Cuba Almost 400m Dollars' Worth of Loans" 2001.

136. Vuoto 2001, Gertz 2001, and "Fidel Castro Discusses Sino-Cuban Ties" 2001.

137. Bain 2008, 71.

138. Pizarro 2009.

139. "China Pledges Financial Aid to Cuba's Castro" 2012.

140. These figures are derived from a review of trade statistics from Barbieri et al. 2009.

141. Rohter 2004 and Ortiz 2012.

142. "China Grants Cuba Almost 400m Dollars' Worth of Loans" 2001 and "Chinese, Cuban Presidents Visit TV Manufacturing Plant in Nanjing" 2003.

143. Chen 2007.

144. Kaplowitz 1998, 67.

145. Gunson 2006.

146. Erikson 2004 and Goodspeed 2006.

147. Harman 2005.

148. McCoy 2000.

149. See Ramírez 2005, 81. The "Bolivarian" ideology is steeped in mythos surrounding Simón Bolívar, the revolutionary responsible for liberating Venezuela from colonial rule of Spain in the 1800s. It is a mixture of populism, socialism, and pan-Latin Americanism that also encompasses Chávez's own predilection for militarism and authoritarianism (Shifter 2006).

150. Aponte-Moreno and Lattig 2012.

151. Snow 2005 and Shifter 2006.

152. Harman 2005.

153. This project did not come to fruition until 2007, as the Cienfuegos Refinery had been reliant on outdated Soviet equipment and technologies that needed to be refitted (Walter 2007).

154. Gott 2000, 29.

155. Rohter 2000b.

156. Rohter 2000a; see also Rohter 2000b and "With Help from Oil" 2005.

157. Erikson 2004, 35.

158. Adams 2002.

159. Erikson 2004 and Kozloff 2007.

160. This sum totaled $752 million in 2004 (Erikson 2004, 36).

161. Rohter 2000b, Adams 2002, and Erikson 2004, 36.

162. "Using Oil to Spread" 2005 and Harman 2005.

163. Kozloff 2007, 7.

164. Shifter 2006.

165. Bulmer-Thomas 2008, 22.

166. Romero 2008.

167. "If Hugo Goes" 2011 and U.S. Energy Information Administration 2012.

168. Rohter 2000b and Goodspeed 2006.

169. Harman 2005.

170. Gunson 2006.

171. "With Help from Oil and Friends" 2005 and Forero 2006.

172. Goodman 2013.

173. Burnett and Neuman 2014.

174. Hufbauer et al. 1990, 12.

175. Roy 2000, 84.
176. Commission for Assistance to a Free Cuba 2006, 6.

Chapter 8

1. Early 2009.
2. For more on this issue, see Morgan and Bapat 2003.
3. This is part of what makes sanctions-busting aid fundamentally different from sanctions-busting trade. If the profit margins are high enough, third-party firms will emerge that will prioritize providing the target with whatever it needs and can pay for.
4. Manyin and Nikitin 2011.
5. See Cortright and Lopez 2002 and Drezner 2011.
6. Lektzian and Sprecher 2007.
7. Volcker, Goldstone, and Pieth 2005, Chapter 4, 48–49.
8. For example, see Peterson and Drury 2011, Biglaiser and Lektzian 2011, and Lektzian and Biglaiser 2013.
9. For more on each of these topics, see the following authors' respective works: Slovov 2007; Andreas 2005, 2008; and Peterson and Drury 2011.
10. For example, see Drezner 2003, Morgan et al. 2009, Krustev 2010, and Whang, McLean, and Kuberski 2013.
11. See Baldwin 1985. There have been some subsequent works that jointly consider sanctions and incentives together (Haas and O'Sullivan 2000 and Soligen 2012), but they do so qualitatively.
12. Lektzian and Biglaiser 2013, 2014, and Spadoni 2010.
13. Drezner 1999.

References

Abdelal, Rawi, and Jonathan Kirshner. 1999. "Strategy, Economic Relations, and the Definition of National Interests." *Security Studies* 9(1): 123–162.

Adams, David. 2002. "Venezuela Cuts Cheap Oil Shipments to Cuba." *St. Petersberg Times*, June 1.

Albright, David, and Corey Hinderstein. 2005. "Unraveling the A. Q. Khan and Future Proliferation Networks." *The Washington Quarterly* 28(2): 111–128.

Alden, Edward. 2003. "Halliburton Agrees to Review Iran Operations." *Financial Times*, March 23.

Ajman Free Zone Authority. 2005. Retrieved on November 1, 2005 from www.afza .gov.ae/.

Alesina, Alberto, and David Dollar. 2000. "Who Gives Foreign Aid to Whom and Why?" *Journal of Economic Growth* 5(1): 33–63.

Al-Gurg, Easa. 1998. *Wells of Memory*. London: John Murray Publishers.

Allen, Susan Hannah. 2005. "The Determinants of Economic Sanctions Success and Failure." *International Interactions* 31(2): 117–138.

Allen, Susan, and David Lektzian. 2013. "Economic Sanctions: A Blunt Instrument?" *Journal of Peace Research* 50(1): 12–135.

Allison, Graham and Philip Zelikow. 1999. *Essence of Decision: Explaining the Cuban Missile Crisis*, 2nd edition. New York: Pearson.

Alnasrawi , Abbas. 2001. "Iraq: Economic Sanctions and Consequences, 1990–2000." *Third World Quarterly* 22(2): 205–218.

Al-Roken, Mohamed. 2001. "Dimensions of the UAE–Iran Dispute over Three Islands." In *United Arab Emirates: A New Perspective*, edited by Ibrahim Abed and Peter Hellyer, 179-201. United Arab Emirates: Trident Press.

Al-Sayegh, Fatma. 1998. "Merchants' Role in a Changing Society: The Case of Dubai, 1900–90." *Middle Eastern Studies* 34(1): 87–102.

Amuzegar, Jahangir. 1997. "Adjusting to Sanctions." *Foreign Affairs* (May/June): 31–41.

Anderson, James E., and Eric van Wincoop. 2004. "Trade Costs." *Journal of Economic Literature* 42(3): 691–751.

Andreas, Peter. 2005. "Criminalizing Consequences of Sanctions: Embargo Busting and Its Legacy." *International Studies Quarterly* 49: 335–60.

———. 2008. *Blue Helmets and Black Markets: The Business of Survival in the Siege of Sarajevo.* Ithaca, NY: Cornell University Press.

Ang, Adrian U-Jin, and Dursun Peksen. 2007. "When Do Economic Sanctions Work? Issue Salience, Asymmetric Perception, and Outcomes." *Political Research Quarterly* 60(1): 135–145.

Aponte-Moreno, Marco, and Lance Lattig. 2012. "Chávez: Rhetoric Made in Havana." *World Policy Journal* 29: 33–42.

Askari, Hossein, John Forrer, Hildy Teegen, and Jiawen Yang. 2003a. *Economic Sanctions: Examining Their Philosophy and Efficacy.* Westport, CT: Praeger.

———. 2003b. *Case Studies of U.S. Economic Sanctions.* Westport, CT: Praeger.

Auerbach, Stuart. 1980. "Despite Curbs, Iranian Stores Still Stocking U.S. Goods." *The Washington Post*, June 2.

Bain, Mervyn. 2007. *Soviet–Cuban Relations 1985–1991.* New York: Lexington Books.

———. 2008. *Russian–Cuban Relations since 1992: Continuing Camaraderie in a Post-Soviet World.* Lanham, MD: Lexington Books.

Baldwin, David. 1985. *Economic Statecraft.* Princeton, NJ: Princeton University Press.

———. 1999/2000. "The Sanctions Debate and the Logic of Choice." *International Security* 24(3): 80–107.

———. 2002. "Power in International Relations." In *Handbook of International Relations*, edited by Walter Carlsnaes, Thomas Risse, and Beth A Simmons, 177–191. Thousand Oaks, CA: Sage Publications.

Bapat, Navin A., and T. Clifton Morgan. 2009. "Multilateral versus Unilateral Sanctions Reconsidered: A Test Using New Data." *International Studies Quarterly* 53(4): 1075–1094.

Barber, James. 1979. "Economic Sanctions as a Policy Instrument." *International Affairs* 55(3): 367–384.

Barbieri, Katherine, Omar Keshk, and Brian Pollins. 2009. "TRADING DATA: Evaluating our Assumptions and Coding Rules." *Conflict Management and Peace Science.* 26(5): 471–491.

Barbieri, Katherine, and Jack Levy. 1999. "Sleeping with the Enemy: The Impact of War on Trade." *Journal of Peace Research* 36(4): 463–479.

Bennett, D. Scott, and Allan Stam. 2000. "EUGene: A Conceptual Manual." *International Interactions* 26: 179–204.

Biglaiser, Glen, and David Lektzian. 2011. "The Effect of Sanctions on United States Foreign Direct Investment." *International Organization* 65(3): 531–551.

Bilirakis, Gus. 1998. "Fiftieth Anniversary of the Berlin Airlift." *Congressional Record*, U.S. House of Representatives. June 25.

Blumenfeld, Jesmond. 1991. *Economic Interdependence in Southern Africa: From Conflict to Cooperation*. New York: St. Martin's Press.

Box-Steffensmeier, Janet, and Jones, Bradford. 2004. *Event History Modeling: A Guide for Social Scientists*. Cambridge, UK: Cambridge University Press.

Bueno de Mesquita, Bruce, and Alastair Smith. 2007. "Foreign Aid and Policy Concessions." *Journal of Conflict Resolution* 51: 251–284.

Bueno de Mesquita, Bruce, Alastair Smith, and Randolph M. Siverson. 2004. *The Logic of Political Survival*. Cambridge, MA: MIT Press.

Bulmer-Thomas, Victor. 2008. "Cuba after Fidel: The New Leadership." *Harvard International Review*, February 8.

Burnett, Victoria, and William Neuman. 2014. "Protesting in Venezuela, with Antipathy Toward Cuba's Government." *New York Times*, March 25.

Campbell, Duncan. 2000. "US Lifts Sanctions on Iran's Caviar and Rugs." *Guardian*, March 18.

Carswell, Robert. 1981–1982. "Economic Sanctions and the Iran Experience." *Foreign Affairs* 60(2): 247–265.

Carter, David B., and Curtis S. Signorino. 2010. "Back to the Future: Modeling Time Dependence in Binary Data." *Political Analysis* 18(3): 271–292.

Caruso, Raul. 2003. "The Impact of International Economic Sanctions on Trade: An Empirical Analysis." *Peace Economics, Peace Science, and Public Policy* 9(2): 1–34.

"Castro Charges Peking Hostility." 1966. *New York Times*, February 7.

Chen, Yinghong. 2007. "Fidel Castro and 'China's Lesson for Cuba': A Chinese Perspective." *The China Quarterly* 189: 24–42.

Cheney, Dick. 2000. Transcript of a Speech before the World Petroleum Congress in Calgary, Alberta, Canada, June 13.

"China and Cuba Sign on Trade." 1962. *New York Times*, April 26.

"China Cuts Back Trade with Cuba." 1966. *New York Times*, January 3.

"China Grants Cuba Almost 400m Dollars' Worth of Loans." 2001. *BBC Monitoring*, April 15.

"China Pledges Financial Aid to Cuba's Castro." 2012. *Agence France-Presse (AFP)*, July 5.

"China Uses Methods of Goebels to Attack Cuba, Castro Says." 1966. *New York Times*, March 14.

"Chinese, Cuban Presidents Visit TV Manufacturing Plant in Nanjing." 2003. *Xinhua News Agency*, February 28.

Chong, Alberto, Mark Gradstein, and Cecilia Calderon. 2009. "Can Foreign Aid Reduce Income Inequality and Poverty?" *Public Choice* 140: 59–84.

Choo, Jaewoo. 2008. "Mirroring North Korea's Growing Economic Dependence on China: Political Ramifications." *Asian Survey* 48(2): 343–372.

Clawson, Patrick. 1998. "Iran." In *Economic Sanctions and American Diplomacy*, edited by Richard Haass, 85–86. New York: Council on Foreign Relations.

Clay, Lucius. 1962. "Berlin." *Foreign Affairs* 41(1): 47–58.

Cockburn, Patrick. 1982a. "United Arab Emirates IV—Foreign Policy—Warring Neighbours Heighten Sense of Vulnerability—An End to the Iran/Iraq War Would Be a Great Relief." *Financial Times*, October 26.

———. 1982b. "United Arab Emirates II—Economy—Moving Strongly but with Markets Curtailed—More Federal Control and New Agency Laws Will Have a Major Impact." *Financial Times*, October 26.

Coll, Steve. 1990. "Smugglers Seek to Bypass Sanctions." *The Washington Post*, September 1.

Commission for Assistance to a Free Cuba. 2006. *Report to the President*, July. Retrieved from http://i.cfr.org/content/publications/attachments/68166.pdf.

Corera, Gordon. 2006. *Shopping for Bombs*. Oxford, UK: Oxford University Press.

Cortright, David, and George Lopez, eds. 2002. *Smart Sanctions: Targeting Economic Statecraft*. Plymouth, UK: Rowman & Littlefield.

Cowell, Alan. 1988. "Dubai Journal; A Barometer of Gulf Riches: How Now the Dhow?" *New York Times*, October 27.

Cox, Dan, and A. Cooper Drury. 2006. "Democratic Sanctions: Connecting the Democratic Peace and Economic Sanctions." *Journal of Peace Research* 43(6): 709–722.

"Cuba Becomes Full member of Soviet Economic Bloc." 1972. *New York Times*, July 12.

"Cuba May Profit from Communist China's Cut in the Purchase of Sugar." 1966. *New York Times*, January 4.

Curovic, Tatjana D. 1997. "Essays in the Theory and Practice of Economic Sanctions." PhD dissertation, Rutgers University.

Dadak, Casimir. 2003. "The 1992–96 Bulgarian Trade Data Puzzle: A Case of Sanctions Breaking?" *Cato Journal* 22(3): 511–532.

Dalgaard, Carl Johan, and Ola Olsson. 2008. "Windfall Gains, Political Economy and Economic Development." *Journal of African Economics* 17: 72–109.

Davidson. Christopher. 2005. *The United Arab Emirates: A Study In Survival*. Boulder, CO: Lynne Rienner Publishers.

———. 2008. *Dubai: The Vulnerability of Success*. New York: Columbia University Press.

Desai, Raj, and Homi Kharas. 2010. "The Determinants of Foreign Aid Volatility." *Global Economy & Development Working Paper 42*. Washington, DC: The Brookings Institute.

"Despite Fighting, Dubai Smugglers Still Manage to Carry Goods to Iran." 1980. *The Wall Street Journal*, October 10.

"Dhows in Gulf Slip by Iraqis in Iran Trade." 1984. *New York Times*, June 10.

"Dhows use Iran to Smuggle Iraqi Diesel: UAE." 1998. *Agence France-Presse*, July 12.

Dixon, William J., and Bruce Moon. 1993. "Political Similarity and American Foreign Trade Patterns." *Political Research Quarterly* 46(1): 5–25.

Dobbs, Michael. 2008. *One Minute to Midnight*. New York: Vintage Books.

Dorraj, Manochehr, and Carrie Liu Currier. 2008. "Lubricated with Oil: Iran–China Relations in a Changing World." *Middle East Policy* 15(2): 66–80.

Downey, Arthur. 1998. "Extraterritorial Sanctions in the Canada/U.S. context—A U.S. Perspective." *Canada–United States Law Journal* 24: 215–224.

Dreher, Axel, and Andreas Fuchs. 2011. "Rogue Aid? The Determinants of China's Aid Allocations." *CESifo Working Paper Series No. 3581*. Retrieved from http://papers .ssrn.com/sol3/papers.cfm?abstract_id=1932086.

Drezner, Daniel. 1998. "The Hidden Hand of Economic Coercion." *International Organization* 57(3): 643–659.

———. 1999. *The Sanctions Paradox*. Cambridge, UK: Cambridge University Press.

———. 2000. "Bargaining, Enforcement and Multilateral Sanctions: When Is Cooperation Counterproductive?" *International Organization* 54(1): 73–102.

———. 2003. "The Hidden Hand of Economic Coercion." *International Organization* 57(3): 643–659.

———. "Sanctions Sometimes Smart: Targeted Sanctions in Theory and Practice." *International Studies Review* 13(1): 96–108.

Drury, A. Cooper. 1998. "Revisiting Economic Sanctions Reconsidered." *Journal of Peace Research* 35(4): 497–509.

———. 2005. *Economic Sanctions and Presidential Decisions: Models of Political Rationality*. New York: Palgrave.

Dubai Airport Free Zone. 2005. Retrieved on November 1, 2005, from www.dafza .gov.ae/en/.

"Dubai: A Booming Entrepot and Growing Diversion Risk." 1996. *The Risk Report* 2(2): 3–4.

Dubai Chamber of Commerce and Industry (DCCI). 2005. *Dubai External Trade Statistics*. CD-Rom. Dubai: Dubai Chamber of Commerce and Industry.

"Dubai Smugglers Still Voyaging to Iran." 1980. *The Wall Street Journal*, October 10.

"Dubai Technology and Media Free Zone Authority: Laws and Regulations." 2005. Government of Dubai. Retrieved on May 1, 2005, from www.tecom.ae/law/index .htm.

"Dubai's Merchants Find Market Niche in Far-off Places." 1989. *Christian Science Monitor*, July 18.

Dubowitz, Mark, and Emanuele Ottolenghi. 2013. "Iran's Car Industry–A Big Sanctions Buster." *Forbes Online*, May 13.

Duncan, Raymond. 1985. *The Soviet Union and Cuba*. New York: Praeger.

Dyer, Jeffrey. 1997. "Effective Interfirm Collaboration: How Firms Minimize Transaction Costs and Maximize Transaction Value." *Strategic Management Journal* 18(7): 535–556.

Early, Bryan. 2009. "Sleeping with Your Friends' Enemies: An Explanation of Sanctions-Busting Trade." *International Studies Quarterly* 53(1): 49–71.

———. 2010. "Acquiring Foreign Nuclear Assistance in the Middle East: Strategic Lessons from the United Arab Emirates." *The Nonproliferation Review* 17(2): 259–280.

———. 2011. "Unmasking the Black Knights: Sanctions Busters and Their Effects on the Success of Economic Sanctions." *Foreign Policy Analysis* 7: 381–402.

———. 2012. "Alliances and Trade with Sanctioned States: A Study of U.S. Economic Sanctions, 1950–2000." *Journal of Conflict Resolution* 56(3): 547–572. DOI: 10.1177/0022002711420961.

Economist Intelligence Unit (EIU). 2005. "United Arab Emirates." *Country Reports*, August.

Eisenhower, Dwight. 1965. *Waging Peace, 1956–1961: The White House Years, Volume 2.* New York: Doubleday.

Eizenstat, Stuart. 2004. *Do Economic Sanctions Work? Lessons from ILSA and Other U.S. Sanctions Regimes.* Washington, DC: Atlantic Council of the United States.

Emadi-Coffin, Barbara. 2002. *Rethinking International Organisation: Deregulation and Global Governance.* New York: Routledge.

"Emirates Vows to Crack Down on Iraqi Oil Smuggling." 1998. *Dow Jones News Service*, January 19.

Entessar, Nader. 1988. "Superpowers and Persian Gulf Security: The Iranian Perspective." *Third World Quarterly* 10(4): 1427–1451.

Erikson, Daniel. 2004. "Castro and Latin America: A Second Wind?" *World Policy Journal* 21(1): 32–40.

Escribà-Folch, Abel, and Joseph Wright. 2010. "Dealing with Tyranny: International Sanctions and the Survival of Authoritarian Rulers." *International Studies Quarterly* 54: 335–359.

Estelami, Hooman. 1999. "A Study of Iran's Responses to U.S. Economic Sanctions." *Middle East Review of International Affairs* 3(3); retrieved from www.gloria-center .org/1999/09/estelami-1999-09-05/.

"Europeans Agree on Steps to Retaliate For U.S. Cuba Curbs." 1996. *New York Times*, July 16.

Faison, Seth. 1995. "Castro All Hugs and Kisses on First Visit to Old Ally." *New York Times*, December 1.

Falk, Pamela. 1987. "Cuba in Africa." *Foreign affairs* 65(5): 1077–1096.

Fares, Aisha. 1994. "Sanctions-Busting Captain Said He Was Coerced to Iraq." *Deutsche Presse-Agentur*, October 24.

Feaver, Peter, and Eric Lorber. 2010. "Coercive Diplomacy: Evaluating the Consequences of Financial Sanctions." London: Legatum Institute.

"Fidel Castro Discusses Sino-Cuban Ties, Terrorism with Visiting Li Peng." 2001. *BBC World Monitoring*, November 6.

Fisher, Mark. 1988. "Dubai's Traders Anticipate Profitable Peace." *The Globe and Mail* (Toronto), September 6.

Fisk, Daniel. 2000. "Economic Sanctions: The Cuba Embargo Revisited." In *Sanctions as Economic Statecraft*, edited by Steve Chan and A. Cooper Drury. New York: St. Martin's Press.

Fisk, Robert. 1987. "Spectrum: 'They Will Deliver to the Devil'—Inside the Arms Trade." *The Times* (London), June 18.

Fletcher, Pascal. 1996. "Cuba Comes Out of Shell to Search for Allies." *The Financial Times*, January 4.

Foley, Sean. 1999. "The UAE: Political Issues and Security Dilemmas." *Middle East Review of International Affairs* 3(1); available at www.gloria-center.org/1999/03/foley-1999-03-03/.

Forero, Juan. 2006. "Cuba Perks Up as Venezuela's Lifeline Foils U.S. Embargo." *New York Times*, August 4.

Foroohar, Kambiz. 2010. "Dubai Helps Iran Evade Sanctions as Smugglers Ignore U.S. Laws." *Bloomberg News*, January 25.

Fujairah Free Zone. 2005. "Company Listing Page." Retrieved on November 1, 2005, from www.fujairahfreetradezone.com.

Galeano, Javier. 2012. "No Cigar: Economic Embargo against Cuba Turns 50." *USA Today*, February 7.

Gause, F. Gregory III. 2000. "The UAE: Between Pax Britannica and Pax Americana." In *A Century in Thirty Years: Shaykh Zayed and the United Arab Emirates*, edited by Joseph Kechichian, 213–231. Washington, DC: Middle East Policy Council.

George, Alexander, and Andrew Bennett. 2005. *Case Studies and Theory Development in the Social Sciences.* Cambridge, MA: MIT Press.

Gerring, John. 2004. "What Is a Case Study and What Is It Good For?" *American Political Science Review* 98(2): 341–354.

Gertz, Bill. 2001. "China Secretly Shipping Arms to Cuba." *The Washington Times*, June 12.

Ghanem, Shihab. 2001. "Industrialization in the UAE." In *United Arab Emirates: A New Perspective*, edited by Ibrahim Abed and Peter Hellyer, 260–276. United Arab Emirates: Trident Press.

Gill, Bates. 2011. "China's North Korea Policy: Assessing Interests and Influences." *Special Report*. Washington, DC: U.S. Institute of Peace.

Gleditsch, Kristian. 2008. "Expanded Trade and GDP Data." Retrieved from http://privatewww.essex.ac.uk/~ksg/exptradegdp.html.

Goodman, Joshua. 2013. "Venezuelan Oil Diplomacy Curbed by Economic Crisis." *New Zealand Herald*, December 2.

Goodspeed, Peter. 2006. "Chavez Dreams of a Continental Shift." *National Post*, January 30.

Goodwin, Thomas. 2006. Transcript of an Interview with Wolf Blitzer. *The Situation Room*, March 6.

Gott, Richard. 2000. *In the Shadow of the Liberator: The Impact of Hugo Chavez on Venezuela and Latin America.* London: Verso.

Gray, Stephanie. "Merchants Make Art of Brinksmanship." *Financial Times*, November 30.

Grimm, Sven, Rachel Rank, Matthew McDonald, and Elizabeth Schickerling. 2011. *Transparency of Chinese Aid: An Analysis of the Published Information on Chinese External Financial Flows.* Stellenbosch, South Africa: Centre for Chinese Studies.

Gundzik, Jephraim. 2005. "The Ties That Bind China, Russia and Iran." *Asia Times*, June 4.

Gunson, Phil. 2006 "Chávez's Venezuela." *Current History* 105(687): 58–63.

Haas, Richard. 1997. "Sanctioning Madness." *Foreign Affairs* (Nov/Dec): 74–85.

Haas, Richard, and Meghan O'Sullivan. 2000. *Honey and Vinegar: Incentives, Sanctions, and Foreign Policy*. Washington, DC: Brookings Institution.

Hafner-Burton, Emilie, and Alexander Montgomery. 2008. "Power or Plenty: How Do International Trade Institutions Affect Economic Sanctions?" *Journal of Conflict Resolution* 52(2): 213–242.

Haggard, Stephan, and Marcus Noland. 2007. "North Korea's External Economic Relations." *Working Paper Series WP 07-7*. Washington, DC: Peterson Institute for International Economics.Hall, Camilla. 2012. "Dubai Jittery over Business with Iran." *Financial Times*, August 12. Retrieved from www.ft.com/intl/cms/s/0/63c880bc-e23f-11e1-8e9d-00144feab49a.html.

Haney, Patrick, and Walt Vanderbush. 2005. *The Cuban Embargo: The Domestic Politics of an American Foreign Policy*. Pittsburgh, PA: University of Pittsburgh Press.

Hansen, Henrik, and Derek Headey. 2010. "The Short-Run Macroeconomic Impact of Foreign Aid to Small States: An Agnostic Time Series Analysis." *Journal of Development Studies* 46: 877–896.

Harman, Danna. 2005. "Chávez Seeks Influence with Oil Diplomacy." *The Christian Science Monitor*, August 25.

Harper, Douglas. 1991. "Dubai Grows as Trade Center." *Christian Science Monitor*, July 29.

Hayes, Jack, Edward Krauland, Meredith Rathbone, and Julia Ryan. 2012. "New Iran Sanctions Threaten Foreign Banks' Access to the United States, Impose Strict Measures on Financial System of Iran" *Stepoe & Johnson LLP Newsletter*, January 4. Retrieved from www.steptoe.com/publications-newsletter-395.html.

Heard-Bey, Frauke. 1982. *From Trucial States to United Arab Emirates*. New York: Longman.

Hiro, Dilip. 1988. "Iran's Unlikely Champions in the Gulf." *Wall Street Journal*, January 26.

Hofmann, Paul. 1965. "Reds' Trade Share with Cuba Shrinks." *New York Times*, June 12.

Hosenball, Mark. 1987. "Trade with Iran: Importing Trouble?" *Wall Street Journal*, September 2.

Hufbauer, Gary, Kimberly Elliot, Tess Cyrus, and Elizabeth Winston. 1997. "U.S. Economic Sanctions: Their Impact on Trade, Jobs, and Wages." *Working Paper Special*. Washington, DC: Peterson Institute for International Economics.

Hufbauer, Gary, J. J. Schott, and K. A. Elliott. 1990. *Economic Sanctions Reconsidered: History and Current Policy*, 2nd edition. Washington, DC: Institute for International Economics.

Hufbauer, Gary, Jeffrey Schott, Kimberly Elliot, and Barbara Oegg. 2007. *Economic Sanctions Reconsidered*, 3rd edition. Washington, DC: Peterson Institute for International Economics.

Huifen, Chen. 2004. "Dubai on S'pore's Heels." *The Business Times*, April 3.

Ibrahim, Youssef. 1980. "Dhows' New Role: Cargo Link to Iran." *New York Times*, October 26.

"If Hugo Goes: Raúl Castro Searches for Other Lifelines." 2011. *Economist*, July 7.

Institute for Far Eastern Studies. 2012. "China Offers Large-Scale Food Aid to North Korea from February." *North Korean Economy Watch*. Retrieved from www.nkeconwatch.com/2012/06/22/china-offers-large-scale-food-aid-to-north-korea-from-february/.

"Iran Hits Back at New US Trade Ban." 1995. *The Advertiser*, May 2.

Iraq Survey Group. 2005. *Iraq Survey Group Final Report*. Washington, DC: Special Advisor to the Director of Central Intelligence.

"Iraq's Shipping." 2002. *Lloyd's List*, September 25.

Irish, John. 2007. "Dubai–Iran Ties Thrive against Odds." *Agence France Presse*, March 22.

Ivanovich, David. 2005. "Halliburon: Iran's Not Worth It." *The Houston Chronicle*, January 29.

"Jebel Ali Free Zone: Free Zone Companies." 2005. Ports, Customs and Free Zone Corporation. Retrieved on November 1, 2005, from www.jafza.ae/frame-fze.htm.

Jehl, Douglas. 1997. "U.S. Finds Hard Feelings in an Allied Gulf Sheikdom." *New York Times*, July 19.

Jentleson, Bruce. 1986. *Pipeline Politics: The Complex Political Economy of East–West Energy Trade*. Ithaca, NY: Cornell University Press.

Johnson-Freese, Joan. 2007. *Space as a Strategic Asset*. New York: Columbia University Press.

Kaempfer, William H., and Anton D. Lowenberg. 1989. "Sanctioning South Africa: The Politics behind the Policies." *CATO Journal* 8(3): 713–727.

———. 1999. "Unilateral vs. Multilateral Sanctions: A Public Choice Perspective." *International Studies Quarterly* 43: 37–58.

Kaempfer, William H., Anton D. Lowenberg, and William Mertens. 2004. "International Economic Sanctions against a Dictator." *Economics and Politics* 16(1): 29–51.

Kaempfer, William H., and Martin Ross. 2004. "The Political Economy of Trade Sanctions against Apartheid South Africa: A Gravity Model Approach." In *The Political Economy of Trade, Aid, and Foreign Investment Policies*, edited by Devashish Mitra and Arvind Panagariya, 233–244. New York: Elsevier.

Kandemir, Asli. 2013. "Turkey to Iran Gold Trade Wiped Out by New U.S. sanction." *Reuters Online*, February 15.

Kaplowitz, Donna. 1998. *Anatomy of a Failed Embargo*. Boulder, CO: Lynne Reinner.

Kaplowitz, Donna, and Michael Kaplowitz. 1992. *New Opportunities for U.S.–Cuban Trade*. Washington, DC: Johns Hopkins University Press.

Karol, K. S. 1970. *Guerrillas in Power: The Course of the Cuban Revolution*. New York: Hill & Wang.

Kastner, Scott L. 2007. "When Do Conflicting Political Relations Affect International Trade?" *Journal of Conflict Resolution* 51(4): 664–688.

Katzman, Kenneth. 2003. "Iraq: Weapons Threat, Compliance, Sanctions, and U.S. Policy." *Congressional Research Service Report* # IB92117. Washington, DC: Library of Congress.

Katzman, Kenneth. 2005. "The United Arab Emirates (UAE): Issues for U.S. Policy." *Congressional Research Services Report* # RS21852. Washington, DC: Library of Congress.

———. 2007. "The Iran Sanctions Act (ISA)" *Congressional Research Services Report* #RS20871. Washington, DC: Library of Congress.

———. 2008. "The United Arab Emirates (UAE): Issues for U.S. Policy." *Congressional Research Services Report* # RS21852. Washington, DC: Library of Congress.

———. 2013. "Iran Sanctions." *Congressional Research Services Report* # RS20871. Washington, DC: Library of Congress.

Keivani, Ramin, Ali Parsa, and Bassem Younis. 2003. "Development of the ICT Sector and Urban Competitiveness: The Case of Dubai," *Journal of Urban Technology* 10: 19–46.

Keshk, Omar M. G, Brian Pollins, and Rafael Reuveny. 2004. "Trade Still Follows the Flag: The Primacy of Politics in a Simultaneous Model of Interdependence and Armed Conflict." *Journal of Politics* 66(4): 1155–1179.

Kharas, Homi. 2008. "Measuring the Costs of Aid Volatility." *Wolfensohn Center for Development Working Paper 3*. Washington, DC: The Brookings Institute.

King, Gary, and Langche Zeng. 2001. "Logistic Regression in Rare Events Data." *Political Analysis* 9(2): 137–163.

Kirk, John, and Peter McKenna. 1997. *Canada–Cuba Relations: The Other Good Neighbor Policy*. Tallahassee: University of Florida Press.

Kirshner, Jonathon. 1997. "The Microfoundations of Economic Sanctions." *Security Studies* 6(3): 32–64.

Kosack, Stephen, and Jennifer Tobin. 2006. "Funding Self-Sustaining Development: The Role of Aid, FDI, and Government in Economic Success." *International Organization* 60: 205–43.

Kozloff, Nikolas. 2007. *Hugo Chavez: Oil, Politics, and the Challenge to the U.S.* New York: Palgrave Macmillan.

Krauss, Clifford. 2007. "Halliburton Moving C.E.O. from Houston to Dubai." *New York Times*, March 12.

Krauland, Edward, Meredith Rathbone, Julia Ryan, Jack Hayes, Anthony Rapa, and Charles Morris. 2012. "Targeting Foreign Evaders of Iran and Syria Sanctions." *Steptoe & Johnson LLP Newsletter*, May 7. Retrieved from www.steptoe.com/publications-8183.html.

Krustev, Valentin. 2010. "Strategic Demands, Credible Threats, and Economic Coercion Outcomes." *International Studies Quarterly* 54(1): 147–174.

Kumar, Himendra. 2010. "UAE Implements Iran Sanctions." *Gulf News*, October 5.

Lake, Eli. 2005. "Halliburton Unit Wins Contract in Iran." *The New York Sun*, July 12.

Lancaster, John. 1995. "Despite Trade Ban, U.S. Goods Still Find Their Way to Iran." *The Washington Post*, June 25.

Lautenberg, Sen. Frank. 2005. "Dick Cheney, Iran and Halliburton: A Grand Jury Investigates Sanctions Violations." Washington, DC: U.S. Senate.

Lee, Don. 2013. "China Tightening Trade with North Korea." *Los Angeles Times*, June 7.

Leeds, Brett Ashley. 2003. "Do Alliances Deter Aggression? The Influence of Military Alliances on the Initiation of Militarized Interstate Disputes." *American Journal of Political Science* 47: 427–439.

Leeds, Brett Ashley, Andrew Long, and Sara McLaughlin Mitchell. 2000. "Reevaluating Alliance Reliability: Specific Threats, Specific Promises." *Journal of Conflict Resolution* 44(5): 686–699.

Leeds, Brett Ashley, Jeffrey M. Ritter, Sara McLaughlin Mitchell, and Andrew G. Long. 2002. "Alliance Treaty Obligations and Provisions, 1815–1944." *International Interactions* 28: 237–260.

Lektzian, David, and Glen Biglaiser. 2013. "Investment Opportunity and Risk: Do U.S. Sanctions Deter or Encourage Global Investment?" *International Studies Quarterly* 57(1): 65–78.

———. 2014. "The Effect of Foreign Direct Investment on the Use and Success of U.S. Sanctions." *Conflict Management and Peace Science* 31(1): 70–93.

Lektzian, David, and Mark Souva. 2007. "An Institutional Theory of Sanctions Onset and Success." *Journal of Conflict Resolution* 51(6): 848–871.

Lektzian, David, and Christopher Sprecher. 2007. "Sanctions, Signals, and Militarized Conflict." *American Journal of Political Science* 51(2): 415–431.

Leogrande, William. 1996. "Making the Economy Scream: U.S. Economic Sanctions against Sandinista Nicaragua." *Third World Quarterly* 17(2): 329–348.

Leogrande, William, and Julie M. Thomas. 2002. "Cuba's Quest for Economic Independence." *Journal of Latin American Studies* 34(2): 325–363.

Lévesque, Jacques. 1978. *The USSR and the Cuban Revolution*. New York: Praeger Publishers.

Levin, Doron. 1981. "U.S. Sales to Iran Resume Gingerly." *Wall Street Journal*, June 10.

Levy, Philip. 1999. "Sanctions on South Africa: What Did They Do?" *American Economic Review* 89(2): 415–420.

Li, Quan, and David Sacko. 2002. "The (Ir)Relevance of Militarized Interstate Disputes for International Trade." *International Studies Quarterly* 46: 11–43

Licht, Amanda A. 2010. "Coming into Money: The Impact of Foreign Aid on Leader Tenure." *Journal of Conflict Resolution*, 54(1): 58–87.

Limão, Nuno, and Anthony Venables. 2001. "Infrastructure, Geographical Disadvantage, Transport Costs, and Trade." *The World Economic Review* 15(3): 451–479.

Lister, Tim. 2012. "EU Steps of Banking Sanctions against Iran." *CNN Online*, March 15. Accessed at www.cnn.com/2012/03/15/world/meast/iran-banking-sanctions/.

Long, Andrew. 2003."Defense Pacts and International Trade." *Journal of Peace Research* 40: 537–552.

———. 2008. Bilateral Trade in the Shadow of Armed Conflict." *International Studies Quarterly* 52(1): 81–101.

Lum, Thomas, Hannah Fischer, Julissa Gomez-Granger, and Anne Leland. 2009. "China's Foreign Aid Activities in Africa, Latin America, and Southeast Asia." *Congressional Research Service Report #7-5700*. Washington, DC: Library of Congress.

"Luring Minds and Money." 2005. *Iran Daily*, February 1, 6.

Malloy, Michael. 2001. *United States Economic Sanctions: Theory and Practice*. Boston: Kluwer International Law.

Mansfield, Edward, Helen Milner, and B. Peter Rosendorff. 2000. "Free to Trade: Democracies, Autocracies, and International Trade." *American Political Science Review* 94(2): 305–321.

Manyin, Mark. 2005. "Foreign Assistance to North Korea." *Congressional Research Service Report #RL31785*. Washington, DC: Library of Congress.

Manyin, Mark, and Mary Nikitin. 2011. "Foreign Assistance to North Korea." *Congressional Research Service Report # R40095*. Washington, DC: Library of Congress.

———. 2014. "Foreign Assistance to North Korea." *Congressional Research Service Report # R40095*. Washington, DC: Library of Congress.

Marshall, Monty G., and Keith Jaggers. 2009. *Polity IV Project: Political Regime Characteristics and Transitions, 1800–2007*. Arlington, VA: Polity IV Project.

Martin, Lisa. 1992. *Coercive Cooperation*. Princeton, NJ: Princeton University Press.

McCoy, Jennifer. 2000. "Demystifying Venezuela's Hugo Chávez." *Current History* 99(634): 66–71.

McGovern, Elena. 2009. "Export Controls in the United Arab Emirates: A Practical Manifestation of a Strategic Dilemma." Washington, DC: Stimson Center. Retrieved from www.stimson.org/summaries/export-controls-in-the-united-arab-emirates-a-practical-manifestation-of-a-strategic-dilemma/.

McLean, Elena, and Taehee Whang. 2010. "Friends or Foes? Major Trading Partners and the Success of Economic Sanctions." *International Studies Quarterly* 54(2): 427–447.

Milhollin, Gary, and Kelly Motz. 2004. "Nukes 'R' Us." *New York Times*, March 4.

Miller, Roger. 2005. *To Save a City: The Berlin Airlift, 1948–1949*. Washington, DC: Air Force History and Museums Program.

Miscamble, Wilson. 1980. "Harry S. Truman, the Berlin Blockade and the 1948 Election." *Presidential Studies Quarterly* 10(3): 306–316.

Molotsky, Irvin. 1996. "U.S. Linked to Saudi Aid for Bosnians." *New York Times*, February 2.

Monreal, Pedro. 2002. "Development as an Unfinished Affair: Cuba after the 'Great Adjustment' of the 1990s." *Latin American Perspectives* 29(3): 75–90.

Montgomery, Alexander. 2005. "Ringing in Proliferation: How to Dismantle an Atomic Bomb Network." *International Security* 30(2): 153–187.

Moravcsik, Andrew. 1997. "Taking Preferences Seriously: A Liberal Theory of International Politics," *International Organization* 51(4): 513–553.

Morely, Morris. 1987. *Imperial State and Revolution: The United States and Cuba, 1952–1986*. New York: Cambridge University Press.

Morely, Morris, and Chris McGillion. 2002. *Unfinished Business: America and Cuba after the Cold War, 1989–2001*. New York: Cambridge University Press.

Morgan, T. Clifton, and Navin Bapat. 2003. "Imposing Sanctions: States, Firms, and Economic Coercion." *International Studies Review* 5(4): 65–79.

Morgan, T. Clifton, Navin Bapat, and Valentin Krustev. 2009. "The Threat and Imposition of Economic Sanctions, 1971–2000." *Conflict Management and Peace Science* 26(1): 95–113.

Morrow, James, Randolph Siverson, and Tressa Tabares. 1998. "The Political Determinants of International Trade: The Great Powers, 1907–1990." *American Political Science Review* 97(3): 649–661.

Most, Benjamin, and Harvey Starr. 1989. *Inquiry, Logic, and International Politics*. Columbia: University of South Carolina Press.

Mueller, John, and Karl Mueller. 1999. "Sanctions of Mass Destruction." *Foreign Affairs* 78(3): 43–53.

Nanto, Dick, and Emma Chanlett-Avery. 2010. "North Korea: Economic Leverage and Policy Analysis." *Congressional Research Service Report # RL32493*. Washington, DC: Library of Congress.

Naylor, R. T. 2001. *Economic Warfare: Sanctions, Embargo Busting, and Their Human Costs*. Boston: Northeast University Press.

Network for North Korean Democracy and Human Rights (NKNET). 2011. "Defector Survey on the Distribution of Overseas Food Aid." Retrieved from https://docs .google.com/file/d/0B8IwVGFnTo5NNGIxN2QwNTctZTIwZSooMGNmLTk4Nm QtMWQ4ODJmN2FiOTRl/edit?hl=en_US&pli=1.

Nincic, Miroslav. 2005. *Renegade Regimes: Confronting Deviant Behavior in World Politics*. New York: Columbia University Press.

Noland, Marcus, and Stephan Haggard. 2005. "Statement Submitted to House International Relations Subcommittees on Asia and the Pacific and on Africa, Global Human Rights, and International Operations." 109th Congress, First Session. Hearing on April 28, 2005.

———. 2011. *Witness to Transformation: Refugee Insights into North Korea*. Washington, DC: Peterson Institute for International Economics.

Nooruddin, Irfan. 2002. "Modeling Selection Bias in Studies of Sanctions Efficacy." *International Interactions* 28(1): 57–74.

O'Clery, Conor. 2004. "Inquiry Launched into US Firm over Iran Links." *The Irish Times*, July 21.

OECD. 2008. "Is It ODA?" November. Paris: Author. Retrieved from www.oecd.org/ dac/stats/34086975.pdf.

"Official against Ban on Re-Export from Dubai." 2005. *Iran Daily*, January 1.

Ortiz, Jaime. 2012. "Déjà Vu: Latin America and Its New Trade Dependency . . . This Time with China." *Latin American Research Review* 47(3): 175–190.

O'Sullivan, Meghan L. 2003. *Shrewd Sanctions: Statecraft and State Sponsors of Terrorism*. Washington DC: Brookings Institution Press.

Pamuk, Humeyra. 2012. "Turkish Gold Trade Booms to Iran, via Dubai." *Reuters Online*, October 23.

Pape, Robert. 1997. "Why Economic Sanctions Do Not Work." *International Security* 22(2): 90–136.

Parrish, Thomas. 1998. *Berlin in the Balance: 1945–1949*. Reading, MA: Addison-Wesley.

Pavlov, Yuri. 1994. *Soviet–Cuban Alliance, 1959–1991*. New Brunswick, NJ: Transaction Publishers.

Peksen, Dursun. 2009. "Better or Worse? The Effect of Economic Sanctions on Human Rights." *Journal of Peace Research* 46(1): 59–77.

———. 2011. "U.S. Economic Sanctions Have a Significant Negative Effect upon Public Health." *Foreign Policy Analysis* 7: 237–251.

Peksen, Dursun, and A. Cooper Drury. 2010. "Coercive or Corrosive: The Negative Impact of Economic Sanctions on Democracy." *International Interactions* 36: 240–264.

Pérez-López, Jorge. 1996/1997. "Foreign Investment in Socialist Cuba: Significance and Prospects." *Studies in Comparative International Development* 31(4): 3–28.

Peterson, J. E. 2003. "The United Arab Emirates: Economic Vibrancy and US Interests," *Asian Affairs* 34 (2): 137–142.

Peterson, Timothy, and A. Cooper Drury. 2011. "Sanctioning Violence: The Effect of Third-Party Economic Coercion on Militarized Conflict." *Journal of Conflict Resolution* 55(4): 580–605.

Phillips, R. Hart. 1960a. "Cuba Says Soviet Will Keep Sugar." *New York Times*, February 16.

———. 1960b. "Red Chinese Sign a Five-Year Pact for Cuban Sugar." *New York Times*, July 24.

Pilger, John. 2000. "Squeezed to Death." *The Guardian*, March 3.

Pizarro, Renato. 2009. "China Grants Cuba a $600M Credit line." *Miami Herald Online*, September 3.

Pollitt, Brian. 1997. "The Cuban Sugar Economy: Collapse, Reform and Prospects for Recovery." *Journal of Latin American Studies* 29(1): 171–210.

———. 2004. "The Rise and Fall of the Cuban Sugar Economy." *Journal of Latin American Studies* 36(2): 319–348.

Preeg, Ernest. 1999. *Feeling Good or Doing Good with Sanctions*. Washington, DC: The CSIS Press.

Preston, Julia. 1996. "U.S. Finds Mexico Is Adamant on Cuba Trade." *New York Times*, August 29.

Protess, Ben, and Jessica Silver-Greenberg. 2012. "HSBC to Pay $1.92 Billion to Settle Charges of Money Laundering." *DealBook*, December 10. Retrieved from http://dealbook.nytimes.com/2012/12/10/hsbc-said-to-near-1-9-billion-settlement-over-money-laundering/.

Purcell, Susan. 1991/1992. "Collapsing Cuba." *Foreign Affairs* 71(1): 130–145.

Rahman, Saifur. 2004. "Iran Wants Aid against Smuggling." *Financial Times*, December 13.

Ramírez, Cristóbal. 2005. "Venezuela's Bolivarian Revolution: Who Are the Chavistas?" *Latin American Perspectives* 32(3): 79–97.

Ras Al-Kaimah Free Zone. 2005. Retrieved on November 1, 2005 from http://rakftz.com/.

Ratliff, William. 2004. *China's "Lessons" for Cuba's Transition?* Miami, FL: Institute for Cuban and Cuban-American Studies, University of Miami.

"Red China and Cuba Sign Pact on Trade." 1963. *New York Times*, February 27.

Rettab, Belaid and Marietta Morada. 2005. "Export/Re-Export of DCCI Members, 2005." *Foreign Trade Series Research Paper*. Dubai: Dubai Chamber of Commerce & Industry.

Rettab, Belaid, Marietta Morada, and Maryam Abdullah. 2005. "Dubai's Foreign Trade over the Years." *Foreign Trade Series Research Paper*. Dubai: Dubai Chamber of Commerce & Industry.

Richey, Warren. 1982. "Neutrality, Trade Links May Make Best Defense." *Christian Science Monitor*, December 1.

Rieff, David. 1996. "Cuba Refrozen." *Foreign Affairs* 75(4): 62–76.

Rodman, Kenneth. 1995. "Sanctions at Bay? Hegemonic Decline, Multinational Corporations, and U.S. Economic Sanctions since the Pipeline Case." *International Organization* 49(1): 105–137.

———. 2001. *Sanctions beyond Borders: Multinational Corporations and U.S. Economic Statecraft*. Lanham, MD: Rowman & Littlefield Publishers.

Rohter, Larry. 1996. "Latin American Nations Rebuke U.S. for the Embargo on Cuba." *The New York Times*, June 6.

———. 2000a. "Chavez Extends a Hero's Welcome to Castro in Caracas." *New York Times*, October 27.

———. 2000b. "Venezuela Will Sell Cuba Low-Priced Oil." *New York Times*, October 31.

———. 2004. "China Widens Economic Role in Latin America." *The New York Times*, November 20.

Romero, Simon. 2008. "Cuban Leader in Venezuela to Build Ties with Chavez." *New York Times*, December 14.

Roodman, David. 2011. "An Index of Donor Performance." Washington, DC: Center for Global Development. Working Paper #67.

Rosenthal, Elisabeth. 2003. "China's Sparkle Bedazzles a Visiting Castro." *New York Times*, February 28.

Rosenthal, Lisa. 2005. "Information Technology in the UAE," American University. Retrieved on May 1, 2005, from www.american.edu/carmel/lr2962a/author.html.

Roy, Joaquín. 2000. *Cuba, the United States, and the Helms-Burton Doctrine*. Gainesville: University Press of Florida.

Rugh, William. 2000. "Leadership in the UAE: Past, Present, and Future." In *A Century in Thirty Years: Shaykh Zayed and the United Arab Emirates,* edited by Joseph A. Kechichian, 235–271. Washington, DC: Middle East Policy Council.

Sadjadpour, Karim. 2011. "The Battle of Dubai: The United Arab Emirates and the U.S.–Iran Cold War." *Carnegie Papers.* Washington, DC: Carnegie Endowment for International Peace.

Salama, Samir. 2004. "SMB Workers Stare at Uncertainty." *Gulf Times,* April 8.

Sanger, David. 1996. "U.S., Enforcing Cuba Curbs, Punishes Canadian Company." *New York Times,* July 10.

———. 1998. "Europeans Drop Lawsuit Contesting Cuba Trade Act." *New York Times,* April 21.

———. 2006. "Under Pressure, Dubai Company Drops Port Deal." *New York Times,* March 10.

Scarborough, Rowan. 1997. "UAE to Honor Pact, Will Buy 80 F-16s from U.S." *The Washington Times,* July 21.

Schraeder, Peter, Steven Hook, and Bruce Taylor. 1998. "Clarifying the Foreign Aid Puzzle: A Comparison of American, Japanese, French and Swedish Flows." *World Politics* 50(2): 294–323.

Schwartz, Harry. 1964. "Moscow–Peking Rivalry Grows." *New York Times,* February 9.

———. 1966. "Red China Hints at Racism." *New York Times,* August 28.

Sedarat, Firouz. 1997. "U.S. Computers Flow to Iran Despite Ban." *Reuters News,* November 3.

Selaya, Pablo, and Rainer Thiele. 2010. "Aid and Sectoral Growth: Evidence from Panel Data." *Journal of Development Studies* 46(10): 1749–1766.

Shaheen, Kareem. 2010. "Dubai's Iranian Traders Feel Heat of Sanctions." *The National,* September 24.

Shambaugh, George. 1999. *States, Firms, and Power.* Albany: SUNY Press.

Sharjah International Free Zone. 2005. "Investor Directory." Retrieved on November 1, 2005, from www.saif-zone.com/main/InvestorDir.asp#.

Shehadi, Philip. 1981. "Economic Sanctions and Iranian Trade." *MERIP Reports* 98: 15–16.

Sheridan, Mary. 2011. "Obama Loosens Travel Restrictions to Cuba." *Washington Post,* January 15.

Shifter, Michael. 2006. "In Search of Hugo Chávez." *Foreign Affairs* 85(3): 45–59.

Shlaim, Avi. 1983–1984. "Britain, the Berlin Blockage and the Cold War." *International Affairs* 60(1): 1–14.

Sieff, Martin. 1994. "Iran Ships Iraq's oil, U.S. Says." *The Washington Times,* December 20.

Slavin, Barbara. 1987. "Dubai Tries to Make Its Mark." *St. Petersburg* [FL] *Times,* September 27.

Sleiman, Mirna. 2012. "UAE, Qatar Stop Trade Finance to Iran over Sanctions." *Reuters,* February 2.

Slovov, Slavi. 2007. "Innocent or Not-So-Innocent Bystanders: Evidence from the Gravity Model of International Trade about the Effects of UN Sanctions on Neighbor Countries." *The World Economy* 30(11): 1701–1725.

Smith, Wayne. 1996. "Cuba's Long Reform." *Foreign Affairs* 75(2): 99–112.

———. 1998. "An Ocean of Mischief: Our Dysfunctional Cuban Embargo." *Orbis* 42(4): 33–544.

"Smugglers Run Blockade along Old 'Pirate Coast.'" 1990. *San Diego Union Tribune*, September 22.

Snow, Anita. 2005. "Cuba, Venezuela Woo Nations on Trade Pact." *Associated Press Online*, April 25.

Snyder, Glenn. 1997. *Alliance Politics*. Ithaca, NY: Cornell University Press.

Soligen, Etel, ed. 2012. *Sanctions, Statecraft, and Nuclear Proliferation*. Cambridge, UK: Cambridge University Press.

Spadoni, Paolo. 2010. *Failed Sanctions: Why the U.S. Embargo against Cuba Could Never Work*. Gainesville: University of Florida Press.

Stern, Laurence. 1974. "Quiet Moves Made on Restoring Relations with Cuba." *The Washington Post*, August 24.

Stewart, Christopher. 2008. "The Axis of Commerce." *Portfolio*, September.

Stinnett, Douglas, Bryan R. Early, Cale Horne, and Johannes Karreth. 2011. "Complying by Denying: Explaining Why States Develop Nonproliferation Export Controls." *International Studies Perspectives* 12(3): 308–326.

Stinnett, Douglas, Jaroslav Tir, Philip Schafer, Paul F. Diehl, and Charles Gochman. 2002. "The Correlates of War Project Direct Contiguity Data, Version 3.0." *Conflict Management and Peace Science* 19(2): 59–67.

Stockman, Farah. 2008. "HP Uses Third Party to Sell Printers in Iran." *The Boston Globe*, December 29.

Stolberg, Alan G. 2010. "Chapter 1: Crafting National Interests in the 21st Century." In J. Boone Bartholomees Jr., ed., *The U.S. Army War College Guide to National Security Issues Volume II: National Security Policy and Strategy*, pp. 3–14. Carlisle, PA: Strategic Studies Institute.

Suro, Roberto. 1987. "Ancient Boats Still Ply a Tense Gulf." *The New York Times*, November 5.

Sutherland, Jon and Diane Canwell. 2007. *The Berlin Airlift: The Salvation of a City*. South Yorkshire, UK: Pen & Sword Books.

Swibel, Matthew. 2004a. "Trading with the Enemy." *Forbes Online*, April 12. Retrieved from www.forbes.com/forbes/2004/0412/086_print.html.

———. 2004b. "Oops." *Forbes*, 173(7).

Szulc, Tad. 1962. "Cuba Troubles Grow Despite Soviet Aid." *New York Times*, August 19.

———. 1965. "Cuba and China Sign Trade Pact." *New York Times*, January 6.

Tanner, Henry. 1964. "Khrushchev and Castro Reach New Trade Accord." *New York Times*, January 22.

Taubman, Phillip. 1997. "America's Hollow Embargo on Iran." *New York Times*, November 13.

"Trade with the UAE 1994." 1994. *Agence France-Presse*, January 26.

"23% of Cuba's Trade Is Still With Non-Reds." 1967. *New York Times*, September 24.

"UAE Stock Exchange Tumbles and Turns in Joy; Iranian Capital Number One Cause." 2006. *Mehrnews.com*, January 3.

U.S. & Foreign Commercial Service. 2005. "FY 2005 Country Commercial Guide: United Arab Emirates." Washington, DC: U.S. Department of State.

U.S. Department of Commerce, Bureau of Industry and Security Export Enforcement. 2010. *Don't Let This Happen to You! An Introduction to U.S. Export Control Law.* Washington, DC: U.S. Department of Commerce.

U.S. Department of State. 1949. "Berlin Backgrounder." *Information Memorandum No. 28* [Declassified Document]. Washington, DC: Office of Public Affairs, Department of State.

U.S. Energy Information Administration. 2012. "Cuba." *Country Analysis Briefs*, May 1. Retrieved from www.eia.gov/countries/cab.cfm?fips=CU.

U.S. GAO. 2007. "Economic Sanctions: Agencies Face Competing Priorities in Enforcing the U.S. Embargo on Cuba." *Report to Congress*, November.

———. 2010. "Iran Sanctions: Complete and Timely Licensing Data Needed to Strengthen Enforcement of Export Restrictions." *Report to Congress*, March.

———. 2013. "Iran: U.S. and International Sanctions Have Adversely Affected the Iranian Economy." *Report to Congress*, February.

"U.S. Opposes Moves to Let Nations in O.A.S. Lift Sanctions against Cubans." 1971. *New York Times*, December 17.

"Using Oil to Spread Revolution Venezuela and Latin America." 2005. *Economist*, July 30.

Valentine, Paul. 1989. "2 Md. Brothers Admit Selling Iran Military Parts." *The Washington Post*, July 12.

Van Bergeijk, Peter A. G. 1994. *Economic Diplomacy, Trade, and Commercial Policy: Positive and Negative Sanctions in a New World Order.* Brookfield, VT: E. Elgar.

———. 1995. "The Impact of Economic Sanctions in the 1990s." *World Economy* 18(3): 443–453.

Van Bergeijk, Peter, and Charles van Marrewijk. 1995. "Why Do Sanctions Need Time to Work? Adjustment, Learning, and Anticipation." *Economic Modeling* 12(2): 75–86.

Vicker, Ray. 1980. "Outwitting the Ayatollah." *The Wall Street Journal*, May 7.

Volcker, Paul, Richard Goldstone, and Mark Pieth. 2005. *Manipulation of the Oil-for-Food Programme by the Iraqi Regime.* New York: Independent Inquiry Committee Into the United Nations Oil-for-Food Programme, United Nations.

Volsky, George. 1979. "Cuba Twenty Years Later." *Current History* 76(444): 54–57, 83–34.

Vuoto, Grace. 2001. "Embraced by the Dragon; China Can't Back Up Veneer of Good Will." *Washington Times*, July 25.

Walker, Tony. 1987. "Iran's Mines Add to Dhows' Troubles." *Sydney Morning Herald*, October 3.

———. 1995. "Castro Makes Belated Pilgrimage to Beijing." *Financial Times*, November 27.

Walter, Matthew. 2007. "Venezuelan Oil Subsidies to Cuba Top $3 Billion, Report Says." *Bloomberg News*, August 2.

Warner, Sen. John. 2006. Interview Transcript. *Meet the Press*, February 26.

Weintraub, Richard. 1987. "Most Persian Gulf Ships Travel without Escorts." *The Washington Post*, August 28.

Weiss, Martin. 2006. "Arab League Boycott of Israel." *Congressional Research Service Report #RS22424*. Washington, DC: Library of Congress.

Whang, Taehee. 2011. "Playing to the Home Crowd? Symbolic Use of Economic Sanctions in the United States." *International Studies Quarterly* 55(3): 787–801.

Whang, Taehee, Elena McLean, and Douglas Kuberski. 2013. "Coercion, Information, and the Success of Sanction Threats." *American Journal of Political Science* 57(1): 65–81.

Williamson, Oliver. 1985. *The Economic Institutions of Capitalism: Firms, Markets, Relational Contracting*. New York: The Free Press.

"With Help from Oil and Friends." 2005. *Economist*, January 15.

Wood, Reed. 2008. "A Hand upon the Throat of the Nation: Economic Sanctions and State Repression, 1976–2001." *International Studies Quarterly* 52(3): 489–513.

Worsnip, Patrick. 1998. "Iran Still Helps Iraq Oil Smuggling, Monitors Say." *Reuters News*, October 9.

Wright, Robin. 1995. "Dubai's Wooden Hulls Will Sunder the Blockade." *New York Times*, May 31.

———. 2008. "Stuart Levey's War." *New York Times*, October 31.

Index

Cuba (*continued*)
    U.S. sanctions against, 3, 6, 13, 15,
        16, 19–20, 73, 87, 92, 136, 158,
        159–206, 183, 212–13, 215
Cuban American National Foundation
    (CANF), 239n85
Cuban Democracy Act (CDA), 184, 186,
    189, 204
Cuban Missile Crisis, 163, 166, 169,
    172–73, 176, 178, 179
Curovic, Tatjana D., 224n1
Czechoslovakia, 169

Dadak, Casimir, 230n43
Davidson, Christopher, 108
defense pacts, 45–46, 47, 71–72, 75–76,
    156, 158, 227n43; *Sender-Third Party
    Defense Pact Hypothesis*, 76, 146,
    149, 151–52; *Target-Third Party
    Defense Pact Hypothesis*, 73, 146,
    149, 151–52; U.S.-UAE defense pact,
    13, 89, 90, 105, 111, 112, 126–28, 208.
    See also alliances
democracy, 82, 85, 143, 144, 211, 227n42;
    democratic peace theory, 76, 229n36;
    government-constituent relations
    in, 33, 39, 76; *Target-Third Party
    Democratic Regimes Hypothesis*,
    76–77, 146–47, 149, 152–53
Deng Xiaoping, 156, 191
Direct Contiguity Data Set, 147
Downey, Arthur, 91
DP World, 133, 234n145
Drezner, Daniel, 148, 219, 225nn5,10,
    226n8, 227n43, 228n3
Drury, A. Cooper, 224n25, 225n10,
    229n36
Dubai: Diera district, 110; DP World,
    133, 234n145; Dubai Airport Free
    Zone, 123, 124; Dubai Internet City
    (DIC) Zone, 124; ethnic Persians
    in, 109–10; Jebel Ali Free Zone
    (JAFZA), 108, 111, 119, 121–22, 123,

124–25, 127, 234n132; Juma Majid
    Co., 115–16; Khan proliferation
    network in, 121, 131, 132–33, 223n6;
    Port Rashid, 108; Redington Gulf,
    116; sanctions-busting activities,
    1–3, 14, 89, 98–101, 102–5, 106,
    107–12, 113, 115–17, 118–19, 121–25,
    126, 127–29, 130, 135, 140, 208,
    223n6, 233n107, 234n128, 235n175;
    Sheikh Rashid, 101, 108; technology
    and information sectors, 124
Duncan, Raymond, 172
duration of economic sanctions, 6, 25,
    32, 43, 54, 148, 212–13; relationship
    to aid-based sanctions busting, 47,
    51–53; relationship to effectiveness
    of sanctions, 47, 215, 228nn52,55
Dyer, Jeffrey, 226n12

East Germany, 169
effectiveness of economic sanctions:
    Foreign Aid Hypothesis regarding,
    42, 50–51; impact of amount of
    foreign aid received on, 10, 14,
    38–42, 43, 45, 46–48, 49–51, 130,
    161, 181–82, 204–6, 210–11, 215–16,
    218, 227n40, 228nn52,53; impact of
    coercion of third-party states on,
    133–36, 137–38, 141, 157; impact
    of Cold War on, 46, 47; impact of
    duration of sanctions on, 47, 215,
    228nn52,55; impact of economic
    development of target state on, 45,
    47, 55; impact of foreign aid volatility
    on, 10, 14, 38–42, 43, 45, 46–48,
    49–51, 52–54, 55, 56, 80; impact of
    international cooperation on, 46,
    47, 131–39, 141; impact of modest
    U.S. goals on, 46, 47, 54; impact of
    number of trade-based sanctions
    busters on, 14, 38, 44, 46–49, 52–54,
    55, 80, 95, 130, 210, 211, 212; impact
    of prior military relationship on,

45–46, 47; impact of prior sender-
target relations on, 45–46, 47, 54–55;
impact of regime type of target on,
45, 47, 227n42; impact of sanction-
busting activities on failure, 3–4,
9–13, 14, 16, 19–20, 25, 26, 28, 29,
30, 31–56, 80, 88, 90, 94–95, 130–31,
204–6, 207, 210–11, 212, 219, 225n10;
impact of third-party support on,
59–60, 228n3; incidence of failure,
5, 6, 9, 223n12; modeling of, 43–56,
227nn35,37,42,43,51, 228nn52–54;
Sanctions-Busting Trade Hypothesis
regarding, 38, 49
Eisenhower, Dwight, 163, 168
Eizenstat, Stuart, 239n93
Entessar, Nader, 232n69
EuGene, 236n7
European Union (EU): relations with
United States, 1, 184, 185–86, 189,
204; sanctions against Iran, 1, 2–3,
138; sanctions-busting activities,
188, 189, 204; trade with Cuba, 188,
189, 204
extraterritorial sanctions: regarding
third-party states, 34, 61, 74–75, 98,
141, 163, 165, 184, 185–86; by U.S.,
34, 74–75, 98, 141, 163, 165, 184,
185–86

firms. *See* nonstate commercial actors
Fisk, Daniel, 239n93
foreign aid: as altruistic vs. political,
80–81; amount received, 10, 14,
26, 38–42, 43, 45, 46–48, 49–51,
62–65, 130, 161, 172–75, 176, 179–80,
181–82, 210–11, 215, 218–19, 227n40,
228nn52,53; as fungible, 19, 38, 39, 40,
41, 55; and government-constituent
relations, 10, 38, 39, 40–41, 42, 55,
228n13; as subsidized trade, 19, 26,
27, 35, 40, 63, 76, 83–84, 169, 172,
173, 174–75, 176, 177, 180, 181, 187,

198; volatility of, 10, 14, 38–42, 43,
45, 46–48, 49–51, 52–54, 55, 56, 80.
See also aid-based sanctions busting
foreign direct investment (FDI), 21, 112,
123, 124, 126, 188, 219
foreign remittances, 21, 167, 186, 187,
219
fossil fuels, 1, 112, 114, 131; *See also* oil
and natural gas
France: exports to Iran, 113, 114;
relations with United States, 74–75,
90, 217; sanctions against Iran, 90;
sanctions-busting activities, 74–75,
113, 114, 143, 144, 155, 211, 217,
231n27
free trade zones (FTZs), 101, 108,
119–20, 121–22, 123–25, 129–30, 140,
234n133
Fujairah, 105
Fulbright, J. William, 164
future research, 207, 217–19

General Electric (GE), 115, 116
Germany: exports to Iran, 113;
sanctions-busting activities, 113,
138, 144, 145, 155, 158, 211
Gleditsch, Kristian: *Expanded Trade
and GDP Data*, 236n3
Goebels, Joseph, 180, 239n78
gold, 1–2, 137, 223n2
Gorbachev, Mikhail, 177
government-constituent relations: in
authoritarian states, 7, 33, 39; in
democratic states, 33, 39, 76; and
foreign aid, 10, 38, 39, 40–41, 42,
55, 226n25, 228n13; and liberal
paradigm, 9–10, 30–31, 65–66; in
sender states, 7, 31, 33, 60, 100, 106,
116–17, 128–29, 183, 212–15, 228n13,
234n133, 239n85; in target states,
7, 10, 18, 31, 32, 33, 34, 37, 38, 39,
40–41, 42, 55, 226n25; in third-party
states, 9–10, 11, 14, 18–19, 21, 22, 25,